BOLLINGEN SERIES XXVII

Pl. 1. *Rezadores* worshipping before the two crosses in front of the church of Todos Santos.

MAUD OAKES

# The
# Two Crosses
## of
# Todos Santos

*SURVIVALS OF MAYAN RELIGIOUS RITUAL*

BOLLINGEN SERIES XXVII

PRINCETON UNIVERSITY PRESS

THIS VOLUME IS THE TWENTY-SEVENTH IN A SERIES OF BOOKS

SPONSORED BY AND PUBLISHED FOR

BOLLINGEN FOUNDATION

First Princeton / Bollingen Paperback Printing, 1969
Second Hardcover Printing, 1969

Library of Congress Catalogue Card No. 68-26669
SBN 691-01757-3 (paperback edn.)
SBN 691-09835-2 (hardcover edn.)

Printed in the United States of America
by Princeton University Press, Princeton, New Jersey

IN MEMORY OF MIMA
AND TO NATACHA

# TABLE OF CONTENTS

Introduction, *by Paul Radin*                                1

Preface                                                     15

Note on the Language                                        22

Prologue                                                    23

## PART ONE

1. The Road to Todos Santos                                29
2. The Mode of Life                                        32
3. From Birth to Death                                     41
4. Religion and Religious Organization                     53
5. The Cerros                                              71

## PART TWO

1. Suspicions and Accusations                              81
2. The Chimanes and Their Organization                     90
3. The Year Bearer Ceremony                                99
4. How to Become a Chimán                                 115
5. The Regalia and Functions of the Chimanes             150
6. The Chimanes in Defence and Attack                     160
7. The Dueños as Naguales and Sorcerers                   170
8. The Chimanes as Soothsayers and Curanderos            178

ix

CONTENTS

9. The Calendar and Its Ceremonies — 188

10. The Fiestas and Dances — 209

11. Farewell to the Rezadores and Tata Julián — 233

APPENDIX

1. Structure of Todos Santos — 239

2. The Indians and Education — 240

3. The Finca System — 241

4. The Todos Santos Costume — 242

5. The Origin of Corn — 244

6. Sacred Places — 245

7. Chart of Days for Casting the Mixes — 248

8. The Calendar — 251

Bibliography — 254

Glossary — 256

Index — 263

# LIST OF PLATES

The photographs were taken by the author except for plates 1, 6, 7, 10, 11, and 12, by Hans Namuth; and plate 13, by Bob Hersey. The author herself refrained from photographing members of the religious body. They posed willingly at her request, however, for Mr. Namuth.

Pl. 1. *Rezadores* worshipping before the two crosses in front of the church of Todos Santos                                    *Frontispiece*

Map of Northwestern Guatemala                     *following page*     18

                                                  *following page*    112

Pl. 2. Todos Santos. On the right stands the *juzgado,* in the centre the two *pilas* or fountains

Pl. 3. The market place at Todos Santos

Pl. 4. A typical house

Pl. 5. The author lived in the whitewashed house; her *mozo* and his family in the house in the foreground. Margarita Elón lived in the one to the rear. Fruit trees and corn fields were all around

Pl. 6. Domingo, the author's *mozo*

Pl. 7. Domingo, his wife Patrona, and their children except for the eldest son, Andrés

Pl. 8. Basilia, the author's servant

Pl. 9. Rosa Bautista, midwife and *pulsera,* sister of "El Rey," the calendar priest

xi

*following page* 176

Pl. 10. *Rezadores* in the church doorway: at the right, Tata Julián, Alcalde Rezador; left, Roque Matías, First Rezador. At the right is one of their staffs of office, and on the steps is a *pichacha* or censer

Pl. 11. "El Rey," Macario Bautista, the calendar priest of Todos Santos

Pl. 12. Tata Julián, Alcalde Rezador, and an *escuelix,* in the doorway of the church

Pl. 13. The two crosses, seen through the doorway of the church

Pl. 14. The Year Bearer Ceremony as it was depicted by the ancient Maya in the Dresden Codex

Pl. 15. The two crosses at the foot of the pyramid of Cumanchúm

Pl. 16. The *mixes,* used for divination. Note the medicine bag of the *chimán* and the quartz, marbles, and dice

Pl. 17. Fiesta: Indians standing in line to pull the bell-rope for good luck on Todos Santos Day

Pl. 18. Fiesta: A rider tying a live rooster to the rope above for the *corrida de gallos*

Pl. 19. A *ladino* with his Indian wife and their son

Pl. 20. Two municipal *mayores*

Pl. 21. A *mayor* of the religious body, with his staff of office

Pl. 22. (a) A Mam woman. (b) An unpainted carved oak mask which belonged to Patrona's grandfather

## LIST OF TEXT FIGURES

1. The Year Bearer Ceremony, from the Codex Troano    102–3

2. Mayan priest or god sitting in his house (?), from the Dresden Codex    108

3. *Chimán's* cross of *costumbre*    138

4. Divination, from the Codex Borbonicus    180

5. Chimán Pascual Pablo's arrangement of copal balls    201

# INTRODUCTION

MAUD OAKES's book is a very disturbing one for the academically trained anthropologist. In order to understand and properly evaluate its peculiar excellences as well as her method, or rather methods, it is best to review in some detail the history of anthropological approaches from 1871, year of the appearance of E. B. Tylor's fundamental work *Primitive Culture*, to the present time.

Tylor's approach need not detain us long. It was that of a cultured English gentleman writing during the heyday of the evolutionary theory. Its great merit was its implied recognition that anthropology was an historical discipline. There was no question, consequently, of how primitive cultures were to be studied.

In the last two generations, however, particularly here in the United States, the situation has completely changed, and the problem of method has assumed a prominence to be met with in none of the other so-called humanistic disciplines. I think the reason for this somewhat frantic preoccupation of anthropologists with methodological problems is not far to seek. Fundamentally it is because, for the last two generations, most anthropologists have never been quite clear in their own minds about what they are dealing with. Is anthropology to be regarded as an independent discipline with its own specifically delimited data and its own methods of attack? Is it simply a branch of sociology? Is it a nondescript no man's land where are to be found facts pertaining to all the basic humanistic disciplines, to philosophy, psychology, economics, political science, and history, not to mention to sciences such as biology?

The techniques and approaches anthropologists adopted depended largely upon the answers to the basic question of what anthropology was and what function it was to serve.

1

To the founder of critical anthropology in the United States, Franz Boas, the matter was relatively simple. To him method meant, essentially, being properly trained to recognize what were anthropological facts, where they existed, and how to record them. In Boas's approach the one important point to remember is that facts possessed an existence of their own, so to speak, and that the observer must be continually on his guard not to entangle his own personality with them and not to impose extensions upon them from above. An arrangement of these facts there had to be—that could not be obviated—but the only arrangement to be tolerated was a serial and linear one and even then this was to be of a strictly provisional character.

Such a point of view was obviously rooted in the post-Kantian philosophy which dominated the thinking of European scholars and scientists throughout the nineteenth and the early twentieth centuries. Its two fundamental defects—its merits need not be discussed here—were its marked antihistorical bias and its practical elimination of the individual as a vital factor in the determination of the facts themselves and of their proper and authentic recording.

The same two basic defects were inherent in the approach of all those to whom anthropology was but an offshoot of sociology. And to the founders of modern sociology, Comte and Durkheim, and to all their lineal descendants, French, German, English, and American, the civilizations of aboriginal peoples were essentially illustrative, to be used in the establishment of cultural typologies and cultural processes. For Boas's facts, therefore, which existed in their own right and which had been effectively divorced from all connections with human beings, the sociologists substituted societies existing in and by themselves and societal progressions equally *sui generis* where cultures developed without any discernible intermediation of individuals.

In many ways the most consistent representative of the sociological approach was Bronislaw Malinowski. In direct contrast to Boas, he considered facts not to be objective realities which any properly trained student could recognize immediately and record, but to be derivative realities which were composed of the extensions and the larger meanings of what seemed to greet one's eye and which only the specially qualified observer could detect. The peoples whose beliefs and practices were being recorded were the very last ones to be interrogated as to the nature and meaning of what they were saying or doing.

With such an approach to the data it is clear that the role of the qualified observer was of predominant significance. In short, we are here at exactly the opposite pole from Boas, for whom the role of the observer had been reduced practically to zero.

It might have been expected that, where the observer played so vital a part in determining what was actually seen, attempts would be made at a critical appraisal of the observer. Yet this was the very last thing, apparently, that believers in the sociological approach ever deemed necessary. Nor has the necessity for such thorough and critical appraisal occurred to the members of the sociological school during its most recent phase, which has been so largely under the influence of Freudian and post-Freudian psychoanalytical thinking and of contemporary psychological and psychiatric techniques. Strangely enough, here it is the individuals being studied who have been subjected to this critical appraisal and not the observers making the study—the very ones of whom we need such a critical appraisal most.

The third of the positions mentioned above—namely, that anthropology is a no man's land open to everyone—presupposes, of course, that it is not a distinct discipline, that it is at best what the late Edward Sapir once called an "interim science." It is, I suspect, the most generally held of positions, though held by very few *professional* anthropologists. It represents a half-truth and is as dangerous and misleading as half-truths so frequently are. But this much can be said for it: those who hold it have never fallen into the errors inherent in either Boas's or Malinowski's point of view. Unfortunately it is academic philosophers who have chosen to roam this no man's land, most of them, in fact, philosophers who, whether they knew it or not, were under the influence of an oversimplified form of evolutionism. They studied aboriginal cultures as they typified a stage of cultural and societal evolution where individuals were still completely identified with the group and where differentiated logical thinking had as yet hardly emerged. The two great representatives of this school of thought are L. Lévy-Bruhl and E. Cassirer. Their influence, not only upon laymen but likewise upon anthropologists, has been profoundly mischievous and has only deepened the methodological morass in which academic anthropology finds itself today.

This brief survey of the history of anthropology during the last fifty years will perhaps explain why among so many critical-minded non-anthropologists there still exists considerable scepticism concerning the accuracy and adequacy of the anthropological record. In a sense the present preoccupation with methodological problems, especially during the last ten years, can be taken to reflect the unconscious awareness by anthropologists of this scepticism and criticism. So, too, possibly, we can explain the eagerness with which some have adopted and utilized the often highly tentative results of such shifting disciplines as psychology and psychiatry are today. This somewhat parasitic alliance with psychology and psychiatry has led anthropology nowhere and simply served to emphasize all its basic confusions. It must be so. These confusions will disappear only when anthropological practitioners take to heart what the great English legal historian Maitland cautioned them more than two generations ago. "By and by," he said, "anthropology will have to become either history or nothing."

It is at this point that we can properly return to Miss Oakes's book, for it is her recognition of this fact—namely, that anthropology is history—which explains many of the virtues of her description of the civilization of Todos Santos. She has assuredly not discovered a new method and she has not experimented with new techniques. What she has done is simply to go about the ordinary humdrum business of the historian, which is, by and large, to describe the activities, emotions, and thoughts of human beings, to remember that these are all set in a temporal framework, and never to permit man and his works to become objects in themselves.

The important thing in Miss Oakes's book, from the point of view of its methodological implications, is the fact that the author is not a trained historian and, indeed, makes no claims of being academically trained at all. If, as most of us believe, a proper, rigorous academic training is a prerequisite for good anthropological field-work, how are we to account for Miss Oakes's achievement? The answer must be that no academic training can give an individual historical insight or the ability to establish rapport with other individuals. The capacity to see things as a true historian sees them—that is, historical vision—appears to be something a person is born with. Proper academic training can improve and deepen this vision and make it more effective. It can do no more. Historical insight and vision are the *sine qua non* for all studies of culture, and the author of *The Two Crosses of Todos Santos* possesses both in a high degree, as we shall see. It is the absence of those qualities among so many contemporary anthropologists which has brought about the marked devitalization of their data. It has then led them to attempt, secondarily, to re-endow the human beings whom they have converted into marionettes with a new life by means of psychological techniques which in their hands have become, I cannot help but feel, something like abracadabra.

As I have just stated, the author of *The Two Crosses of Todos Santos* makes no claim to being an historian. Indeed she specifically tells us in her preface that she is not concerned with the historical questions her data raise. This disclaimer, fortunately, is completely belied by her results. Whether she is aware of it or not, her treatment is entirely historical, and she goes about her task as scholars who are deeply concerned with cultural-historical problems have done from time out of mind. Since we are dealing here both with a contribution of a challenging nature to our knowledge of a particular Indian culture and with an example of historical method applied in a highly individualistic manner, I am going to recapitulate the steps, conscious and unconscious, of her approach. Be it remembered, however, that what an observer of culture says he is doing and what he actually is doing are frequently two entirely different things. This holds true not only for Miss Oakes; it holds true for the overwhelming majority of anthropologists.

Miss Oakes seems to have begun her investigation by asking herself a number of questions, having first attempted to determine objectively what kind of questions could be answered. Asking questions is, of course, orthodox procedure. But Miss Oakes realizes that questions must not be asked as such and that one must be certain that the answers received are answers to the questions put. In historical investigations, such queries must be specific, and some preliminary tests must be made to determine the extent to which they can be answered. This is precisely what Miss Oakes did. She asked herself a specific question: What religious practices did the Mayan-speaking inhabitants of the interior of Guatemala observe during the years 1945–1947? Such a delimitation of the field of investigation is common practice among all contemporary sociologists and anthropologists. However, in contradistinction to other workers, Maud Oakes did not stop there. She immediately asked herself another question, one that it is imperative for all students of culture to put to themselves if they wish to obtain full and authentic answers to their queries: For what segment of the history of a people do the observed practices hold true?

Now, it is not a childish interest in chronology that prompts such a question nor is the second question separate and distinct from the first. It is actually contained in the first. And this is exactly what sociologists do not seem to understand. They seem to be under the strange misapprehension that all types of seriation are one and the same and that spatial distribution has the same validity—is, in fact, the same thing—as temporal sequence. When they contend that the insistence upon investigating the past while studying the present is but a form of antiquarianism, they are either confusing history with the scissors-and-paste historians (who really are simple annalists or antiquarians) or assuming that there exists a sociological reality independent of and not based upon an historical reality. What such a position leads to we all know. In the last analysis, all the great proponents of this viewpoint, Durkheim,

Pareto, Mannheim, Lévy-Bruhl, Max Weber, have been forced to take refuge in some form of subjective idealism where they are effectively protected from the disturbing propinquity of a factual record.

But to return to the author of *The Two Crosses of Todos Santos.* Having answered her second question (to the effect that the present-day practices of the Mayan shamans in Central Guatemala represent the essentially uncontaminated continuation of a pre-Spanish, pre-Christian tradition), she proceeded, by visiting a number of villages, to determine objectively where in Central Guatemala this pre-Spanish tradition has been preserved most faithfully.

Such provisional and premature assumptions are inherently quite dangerous unless one is prepared, if necessary, to abandon them when they are not subsequently proved by facts. Yet wrong hypotheses are at their worst possibly better than none at all, if they subsume some of the facts and if the observer is intellectually equipped to make them.

Miss Oakes was so equipped both because of her natural gifts and because of three years of experience studying the religion of the Navaho Indians. How well she understood both the nature and limitations of her hypothesis is best proved by the fact that, as far as I can detect, it did not lead to a subjectively determined selection of the data, which is, of course, always the great danger. For her, apparently, an hypothesis was simply a question or a series of questions which she wished to have answered and which served as a spur for intensifying her search for facts and their interpretations. In other words, it is not something which must be proved at all costs. Here, I must admit, her lack of the usual academic training was an asset. Had she possessed it, it might have proved her ruin, since her hypothesis, the assumption that the religion of Todos Santos was basically uncontaminated by Christian influence, was not correct. However, inasmuch as she used her hypothesis as she did and knew nothing about subordinating her data to a theory, the harm done by postulating the uncontaminated persistence of a pre-Spanish Mayan culture in Todos Santos was relatively slight.

It may offend some of us that in her presentation Miss Oakes never removes her scaffolding, so to speak, but this is at worst an artistic blemish. Besides, it is not only refreshing but methodologically instructive to be shown how a person who has never been taught the academic art of hiding his method of workmanship actually proceeds day by day.

We now come to the heart of Miss Oakes's method, which is something that concerns all anthropologists, namely, the manner in which she established contact with the inhabitants of Todos Santos in order to procure the specific type of information she was seeking.

Now, the techniques employed by anthropological field-workers to establish rapport with aboriginal peoples must, from the very nature of the situations encountered, be highly individualistic. They are certainly not amenable to precise formulation. It has consequently been argued by some scholars, and with a certain degree of justice, that since this is so, and since so much depends upon the personality of the observer, objectivity of recording is practically impossible. To reduce the degree of error which is presumed to be inevitable under such conditions, many field-workers have recourse to the numerous projective techniques devised by psychologists. In short, instead of attempting to discover how much the observer's personality interferes with his understanding of the facts he is recording and of his method of recording them, and instead of learning how to make allowances for it, they reduce the role of the observer to a bare minimum. This is again, of course, a typical sociological approach, and it ends, characteristically, by devitalizing both the cultures investigated and the investigators. Whatever the anthropologists addicted to this approach are doing, it is clear that they are not describing culture.

Fortunately the number of such extremists is small. For good or ill, in anthropology, the personality of the observer and his method of establishing contact with the peoples he is studying will always be the determining factors in the record he will procure. It is of importance and value, therefore, to be able to examine the impingement of a personality upon a group. The opportunity to do so is rarely vouchsafed us. In the case of Miss Oakes, however, we possess it. She tells us with remarkable frankness, in her preface, how she went about her work. Her technique is a combination of procedures every academic anthropologist is taught to use and of others that, on the face of it, should have led to disaster both for her work and for herself. Yet not only did these unorthodox procedures not lead to disaster but they enabled her to obtain data on the Mayan culture of Guatemala that, up till then, had been completely hidden from us.

Miss Oakes began by taking note of the antagonism and ill will existing between the *ladinos* and the Indians and throwing in her lot with the latter. Indeed, she ostentatiously isolated herself from the former, with the exception of one person. Now, the tendency of most ethnologists is to keep clear of such situations, for they are always dangerous. I was faced with a similar one among the Winnebago and I spent most of my time trying to prevent just such a taking of sides—quite unsuccessfully, I might add. Yet I feel certain today that nothing was gained thereby and that Miss Oakes's procedure was the more correct. She made her decision, it would seem, on the basis of a careful weighing of the facts for and against, and of a personal liking for the Indians and a general dislike of the *ladinos* and what they stood for. Yet that her unusual success with the Indians was due to the external procedure of living apart from the *ladinos* and of letting the Indians realize she disliked the *ladinos* I for one very much doubt. It was due primarily to only one factor—who she was.

That she did not "spy" upon the Indians when they were performing their sacred rites, that she did not frequent their sacred places, that she took no photographs without their permission, that she always treated them with courtesy (that is, as equals, humanly speaking)—all this is accepted academic anthropological technique. It is simply common sense and can be learned. Whether, however, success is due in any large measure to the observance by field-workers of such procedures is another matter. I have known observers who disregarded them and obtained excellent material and others who observed them scrupulously and were entirely unsuccessful.

Miss Oakes is much closer to explaining her success when she states that she let her instinct guide her. Here we are once more within the domain where intangible factors determine. But it is just these intangible factors that, in the last analysis, decide whether one is or is not a good field-worker. Instinct is manifestly not the satisfactory term to be used here. What we are actually dealing with is an emotional and intellectual awareness of individuals and of situations, an awareness which is somehow unconsciously communicated and which then evokes a sympathetic response. There must be a reciprocal relationship. Not only does one select; one is selected. The one without the other produces inadequate results.

It is the fatal error of many observers, to the serious detriment of their work, that they fail to realize this. Either they convince themselves that they are selecting their informants, and then always remain on a superficial plane, with only an external relationship to the cultures they are describing; or they convince themselves that *they* are being selected, and they then are overwhelmed by the data and become mystically inarticulate. Where the relationship is recognized as reciprocal, however, both dangers are warded off, for it is the psychological characteristic of this relationship that both observer and observed maintain their individuality and yet become emotionally and intellectually involved. Only observers given to critical self-analysis are likely to recognize that a true rapport has been established. For most observers it is suddenly there, and attempts are then made to explain it.

This is precisely what Miss Oakes has done. After stating, for instance, what care she had taken in the planning of her approach to the Indians, she tells us that the two most important factors in establishing her relationship of trust and friendship with them were quite unplanned. One was her asking her Indian maid to eat with her, the other her taking upon herself the role of village doctor during an epidemic. Now, however important these two events may have been in deepening and extending her contact, it is evident that that contact had been actually established before either had taken place. One can be reasonably certain that had it not already existed her role as village doctor might have proved catastrophic for her work.

What personal traits, intellectual and temperamental, an observer must possess to enable him to establish the desirable relationship with those being observed possibly only the latter, if anyone, can properly tell us. However, a few things seem clear. First, as I have already insisted, we must accept the fact that no academic training can give it to us. Nor is it a reflection upon the worth or the intellectual attainments of an observer if he is unable to establish such a contact. It is only a warning that he should actually be doing something else. Few observers, quite naturally, can accept such a rejection; most, though rejected, continue quite bravely and doggedly with their work. Their monographs, how-ever, indicate only too clearly what serious handicaps they are working under. The second thing to be pointed out is that a correlation does seem to exist between the establishment of a proper contact and the possession by the observer of a number of specific traits: deep-rooted respect and affection for human beings, true humility in the presence of the task to be attempted, a clearly communicated purpose, dogged per-sistence in accomplishing it, and, finally, personal courage. Although I have enumerated these traits serially as though they were distinct and independent, actually they are closely interconnected. The first two I regard as basic. If one possesses these, the others will follow almost auto-matically.

Now, it so happens that Miss Oakes possesses those traits to an aston-ishing degree. Thus the conditions for her establishing contact with the inhabitants of Todos Santos were present from the very first moment she could communicate with them.

Miss Oakes set herself one of the most difficult of all tasks, the study of an esoteric religion. She felt herself, quite rightly, qualified for that task by her three years of experience studying the esoteric religion of the Navaho. The inquiry could be made, of course, only with the help of the accredited shamans, the *chimanes,* of Todos Santos. The question which then presented itself was, How was she to proceed? Had she been more egotistic and less humble in her attitude toward her work she would have attempted to contact these *chimanes* directly. That would have been the ideal thing to do. She convinced herself quickly, however, that this was impossible and that an intermediary was essential. She selected one, a non-Indian, a *ladino,* with whom the Indians were on exceptionally good terms and who worked for her. This should have made her task doubly difficult. She herself realized the dangers this presented—fortunately for her, not all the dangers. In her almost obsessive fear that she might lose the goodwill of those Indians with whom she had established a friendly relationship, she did everything in her power to disguise the fact that her intermediary was putting questions to the *chimanes* that she herself was afraid to put to them. She seems to feel that she succeeded in disguising this tactic.

I am afraid that here she is labouring under a complete delusion. That the *chimanes* who answered her intermediary's questions felt it advisable to convey the impression that they were unaware that Don Pancho really was an intermediary in Miss Oakes's behalf, and that they behaved so, I do not doubt. The whole thing was manifestly a fiction. Actually the *chimanes* were answering the questions because they knew they were Miss Oakes's, and because she specifically was involved. I feel quite confident that they would not otherwise have answered them.

Nevertheless all Miss Oakes's precautions were not only advisable but essential for her success. The information she was seeking could probably have been obtained only by having recourse to just such a fiction, namely, by pretending that she was not asking the *chimanes* any questions and they were not answering any. Here Miss Oakes was really letting her instinct guide her, as do all good anthropologists. Apparently it is difficult for an anthropological observer to believe that his success is due to the impact of his personality upon other people and not upon some carefully thought out programme.

However, I do not wish to convey the impression that personality, historical vision, and such natural gifts are the only requirements for good and penetrating anthropological field-work. One should, in addition, possess specific knowledge which can be acquired only by directed education. It is the failure of gifted amateurs to recognize this that so frequently vitiates their results. It is, for instance, dangerous in the extreme to study religion and religious organization as such without a thorough knowledge of its interconnection with the economic and political organization. If Miss Oakes has not fallen into serious errors here it is because she knew the dangers and permitted this aspect of the culture of Todos Santos to be described by the Indians themselves.

The same holds true for the extent of Spanish and Christian penetration. It is quite evident that the religion of the Indians of Todos Santos, like that of all Indians of the Latin-American countries, is a blend of old and new. To a real understanding of the type of blend it is, no natural gifts can help. One must have knowledge, very specific knowledge, which takes years to acquire. Miss Oakes sensed this and has given a symbolical expression of it in her magnificent prologue. But an historian demands more.

In conclusion a few words are perhaps necessary about the manner in which Miss Oakes has chosen to present her information. It consists of a series of vivid pictures crowded with people and events intimately connected with herself. This is a method of presentation definitely taboo in professional circles because, with some justification, it is generally associated with authors of romantic proclivities who are attempting to give an account of their own strictly personal adventures. But Miss Oakes is, most emphatically, not a romanticist. There is no trace of romanticism in her book. Being an artist, she has instinctively given her account something of the form of a drama.

Such a presentation has its recompenses and Miss Oakes shows what these are. She shows that they can be united with close observation and historical penetration of a quality that the average anthropologist might well emulate.

PAUL RADIN

# PREFACE

THE MATERIAL of this book was collected during a stay of seventeen months in the Mam[1] village, or pueblo, of Todos Santos Cuchumatán,[2] in the Cuchumatanes Mountains of northwest Guatemala. (*See map, p. 18.*) I lived there from November 20, 1945, to April 20, 1947, though I had made two previous visits, in August and in October of 1945. My purpose was to gather what material I could on the practices of the shaman-priests or, in Mam, *chimanes;* I was not concerned with historical problems that the data might raise.

After visiting many villages in Guatemala, I finally chose Todos Santos, for the following compelling reasons:

1. The character of the Todos Santos Indians themselves.

2. The situation of the village: there were no roads to it, only trails, hence it was little touched by the machine age.

3. The fact that in the village there was no resident Catholic priest; a visiting priest came only a few times a year.

4. The fact that the Indians, to all intents and purposes, still carried on their ancient religious practices and used the Mayan calendar.

My original idea had been to incorporate all I obtained in one book, consisting of a day-by-day account and of the ethnological data. On the completion of the work, however, I realized that my material was much too diversified, and so I have written two books: this one, which contains all the ethnological material and is intended more for the specialized student; and a second, in preparation, containing the day-by-day

---

[1] The Indians of Todos Santos and the area round about are Mames, descendants of one of the Mayan peoples. In their language, *mam* means "grandfather" or "ancestor."

[2] Recinos gives (pp. 185–86) an excellent description of Todos Santos. (For full references, see Bibliography.)

record of my life at Todos Santos and only the most relevant ethnological material.[2a]

Knowing the ill will and antagonism that existed between the Indians and the *ladinos*,[3] I chose a house apart from the latter, so that I was surrounded by Indian neighbours only. I made it my policy to acquire no close friends among the *ladinos* except Francisco Palacios (Don Pancho) and his wife, the village schoolmistress.

In my investigation I made a point of never spying on the Indians when they were making *costumbre*[4] and of not visiting their sacred places too often. After I moved into the village I never took a photograph without their permission and never put questions to them unless I could do it in a natural way. I tried to let my instinct guide me in my relations with the Indians. I was particularly careful always to receive them with courtesy when they called at my house.

My work was made possible by a grant from the Bollingen Foundation, which generously put no time limit on my investigations. This freedom proved most valuable, for I feel that in a project of this kind one should never be pressed for time. If one is pressed, the Indian feels it and is apt to shut the door when one comes or give misinformation.

After working three years with the Navaho Indians of New Mexico, I learned that one must have patience, infinite patience, and that one must wait for what one wants till the opportune time comes. I must admit that at times I almost gave up hope.

Two things that happened without any planning on my part helped me to establish a basis of trust and friendship with the Indians. First, I asked my Indian maid to sit at table with me. This scandalized the *la-*

2a *Beyond the Windy Place* (New York: Farrar, Straus, 1951).

3 *Ladino:* "In Guatemala, a person of Spanish language and culture as contrasted with one who follows Indian ways of life."—Redfield, p. 392. The Indians call themselves *ine* when speaking in Mam to one another, *naturales* when speaking to outsiders; they call alien white persons *gringos,* though without the derogation that term has in other parts of Latin America. I, of course, was a *gringa.*

4 "*Costumbre* means literally 'custom.' It is used in Santiago Chimaltenango and throughout this region [which includes Todos Santos], to mean prayer, ritual, ceremony, etc."—Wagley, 1941, p. 16, footnote.

*dinos.* My Indian friends told me later that this action of mine made an impression on them and, at the same time, made them curious about me.

Second, for a considerable period of time, I was the village "doctor," helping *ladinos* as well as Indians.[5] Within a year of my arrival—by October and November of 1946—I was treating and dispensing medicine to an average of four hundred people a month, though admittedly this was during an epidemic. I had to make frequent trips by horse to visit those too sick to come to me. As "doctor" I gained an entrée that nothing else could have given me, not only into the homes but into the esoteric side of life as well, for I came to be considered a *chimán*. Indeed, in December, 1946, I was accused of being both a *bruja,* or sorceress, and a *dueña de cerro.*[6] This reduced the number of my patients by half and was rather an uncomfortable experience, but it brought me information I otherwise might not have obtained.

There were two other bits of good fortune: first, in March, 1946, I attended and participated in a Year Bearers Ceremony (a survival of an ancient Mayan ceremony) held near Santiago Chimaltenango, which gave me information that was invaluable for later work; and second, a neighbour and friend whom I had cured of an eye infection was elected Alcalde Rezador, or Chief Prayermaker, for 1947.

After I had been in Todos Santos for a few months, I realized that the religious organization of the community, together with the *chimanes,* constituted a group that was esoteric not only to the *ladinos* and me but to the ordinary Indians as well. To establish contact with them without

[5] My only training in this role had been two years of volunteer work in the emergency ward and the operating room of a hospital some years ago and two Red Cross first-aid courses in 1940–41.

[6] A *dueño* or *dueña de cerro* ("mountain guardian or master or mistress") is a name the Mames give to a supernatural being or spirit supposed to dwell on the mountain, occasionally coming down to the village on supernatural business. There are *dueños* also for rocks, springs, rivers, and other natural formations. The *dueños* of other parts of Guatemala are considered dangerous and even evil. The "masters" can be male or female (the volcano Tajumulco has a *dueña*), and the latter are supposed to be golden-haired and fair-skinned and to ride a white horse. In a general way, the description suited me and my horse and contributed to the idea that I was a *dueña*. For a discussion of *dueños,* see pp. 74 ff.

17

losing the confidence and friendship I was slowly gaining among the Indians would, I realized, be difficult. I decided that my only course was to have an informant who could ask questions I myself did not want to ask for fear of losing the entrée I had so painstakingly gained. This informant would work in such a way that the Indians would not suspect his connection with me. I realized that the ideal person was Don Pancho, the only *ladino* liked and respected by the Indians. He, also, treated the sick, and he sold medicine.[7] He was already giving me lessons in Spanish conversation, and our conferences need not arouse suspicion. I explained to him the nature of my general project, which I was keeping secret, and told him that I would, on occasion, need an informant. He offered at once to accept this role, and without pay. I insisted on paying him, however, because he was poor and because I felt guilty for taking his patients away from him. (I not only took away his patients, in fact, but treated them and gave them medicine for nothing.) Don Pancho was the only one of my informants whom I paid.

I present my material exactly as the Indians gave it to me, for I feel that I can so give a true insight into their character.

With certain exceptions, I wrote down none of the information in the presence of my informants but always immediately after they had departed. I knew if they saw me writing they would become suspicious and would probably stop the natural flow of conversation. The exceptions are the lists of names, the Mam words (in this case my writing was understood, for all knew I was trying to learn their language), the days of the calendar and their interpretation, and the prayers recorded by Don Pancho.

[7] Don Pancho was a rare thing among the *ladinos* I met—a man of genuine goodwill toward the Indians. His wife, the schoolmistress, was blessed with the same virtue. Don Pancho had formerly lived in Huehuetenango and had a very little income from a piece of property there (a house, rented out as a saloon). He had hoped to study medicine and when his career was frustrated he had read widely in medical literature. He had drifted from one job to another—Army officer, policeman, *aguardiente* dealer during fiesta season—and when I knew him had no job other than his haphazard "practice" among the Indians.

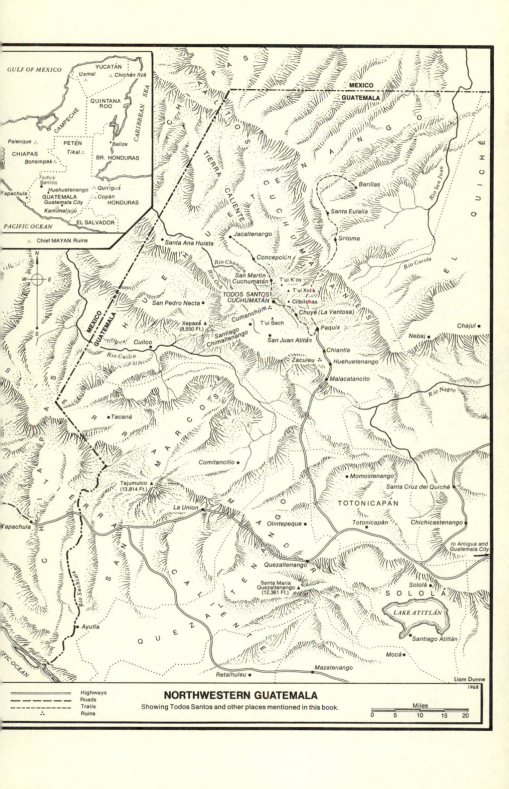

**NORTHWESTERN GUATEMALA**

Showing Todos Santos and other places mentioned in this book.

Miles
0 5 10 15 20

Highways
Roads
Trails
Ruins

Liam Dunne
1968

# INDIAN INFORMANTS

1. DOMINGO CALMO, *chimán* and *principal*. He was about seventy years old. He and the following two *chimanes* were the most important ones of the village, with the exception of the Chimán Nam, who was the calendar priest of the village. Domingo was a man of great intelligence and dignity, and spoke Spanish fluently. He was both respected and feared in the community, for, as it proved later, he was a *brujo* as well as a *chimán*. Outwardly he became a good friend to me, for I treated his deafness and cured his wife of a skin infection. But he was wary about giving me information.

2. RAFAEL CALMO, *chimán* and *principal*. (Not related to Domingo Calmo.) He had been Alcalde Municipal twice. He was about eighty years old, intelligent and cunning. He, too, was both respected and feared for he was even more of a *brujo* than Domingo Calmo. His Spanish was not fluent. He gave information to Don Pancho but not to me because he felt I was even more of a *bruja* than he a *brujo*.

3. PASCUAL PABLO, *chimán*. He was about seventy-five years old, a very intelligent man of great dignity. He was the only *chimán* who dressed in the *ladino* manner. He had the reputation of being a good man and was much respected in the community. He spoke Spanish, but not fluently.

4. PONCIANO RAMÍREZ, known as Tata Julián, Alcalde Rezador (Chief Prayermaker). He was about seventy-five years old, and had once been Alcalde Municipal. He was extremely intelligent and spoke Spanish fluently. He had attended high school for a year and a half in Guatemala City. He had the reputation of being an upright man and was greatly respected. He possessed both dignity and a sense of humour, and was a real friend and a willing talker. (*See plates 10 and 12.*)

5. ROSA BAUTISTA, midwife and *pulsera*. She was about sixty years old, the sister of El Rey, Macario Bautista (see below). Rosa, known as a good woman and greatly respected by the community, had considerable

19

intelligence and a sense of humour. Because her father and her brother were calendar priests and both her husbands had been *chimanes,* she had an amazing amount of ceremonial information. She became my good friend, and talked freely. (*See plate 9.*)

6. DOMINGO CALMO, my *mozo.* (Not related to the *chimán* of the same name.) He was thirty-eight years old, a good story-teller, intelligent, but in certain ways extremely childish. He was good-humoured, willing, honest, and a faithful friend. He interpreted for me with non-Spanish-speaking Indians. (*See plates 6 and 7.*)

7. PATRONA, wife of Domingo and half-sister of Rosa and Macario Bautista. She possessed great ceremonial information, was a very faithful friend, and talked freely. Her Spanish was not fluent. (*See plate 7.*)

8. BASILIA ELÓN, my servant. She was twenty-two years old, intelligent, and spoke Spanish fluently. She had a sense of humour and proved to be a good friend. However, she was more interested in *ladino* than in Indian ways, and had two *ladino* lovers. (*See plate 8.*)

9. MARGARITA ELÓN, my neighbour. (Not related to Basilia Elón.) She was the wife of Satero, a well-known dancer and the richest man in Todos Santos—he was the only Indian *finca* (plantation) agent, and also was a butcher. These were the only neighbours with whom I had difficulties. Both were materialistic and ruthless in their dealings with their fellow Indians. They were at the same time respected and hated by the community. Both had a great deal of ceremonial information. (*See plate 22a.*)

10. MACARIO BAUTISTA, Chimán Nam and calendar priest, known as "El Rey." He was reputed to be one hundred and ten years old and was almost blind. He was the most respected man in Todos Santos. He was friendly to me but reticent. (*See plate 11.*)

I should like to mention briefly the following Indians who also were helpful: Manuel Pablo, a very good friend; Abelino Ramírez, a *principal,* a very old man, very friendly and talkative; Victor Pablo, a very old man, who had been Alcalde Municipal, very friendly; Pascual Carillo, very friendly. At Santiago Chimaltenango there were Manuel Andrés, a *chimán,* about sixty-five years old, who lived in a section called Florida, and though he spoke no Spanish, was most friendly; and Catalina Aguilar, the only woman *chimán* I met, who spoke little Spanish but was friendly. In San Juan Atitán there was the *chimán* Pedro Pérez: he knew little Spanish, was ninety years old, was (I was told) the calendar priest of the village, and was friendly but cautious.

The *ladinos* I should like to mention are Francisco Palacios, called Don Pancho; his wife, Ester; and José Miguel del Valle y de Castillo, postal official, telegraph operator, and a lover of my maid Basilia.

.     .     .

Both to Gerstle Mack and to Paul Radin I owe grateful acknowledgment for editing the manuscript, and to the latter for advice and suggestions. To Maria Matheu and to Antonio Goubaud Carrera, director of the National Indian Institute of Guatemala, I am indebted for invaluable help at the outset of my work in Guatemala and for their continued interest and encouragement.

Maud Oakes

*Big Sur, Spring, 1950*

NOTE

For the paperback printing, minor corrections have been made, and a new map of Northwestern Guatemala has been supplied.

## NOTE ON THE LANGUAGE

This is not offered as a linguistic study, but I have recorded the Mam words to the best of my ability. My ear, however, is untrained. Following is a list of the letters I use whose pronunciation differs from English.

### CONSONANTS

| | |
|---|---|
| j | as *ch* in German *ich* |
| x | as *sh* in English *shut* |
| ch' | as *ch* in English *chalk*, glottalized |
| k' | as English *k*, glottalized |
| t' | as English *t*, glottalized |

### VOWELS

| | |
|---|---|
| e | as in English *re* (the musical note) |
| i | as in English *mi* (the musical note) |

The Spanish words follow the customary American-Spanish pronunciation.

# *PROLOGUE*

*In front of the church at Todos Santos stand two crosses, one tall and commanding in appearance, made of ancient wood,[1] the other short and squat, made of stones and adobe, whitewashed. The candle drippings and ashes show that much* costumbre *has taken place here and it is the same at Cumanchúm, the ruins above the village, where there are two similar, smaller crosses.*

*The two crosses symbolize the Indian and the* ladino. *A year had to pass before I learned from Tata[2] Julián, the Chief Prayermaker, the story that lay behind them. This is the story as he told it:*

You ask me, Señorita, why there are two crosses in front of the church here and the ruins at Cumanchúm. This is why.

Six or eight years ago, before I was Chief Prayermaker, there was only one cross in front of the church here and only one at Cumanchúm. This was when the *ladino* Armando Palacios was Intendente of this pueblo. One day he gave an order to pull down the old cross, the tall one of wood in front of the church, and to put up one of stone in its place. No one dared go against the orders of the Señor Intendente. But the Chief Prayermaker went to him and begged him not to pull down that cross, for it was the cross of our ancestors and belonged to them. Moreover, he told him, they wanted no cross of stone.

But the Intendente would not listen. The old cross here was pulled down and so was the one at Cumanchúm. They were cast aside, the one at the church among a pile of old wood. Then new crosses of stone were erected to replace them.

---

[1] In Mam, the cross is *nim cruz.* (*See plates 1, 13, and 15; for Tata Julián, plate 12.*)
[2] A Mam title of respect, also "Ta"; the feminine is "Na" or "Nana."

23

Soon after, a wind came up, and this wind never stopped. The weather became cold, very cold, the coldest in many years. The sheep died from lack of food. No rain fell and all the corn dried up. The women had to walk long distances to get their water.

The prayermakers thereupon went to the mountain tops to pray for rain. Yet no rain fell. Finally all the people went to the Chimán Nam and to the other *chimanes*[3] to do *costumbre* for rain. All the *chimanes* came together and asked their tables[4] why the *dueño de cerro* was punishing them, what sin they had committed to cause this lack of water. The *dueño* answered:

"You have cast down the big cross, the cross that was born long ago when Santo Mundo was born, the big cross that came with the creation of the world. For this that you have done you are now being punished. God has sent this, our Santo Mundo has given you this drought. Put the big cross up again in the same place. Otherwise all the people and all the animals will die."

Then the *chimanes* went in a group to the church, accompanied by a great many people. I was among them. We gathered together some wood that we found near the church to help brace the ancient cross when we would put it up. We were afraid that the Intendente Armando would suddenly appear. He was not there, but another *ladino* had taken his place.

"What are you doing?" he asked us.

"Nothing, Señor."

"You are about to use wood and I will have you put in prison if you do, for it is a crime to use wood without permission."

"Señor Intendente, the Intendente who was here before you pulled down the big cross. It is lying here in the grass, this cross, the one made of ancient wood. Señor Intendente, we have no water; the earth is dry; all the animals are dying. We *chimanes* asked the Spirit what sin we had

---

[3] A shaman-priest—literally, "ancestor" or "grandfather." In Mayan the word was *chilane*. The Chimán Nam is calendar priest of the pueblo.

[4] Each *chimán* owns a table, considered holy, which serves for casting the sacred beans of divination and as an altar.

24

committed to cause this lack of rain. 'You have cast down the ancient cross,' said the Spirit, 'that is the sin you have committed. Put it up again. Otherwise all the people and animals will die; all the corn will die and you will be without food.'

"That is why we *chimanes* and the people of the pueblo have come together. That is why we have collected this wood, for we are going to put up the cross, first making a good foundation for it. If you want to put us in prison, very well. But send us to Huehuetenango, for it is better there. If you imprison us, you will win and we will win. Send us to prison; we have no fear."

When the Intendente fully understood our words, he heeded and he said nothing. There were fifty *chimanes* there and over a hundred people. And so we put up the cross. In a short time the rain came, the village had water, and the people were contented. Our big and ancient cross directed us to put back the small one that had been thrown down at Cumanchúm. This we did. The stone crosses were left, however, and that is why we have two. An evil man is that Armando. But he will surely pay, little by little, for what he did. His house will burn down; he will lose all his money. God will assuredly punish him. One cannot quarrel with Tata Dios. He is great and he is strong. There is not a moment that Santo Mundo is not in command of everything.

*PART ONE*

# 1

## The Road to Todos Santos

THE MAM VILLAGE of Todos Santos Cuchumatán[1] lies eighty-two hundred feet above sea level in a valley of the Cuchumatanes Mountains, within the Department of Huehuetenango in northwest Guatemala. It is on the ancient trade route between Mexico and the town of Huehuetenango. (*See map, p. 18.*) In the outskirts of that town stand the ruins of Zaculeu, ancient religious centre of the Mames. Near Todos Santos also there are ruins, seemingly of the same period as those of Zaculeu.[2]

I travelled by bus from Guatemala City northwestward to the town of Huehuetenango. There are two routes onward to Todos Santos. One, a journey of about four hours, is by car to Paquix, a handful of houses on the plateau three thousand feet above Huehuetenango, thence by foot or horse to Todos Santos. The other, taking about eight hours, is by horse all the way.

The road from Huehuetenango to Paquix is amazingly beautiful. It climbs steeply upward until it reaches the windy plateau where the pitiful hamlet of Paquix is situated. Here the Indians grow potatoes and pasture their sheep. Everywhere the trees have been stunted and gnarled

---

[1] There are descriptions of the journey to Todos Santos as of the 1640's by Thomas Gage (p. 174) and as of the 1840's (a vivid one) by John L. Stephens (vol. 2, p. 235). (For full references, see Bibliography.)

[2] The excavation and restoration of Zaculeu have been done under the auspices of the United Fruit Company. In a pamphlet guide to the ruins of Zaculeu, Stanley H. Boggs says that "it is possible that Zaculeu, seemingly abandoned about the time of the Quiché conquest and still possessing a Quiché name, is actually the ancient Chinabahul [Xinabahul] of the Mames." Judging from the pottery found, the site goes back to the eighth to tenth centuries A.D. and was occupied up to the invasion of Pedro de Alvarado, in 1525. The results of the excavation are to be published by the United Fruit Company.

by the winds. Immense, strangely formed rocks dominate the landscape and cacti grow in profusion. Here I left the road, which continues northward, and I struck out on horseback along the trail.

From Paquix to the pass at Chuyé, called La Ventosa, "windy place," the trail mounts through a country of wind-blown trees and rarely a piece of good pasture land. Potatoes are grown but the earth is too poor for corn.

As one crosses the pass and starts down the canyon toward Todos Santos, the trail winds through tall masses of pines, firs, and hemlocks. In the spring and the rainy season, flowers are everywhere and noisy brooks rush to join the growing river of Todos Santos, or the Rio Chanjón. Higher up, the cleared land is seeded with potatoes and, farther down, corn. One sees numerous flocks of sheep and of goats and the corrals where at night they are protected from the coyotes that roam the mountains, and where also their droppings are preserved, to fertilize the potatoes.

As I was descending this trail on my first visit to Todos Santos, I snapped a photograph of an old shepherd who was climbing the trail with his sheep. I was immediately taught a lesson I did not forget, for he cried out, in an agonized voice, "What have you done to me?" He made me feel as if I had stuck a knife into him.

As the trail continues downward, the mountains rise higher and higher on each side, so that by the time one reaches the valley they tower above almost threateningly. There are corn fields on all sides, some climbing up seemingly impossible slopes. Stone walls grown with blackberries and elderberries line the trail.

Passing Indians ask where you are going and where you have come from. Their mules, and often the Indians too, are heavily loaded. Cattle and pigs are driven along the trail by *ladinos* coming from the lowlands to the Huehuetenango market.

Then the trail climbs a hill, and from its summit one sees the village of Todos Santos spread out below.

The trail passes through the centre of Todos Santos and is its main street. On it are the homes of the *ladinos* and the few *tiendas* or shops of the village. At its far end are the church and the covered market place, and opposite them the plaza, with its two *pilas* or fountains, and the *juzgado* or town hall, housing in one small room both post office and telegraph office. (*See plates 2 and 3.*) The rest of the village straggles up-hill toward the southwest, where the ruins of Cumanchúm are situated, or downhill toward the river.

Todos Santos is an attractive village, with its whitewashed houses and their high thatched roofs, Chinese in impression, in all the wonderful shades that straw turns as it weathers. The *juzgado*, church, and school, however, have tile roofs. Each plot of land is enclosed by stone walls or by fences of wood or of dried corn stalks. Everywhere, apple and peach trees sprawl over walls and fences. (*See plates 4 and 5.*)

The climate is most agreeable. There are two seasons: the dry season, called *verano*, summer, from mid November to mid April, and the rainy season, called *invierno*, winter. During December and January it can be very cold, so cold that ice forms in the *pilas*. Except for two dry periods, called *canículas* ("dog days"), in late July and August, it rains continuously during the winter—that is, from mid April to mid November.

# 2

## *The Mode of Life*

THE MAM INDIANS of Todos Santos are notably handsome and likeable people. Compared to other Maya groups of Guatemala, they are taller, finer featured, and their faces are more heavily bearded.[1] They possess a dignity and pride that seem almost arrogant. Though they are a conquered race, one is not conscious of it as with other Guatemalan Indians. They are hard-working, intelligent, good-humoured, kind, thoughtful, superstitious, childish. Essentially peaceable, occasionally they can become quarrelsome, and they will stand up for their own rights within reason. Outwardly friendly and well mannered, they are actually cautious, as they have every reason to be. As friends they are hospitable, generous, honest, loyal, trustworthy, and completely dependable.[1a] Being hard bargainers themselves, they have no respect for anyone who will not bargain. As enemies they can be sly and cunning and will go to any extreme.[2]

When they are drunk the Indians vacillate between joviality and

[1] To the Indians of Todos Santos beards signify wisdom. Morley (p. 21) says: "Indeed, beards and moustaches were held in such little esteem by the Mayans in ancient times that Maya mothers burned the faces of their young sons with hot cloths in order to keep their beards from growing. . . . Notwithstanding this practice, however, there is plenty of evidence both from the sculptures and the painted pottery of the Old Empire that beards, something like modern goatees, though longer, were worn; it has been suggested that the bearded figures in Old Empire reliefs were confined to the upper classes, the lower classes only being beardless."

[1a] Every Indian who had borrowed money from me paid me back in full before I left Todos Santos.

[2] La Farge, in *Santa Eulalia* (p. 16), notes "local enmity toward the Todos Santos Indians, and the latter's habit of waylaying and occasionally killing lone travelers. . . ." Further (p. 18), he states: ". . . the Mam settlements of San Martín and Todos Santos are regarded with outright hostility, partly on account of the depredations which the villagers have committed and their notoriously bellicose temperament."

melancholy. They all get drunk especially during fiesta time, and then they are willing to sign contracts to work on the coffee *fincas* or plantations, to will away their possessions, to do anything to buy just one more *trago,* one more drink. And while in this state they are preyed upon by the agents of the *fincas* and their touts, the *caporales.*

From the time they are children the Indians learn to hate the *ladinos* with a hate that smoulders but is rarely permitted to erupt. During my first year in Todos Santos, the Alcalde Municipal, an Indian, got very drunk one night. He walked up and down the main street of the pueblo, pounding his chest and exclaiming, "Today a *ladino* asked me for a horse to take him to Chiantla. I told him there were no horses. Actually there were horses. I, the Alcalde, told the *ladino* he could walk. And he walked." Tata Julián, the Chief Prayermaker, once said to me, "Señorita, I am an old man, I have lived all my life in this pueblo, but not once has a *ladino* given me anything, not even a cigarette." (Yet there were three instances of intermarriage in the village of Todos Santos, and in each case the Indian gave up the native dress for *ladino* clothes.)

My experience has been that the Indians do not class alien whites with the *ladinos.* They do not hate white people; they fear them. When I first came to the pueblo, the children, especially the girls, screamed with terror when they saw me coming and ran away. On one occasion, a boy of about ten said to me, "Is it true, Señorita, that you *gringos* kill people?"

My servant Basilia spoke in a similar strain. One day she said, "Señorita, is it true that if a *natural* went to your country, the people would slit his throat?" When I asked where she had heard such a thing, she answered, "All my life I have heard it." At another time, when I spoke of a friend who had died, she said, "Why, Señorita, I thought that no one died in your country." On questioning her, I found that Basilia thought that only *naturales* and some *ladinos* died.

This same belief in the mysterious powers of the *gringos* cropped up in a conversation just before I left Todos Santos. I was telling several older men that I was going to fly from Huehuetenango to Guatemala

City and that it would take only two hours. They asked me, as they had many times before, to describe the plane and tell how it was run. I told them about the pilot, and said that any man could learn to be one. "Most certainly not," was their reply. "Only a *gringo* could be a pilot; no *ladino*, no *natural*; only a *gringo*." In short, they are awed by us, they fear us, they look upon us in fact somewhat as *supernaturales*.[2a]

The basic unit of social organization in Todos Santos is the patriarchal family. Though the Indian's communal and family ties are equally strong, his feeling for his family is more specifically expressed. The oldest living male in the family is chief, owning the land and other property. His sons and nephews work for him, living on the family land whether single or married. If the sons have outside work they hand over their earnings to the chief just the same. The mother, while owning nothing, holds a position of great respect. The degree of authority and freedom she has depends on her intelligence. Old people are looked after with great care and treated with the utmost respect, for the Indians believe that with age comes wisdom, and with wisdom, authority.

The *municipio* or township containing the village is also called Todos Santos;[3] it comprises the pueblo or village of Todos Santos and seven *aldeas* or hamlets and has in all 6,400 inhabitants, of which 150 are *ladinos*. About half the *ladinos* live in the *aldea* of San Martín

---

[2a] The Indians believe that a stranger, *gringo* or otherwise, can cast evil by a look or a thought. Most of them cover a baby when a stranger appears, for fear that his gaze may harm the child.

[3] It is helpful to note La Farge's definitions in *S. E.* (p. xv): "*Tribes* generally, but not always, coincide with townships. They are units, speaking a common dialect, having a common ceremonial center, and recognizing a common loyalty as against all other neighboring groups. *Townships* are the Spanish *municipios,* to which our cognate, 'municipality,' does not apply so well as does the Anglo-Saxon term. They are the units of government and a subdivision under the department [i.e., of Huehuetenango, which in turn comes under the national government]. *Villages* (Spanish *pueblo*) are the recognized seats of government of townships containing the *juzgado* or town hall, jail, market, church, other governmental offices if any, and generally some slight concentration of population. The village gives its name to the township. *Aldeas* . . . are administrative subdivisions of townships."

Cuchumatán. The village of Todos Santos itself is divided into eight *cantones* or wards.[4] Todos Santos township has the following officials:

The Alcalde Municipal (formerly Intendente) or Mayor Municipal, who is also *juez de paz* or justice of the peace.
The *secretario* or secretary.
The *síndico* or syndic.[5]
The *tesorero* or treasurer.
Four *regidores* or councilmen.
The *comisario de la policía* or commissioner of police.
Six *policías* or policemen.
Twenty-two *auxiliares* or auxiliaries.
Thirty *mayores* or chiefs.

When I arrived in Todos Santos, in 1945, the Intendente, the *secretario,* and the *tesorero* were *ladinos,* appointed by the departmental authorities at Huehuetenango. In January, 1946, however, after a reform government took office at Guatemala City, the Indians were allowed to vote, and naturally they elected an Indian mayor, called the Alcalde Municipal. *Ladinos* remained as *secretario* and *tesorero.* The other offices were held by Indians.

In the more populous *aldeas* of Todos Santos township, the officials consisted of four *auxiliares* and four *mayores;* in the smaller *aldeas,* there were none, or only two or three of each.

All civil officials (other than those appointed) are elected for a year. The *principales,* the Chimán Nam, and the Alcalde Rezador—all religious dignitaries—decide who is to be put up for election except for the posts of *secretario* and *tesorero.* If an official does not execute his job

---

4 The figures are from the government census of 1946. "The town [Todos Santos] is composed of 250 houses, most of which are clustered together within about one square mile, although the municipality with its outlying settlements covers about 59,044 acres. As San Martín Cuchumatán has recently been reduced from the status of a pueblo to a mere *aldea* of Todos Santos, its 9,071 acres give a total of 68.145 acres to the municipality of Todos Santos Cuchumatán."—Stadelman, p. 101. For details of village organization, see the Appendix, p. 239.
5 A kind of business manager for the pueblo. A Spanish-speaking Indian held the post while I was in Todos Santos. It was probably an appointive office, though unfortunately I did not learn much about it.

35

properly he can be dismissed by the local or the Huehuetenango government. Early in 1947, the Huehuetenango authorities removed the Indian who was Alcalde Municipal because of his drinking and inefficiency.

The Alcalde Municipal receives a salary of thirty dollars a month,[6] and besides his civil duties he has ritual obligations which he carries out under the direction of the Chimán Nam. The *auxiliares* and the *mayores* (*see plate 20*) donate their services, as it is taken for granted that, once elected, it is their duty to the community to serve. Their responsibilities do not entail daily work. They all take turns in alternate weeks. Their position enables them to make a little money on the side selling wood and fodder to travellers and carrying messages.

The language spoken by the Indians is Mam, one of the languages of the Mayan stock.[7] Most of the Indian men also speak Spanish; they have to, for Spanish is essential to their work as traders. Few of the Indian women speak Spanish, though all of them know a few words. Most of the *ladinos* speak Mam; it is commercially useful for them to.

In the pueblo there are two schools, nominally under government supervision, one for boys and one for girls. In 1947, a small school was opened in the *aldea* of El Rancho. Indians and *ladinos* attend the same school. The teachers are *ladinos* and instruction is in Spanish only. School is supposed to be compulsory, but, while most *ladino* children attend, I should guess that less than one quarter of the Indian children do. There are two grades, and the children have no more than started to learn how to read and write when they stop and their schooling is

[6] The Guatemalan quetzal (containing 100 centavos) = the U. S. dollar. For simplicity, I use U. S. values in this book.

[7] "More than one hundred thousand Indians occupy this Highland region [Cuchumatanes Mountains]; a few *ladinos* . . . also live in each village. . . . All of these Indians speak languages of the Mayan stock; Mam, Chuj, and Chanabal (Jacalteco) languages are represented."—Wagley, 1941, p. 7. See also Recinos, p. 123. Morley (p. 17) gives an excellent table showing classifications, distribution, and numbers of people in the Mayan linguistic stock.

over. Occasionally a *ladino* and very infrequently an Indian may go on to a higher school in one of the larger towns.[8]

Aside from a game not unlike American marbles which the boys play with adobe or beeswax discs the size of a fifty-cent piece, neither children nor adults have organized games of any kind. The dancing and racing at fiesta time, however, have a little of the character of games.

The Indians have only a few sources of income: to work for a *ladino*, perhaps as a farm worker or porter; to go to the *tierra caliente*—the "hot country," the land below twenty-five hundred feet,[9] to the east or south —and work on a coffee *finca;* to become a *caporal* or handyman for a *finca* agent. *Caporales* are paid twelve dollars a month and have to be on constant call. Their chief function is that of tout, to entice fellow Indians to sign contracts to work on a *finca*. To hire *finca* hands, there were ten agents in the pueblo of Todos Santos. One of them was an Indian, my neighbour Satero, husband of Margarita. Satero earned fifty dollars a month. If agents conscript more labour than is expected, they are paid more.

In 1946, for work on a *finca,* under contract, an Indian was paid one dollar a week plus corn for food and a hut in which to sleep. He usually came home with malaria, tropical ulcers, dysentery, or venereal disease. An Indian working at home on his own can sell potatoes, corn, wood, or corn stalks. If he has a mule he can get more for his potatoes and corn by taking them to Huehuetenango or Quezaltenango. He can also hire out his mule's services. For taking a mule-load of cargo to Huehuete-nango, for instance, a man is paid one dollar and twenty cents. This is a trip of about eight hours each way. The round trip involves two days, and the Indian has to pay for not only his own food but his mule's fodder as well. The price to Chiantla is one dollar. For labour in the field or around the house, a man is paid fifteen to twenty cents a day. For work

---

[8] As to the Indians' attitude toward education, see the conversations with my neighbours given in the Appendix, p. 240.

[9] According to Recinos (p. 52), below 760 metres elevation. (For an example of how the *finca* system of labour recruitment works, see the Appendix, p. 241.)

as a porter—carrying cargo on his back—he is paid fifteen to thirty cents a day, depending on the load.

Every male Indian in the village and the *aldeas* has to contribute to the community from one to two weeks of free labour or its equivalent in money each year. The work usually consists of repairing the roads and trails. The *ladinos* give no free work or money.

The Indian women of Todos Santos rarely take work outside the home. Occasionally a *ladino* family—and one prosperous Indian I knew of, Margarita Elón—may hire a maidservant. A maidservant's wages are sixty cents a month, in addition to two meals a day and an apron. She sleeps out and has to pay for her own clothes. (Material for a blouse costs around four dollars and a half, a skirt two dollars and a quarter, a belt two dollars. So it is just a vicious circle.) A maid's work starts early in the morning. For sixty cents a month, she cooks, grinds the corn for *tortillas*, carries water from the *pila*, cleans the house, washes the clothes.

Most Indian houses are made of adobe bricks, though some are built of boards. The roofs are thatched and are pitched extremely high. Each family has its own sweat-bath—a stone and adobe hut in the yard, large enough for two—and each person uses it at least twice a week. The typical Indian house contains one room. Well-to-do Margarita Elón had but one room, though she had a second little *house* in her yard. (*See plates 4 and 5*.) A new house is always blessed by the family's *chimán*, although once I witnessed the blessing of a house by the visiting Catholic priest.

The costume of the Todos Santos Indians is one of the most picturesque of Guatemala. The men's red-and-white-striped cotton trousers have earned them the name "Uncle Sam's Boys" in tourist circles. They wear warm woolen coats of several kinds, most notably the long black *capixaij*. The women dress almost entirely in cotton. Most of the woolen and cotton cloth is woven in the village—the woolen used to be all woven

38

by the men though nowadays most of it is imported, as are straw hats and sandals.[10]

The Indians of Todos Santos subsist mostly on corn, beans, and potatoes. In addition they eat the squash called *chilacayote,* apples, and peaches. Meat is a luxury. On the rare special occasions when it is served, it is likely to be sheep, goat, pig, turkey, or chicken. The Indians drink much coffee, sweetened with *panela,* an unrefined brown sugar. They also drink much *atole,* a beverage made of ground corn added to boiling water, which is often carried on journeys by the men.[11] *Bebida,* one of the ceremonial drinks, delicious and very rich, is made of ground corn, ground cacao, and *panela,* stirred into boiling water.[12] *Batido,* another ceremonial drink, is made without cacao but is richer than *atole.* The local intoxicant is *aguardiente,* a powerful[13] brandy made from sugar cane. Wine or other alcoholic drinks are little known to the Indians. The *ladinos* also drink what is called "coyote beer," and occasionally soda pop.

The Indian's life depends upon corn. He believes that the gods control both the weather and the fate of the corn. To ensure the corn's proper growth, prayers and offerings to the gods are as important as the

[10] For a detailed description of the Todos Santos costume, see the Appendix, p. 242. (Several of the plates depict the Indian dress vividly.)

[11] According to Friar Diego de Landa (p. 34), the second Spanish bishop of Yucatán, who in 1566 set down a remarkable record of Mayan life before and after the Spanish conquest, the same beverage was drunk and was carried along by travellers in ancient times. (As for Landa, Gates says in the introduction of *Yucatan Before and After the Conquest* [pp. iii, iv] that the Bishop's position in history "rests upon two of his acts, one the writing of [this] book . . . and the other the famous Auto da fé of July 1562 at Maní, at which, in addition to some 5,000 'idols,' he burned as he tells us twenty-seven hieroglyphic rolls, all he could find but could not read, as 'works of the devil,' designed by the evil one to delude the Indians and to prevent them from accepting Christianity when it should in time be brought to them. . . . He burned ninety-nine times as much knowledge of Maya history and sciences as he has given us in his book.")

[12] Cf. ibid., p. 34: "Out of maize and ground cacao they make a sort of froth that is very delicious and with which they celebrate their festivals."

[13] I do not know the proof, but the effect is hair-raising. The tax on *aguardiente* is an important source of revenue for the Guatemala government.

seeding itself.[14] Every available plot of land in the village is planted to corn. The greater portion of the land owned by the Indians lies outside the village, mostly to the east or between Todos Santos and San Martín, which is corn land, or in the district around La Ventosa, where only potatoes are grown.

In the past the Indians were self-sufficient; today they are not. The soil is wearing out, they are losing their land to the *ladinos*, and the cost of living goes always higher.

[14] Stadelman, p. 123; Wagley, 1941, p. 43. For a legend on the origin of corn, see the Appendix, p. 244.

# 3

## From Birth to Death

WHEN A WOMAN believes she is pregnant she goes to a midwife to have her belief confirmed. (*See plate 9.*) Then husband and wife go to their *chimán*, or send for him. The *chimán* prays for the woman and child-to-be at three places—at the cross outside the church, at Cumanchúm, and at his own table. The husband and wife go to the church with candles. During her period of pregnancy the woman should go to the church with her candles every fifth day. Husband and wife should go there every twentieth day, on the day named *k'mané*, taking their candles with them.

When labour pains commence the midwife is called in. She usually attempts, not always accurately, to foretell the baby's sex. She usually rubs the mother's belly with camphor and vaseline, or some other form of grease. Often she gives the woman herbs to drink which facilitate delivery. If the woman has a difficult time the *chimán* is summoned. He calls on his gods or beseeches San Francisco on Santa Lucía to take care of the woman and begs them that death be warded off. He promises that when she is well she will carry a flower to the church. Then he prays that the baby may have a long life and promises that, twenty days after its birth, the new mother will carry a flower to the church for the saints or gods.

When it is time for the baby to be born the midwife tells the husband and other male members of the family to wait outside. After delivery, the navel cord is cut and wrapped in a special cloth and kept. The afterbirth is carefully destroyed. The baby is bathed in warm water and

41

wrapped in clean cloths. The midwife massages the woman's belly and, if necessary, presses on the uterus.

The father goes to the *chimán* to see what name the child is to bear.[1] Then the *chimán* consults his count of the days (sacred calendar), and ascertains the day of the child in this count. After that he casts the *mixes*[2] and tells what luck the child will have in its life. A child born during the last five days of the year will have very bad luck.

On the day of the baby's birth, after being delivered, the mother takes a sweat-bath with the aid of the midwife. For twenty days, such a bath must be taken every second or third day. The actual day is determined by the midwife. During the twenty-day period the mother does no work. If she has no female member of the family to help her, a neighbour is called in. The mother may not leave the house or participate in any matter of outside interest, and she must think only "good thoughts."

Five days after the birth of the baby, the father kills a young goat or a lamb for the family to eat.

When the baby is twenty days old, the *chimán* takes the umbilical cord, wrapped in its special cloth, and if it is a boy, he goes to the mountains and puts the cord in the hollow of a tree or ties it to a limb; if a girl, he goes to a marshy or wet spot and there, with his planting stick,[3] makes a hole in the earth, puts the cord in, and covers the opening with a small rock. Both copal and candles are burned by the *chimán* at Cumanchúm and at his table. The mother burns candles at the church.

At this same time *bebida*, the ceremonial drink, is prepared and drunk by the members of the family and close friends. Both Margarita and Patrona brought me *bebida* in *jicaritas*, gourd cups, on the twentieth day after the birth of their babies.

Some of the children are also baptized by the Catholic priest from Chiantla, on one of his occasional visits during the year.

---

[1] Or, for the price of ten cents, the father could choose a name from a list that the civil secretary would read to him.

[2] The sacred beans or seeds, also called *mix bel. Mix* also means "turkey." (*See plate 16*.)

[3] Used for planting corn. A similar stick is carried by the Prayermakers and the *mayores civiles;* see pp. 63 ff. Friar Diego de Landa told (p. 39) of the Indians' using planting sticks in his time.

Marriages are usually arranged by the parents. The girl is "sold" by her father. The marriageable age for a girl is between twelve and sixteen, for a boy between sixteen and twenty. Before a father selects a particular girl as his son's wife he usually consults a *chimán*, who in turn consults his *mixes*. These will indicate the most suitable wife among the girls the father has in mind, and also the best day for the young man's father to approach the girl's father.

Daughters have a specific bride-price, ranging between fifty and a hundred dollars, depending upon the circumstances of the family. One third or less is paid in cash and the rest in corn and animals. If the woman proves barren or is not a good wife or worker, she can be returned to her father, who must then pay back the money. Virginity is not important.

The Indians observe no specific marriage ceremony, other than feasting, and there is rarely if ever a civil ceremony. The young couple will probably start out living in the house with the man's parents, and the new wife usually works for her mother-in-law. Monogamy generally prevails.

Divorce is simple, merely a mutual separation. The father usually keeps the children. I know, however, of several cases where the mother was left with the children and had to support them. In the old days, an unfaithful wife was taken before the Alcalde, and if found guilty, was hung up by her tied wrists and beaten. Nowadays the Indians do not practise this custom, although a husband will often take his erring wife to the Alcalde for judgment.

When an Indian dies the family is obliged to notify the *juzgado* and make a payment of fifty cents, which ensures the deceased a place in the cemetery. Poor Indians or those who live in distant *aldeas* avoid notifying the *juzgado* so as to escape this expense and the trouble of carrying the body to the cemetery. Instead they secretly bury the body nearby.

As soon as the *juzgado* is notified of a death, the church bells toll, whereupon the body is bathed, dressed in its best clothes, and laid on a *petate* or straw mat on the floor. Two lighted candles are placed at the head of the corpse and two at the feet. If the family is too poor for four candles, only the two at the head are kept burning. A cup of coffee for the deceased's journey is placed at the right of the body. The use of flowers and cut coloured papers for decoration is a custom borrowed from the *ladinos*.

Family and friends sit up with the body all night. People come and go, bringing presents of candles, money, or food. Coffee, food, and *aguardiente* are served several times during the night and a guitarist plays all night long. Abelino Ramírez, a *principal,* is called in to sing the *salve* over the body four times during the night (only twice if the deceased is a child).

One day, when Simona, my servant for a time, and I were having lunch, the church bells tolled. A few seconds later a wasp flew into the room, and Simona said, "It is the spirit of the dead." Then, after a few minutes, she exclaimed, "Señorita, when someone dies in a family, they eat little that day." "What do they eat?" I asked. "Just *tortillas* and a cup of blood." "Blood of a cooked animal or of a freshly killed one?" "Blood of a freshly killed one, an animal killed that very day," she answered.

The most dramatic ceremony connected with death is the wake. In March, 1947, I attended the wake of the two-year-old son of my *mozo* Domingo and his wife Patrona. (*See plates 6 and 7.*) The child died in the morning, and immediately after its death Patrona and the children commenced wailing. Domingo was away working in his corn fields near San Martín, so I had the Alcalde Municipal send a *mayor* for him.

Neighbour women washed the body of the child, dressed it in its best, and laid it on a *petate* on a table. Two candles were kept burning, all day and night, one at each side of the child's head.

Wailing went on all afternoon. It sounded like the wind in the trees, a lonely, sad sound, not human, more like the universal wail of nature.

At eight o'clock in the evening I and Basilia, my servant (*see plate 8*), went over to Domingo's house. We carried candles, two bottles of *aguardiente*, and plenty of cigarettes. Outside on the porch were two little pigs, boarded up behind the bench so that the coyotes would not get them. Inside, grouped in a semicircle, were Tata Julián, the Chief Prayermaker; Patrona's sister, a wonderful old woman; Andrés, a neighbour, with his guitar; another old woman, a neighbour, with her grandchild; and the immediate family—Domingo, who had just returned, his son Andrés, the three younger children, and Patrona.

The dead child was lying on the table, to the right of the door. On his head was one half of a red bandanna, and tied over his mouth was the other half. His hands were crossed, and there were flowers in them. Flowers had also been placed about his body. A wand, with coloured paper streamers hanging from one end, had been placed along his left side. Next to his right hand stood a cup of coffee, and on each side of his head a lighted candle.

Poor Patrona was wailing, as was also Victoria, aged ten. Domingo thanked me for sending a man for him and told how the man found him and how he had broken the news. He went into the most minute details of the matter, with the gusto of a true story-teller. Finally he said, "The night before last, I dreamed that the brother of my neighbour who had died five years ago came to me and began quarrelling with me and trying to hit me. I told him, 'I have no quarrel with you. Why do you talk and act in this way?' I called out to some men and said, 'This man is crazy. He wants to fight with me but I have no desire to fight with him, so take him away.' Then the man said to me, 'Domingo, I do not want to fight with you. I just want the new lasso in your hand.'

"Señorita, I looked down and saw that in one hand I had a small new lasso, a new one like the one you bought at the fiesta at Chiantla. In the other hand I had an old one. The man grabbed the new lasso out of my hand and then I awoke."

Tata Julián thereupon interpreted the dream: "The new lasso was the baby. The man had come to take the spirit of the baby."

We all agreed, and I passed everyone cigarettes. After a while,

Domingo said, "Last night I could not sleep. An owl hooted all night, so I knew something bad had happened to my family."

"Yes," I said, "it is the same in my country; owls are bad luck."

"Yes, truly, owls and vultures," said Tata Julián.

Patrona said, "Señorita, your dogs and mine barked all night."

"That is true," broke in Basilia, "and the cat kept jumping in and out of the window."

We were silent. Then Domingo said, "If there is a chameleon in this room it is bad luck, for the spirit of the dead will go into the chameleon."

We drank coffee then and smoked. Tata Julián, who was sitting on one side of the dead child, commenced to pray. He leaned forward from the stool on which he sat, crossing his hands on the head of a cane, the tip of which rested on the earth between his long legs, encased in their red-and-white-striped pants. He muttered his prayers in a low voice—a mixture of Mam and Spanish Catholic names, for he was taking the place of his brother Abelino, who usually officiated at funerals but was too sick to come. On the top of the red bandanna covering his head he wore a straw hat, and under it his long face was kind and gentle and strong in its earnestness and dignity. He chanted on and on. The others paid no attention to him.

Patrona continued to wail while Domingo talked to us. I watched his face, even though my eyes smarted from the smoke that filled the room. The fire was laid on the earthen floor, and its smoke eventually found its way out through a hole in the roof. As Domingo talked his eyes glistened and his face glowed and seemed to give forth a kind and good force. Patrona's face stood out strong and pure. Her nose was aquiline and aristocratic like Domingo's. Both seemed pure Mayan, both were handsome.

The face of Andrés the guitarist was kind and stupid. The little old neighbour woman, with wide-awake bright eyes like a bird's, bustled about tending the fire and stirring the pots of various sizes. The children all sat near the fire. Their wide intelligent eyes missed nothing.

Next to the fire a pole was pushed in the ground, and on top of this

46

was stuck a lump of clay on which were laid burning pieces of *ocote*, fat pine slivers. These, with the candles, gave all the light. Under a platform of boards that served as a bed was a mewing litter of newly born kittens. In another corner a hen was setting, her chicks under her. Hanging from the beams, down the sides of the room, were rows and rows of corn ears, gleaming yellow.

It was Patrona who now spoke: "Señorita, this is a doubly sad time for me because my brother died just a few days ago near Concepción."

"That is indeed sad, Patrona," I said. "Was he young?"

"Yes, he was about thirty-five years old. He died because of an animal inside him that was jumping about in his stomach. That is what he died of. No one could cure him."

Domingo said, "The people of Concepción are bad people. The *brujos* there can cast spells."

Tata Julián said, "Yes, they can put an animal inside you. Wicked indeed are the people of Concepción."

They asked me if I knew how to cure such a condition, and I said, "Yes, it is an animal called *tenia* or tapeworm, and it can be cured by the sick one swallowing a bottleful of white medicine. The animal does not like this and leaves the body, as in *chor*, dysentery. When the animal comes out one must watch to be sure it comes out with its head, for if the head is not there, it is inside, and more animals will grow from it."

Then Domingo opened a bottle of *aguardiente* and passed the first glass to me. I held it towards my host and towards the others[4] as I sprinkled three drops on the earth and one outwards. This is customary among *chimanes* and other old, wise men. Then I drained the rest in one gulp, as is the general custom. Tata Julián was given the next glass and he did the same. The others, one by one, drained their glasses. It was all done with great formality and feeling.

The guitarist now played and we talked of death. Domingo noticed

---

[4] It is customary to say *"t'on dios ta"* if addressing a toast to a man; to a woman, *"t'on dios na."*

that the dead child's eyes were open a bit and he said, "Señorita, he is looking at us. That means bad luck, Señorita."

But I said, "No, the spirits of children go to the Sky God. The spirit of your son will soon be with the rest of those of your family who have died."

"Señorita, five have died; this now makes six. Yes, Señorita, they are now with the great mother who has many breasts,[5] and enough milk in them all for every child."

"Yes, Señorita Matilde,"[6] said Tata Julián, "she has enough milk for every child."

Patrona now began to sob and wail again. "Señorita," she exclaimed, "I hope this is not the commencement of bad luck."

"Certainly not," I reassured her.

We had another round of drinks, though against my desire, for their *aguardiente* is so very raw and strong.

Tata Julián then sang the *salve,* which his brother usually sang at funerals. It was a mixture of Mam and Spanish Catholic phrases and saints' names intermingled with those of the holy mountains and the Alcaldes del Mundo.[7] He sang for about ten minutes, distressingly off key. The others paid no attention to him and went right on talking, but I listened, and when he finished he gave me a grateful smile.

He asked me what I felt about life after death. I told him I believed in another life.

"What does God look like?" asked Tata Julián. "Does He look like the pictures the fathers distribute or does He look like the idols in the church?"

"We do not know what He looks like," I said, "for no one has ever seen Him. People paint His picture and make figures of Him, but it is

---

[5] No more information could I gather on the "great mother."

[6] As "Maud Oakes" was difficult for the Indians to pronounce, I had asked them to call me Matilde Robles.

[7] The four most important days of the Mayan calendar, and also deified as the Year Bearers. See p. 77.

just what they see in their heads that they paint. God is God, and it is not important what He looks like."

As I said this a moth flickered about the room, and Tata Julián said, "That is the spirit of the child." Everyone looked and said, "Yes, that is the spirit of the baby."

Then they discussed what the baby should be wrapped in when it was put in the coffin. "The woolen cloth it is now wrapped in is new and could be used by my other child," said Patrona.

I interrupted. "I have a piece of material that is blue and red, and you can have it if you want it."

They decided to put a second shirt on the baby, as it had possessed two. This I felt was grotesque and horrible. Nevertheless they went on and pulled all the flowers and coloured paper off the baby and removed the candles. They took the bandannas from its head and mouth, and tried to pull the stiff little arms through the shirt. It was an unearthly scene, for throughout all this Patrona and Victoria kept up their wailing. With deft fingers Basilia dressed the baby and laid it on the table again. Then the old woman pulled on each toe and each finger hard and pinched its nostrils, and tied the bandanna back over its mouth. She then closed its eyes and tied the other half of the bandanna over its head. She put around its neck a necklace of nasturtiums and pansies, made by Basilia and myself, and she put back all the other flowers and cut paper.

Tata Julián asked me, "Señorita Matilde, in your country, how long does the spirit stay on earth before it goes to the Sky World?"

"Three days," I told him. "And how many days does it stay here?"

"Nine days the spirit hovers about,[8] sometimes as a moth or a fly, and on the ninth day at night another ceremony has to be given, like this one but just for the family, and then the spirit goes."

Bowls of smoking hot beans stewed with herbs were now served, and coffee and *tortillas*. If this had been a rich family, boiled meat and potatoes would have been added. After the coffee we had another smoke,

---

[8] To the Maya, nine was the number of the lowest world ruled over by the Lord of Death.

and Tata Julián asked, "Is it true, Señorita Matilda, that there are people called *mojas*[9] who live some place in the centre of Guatemala, people who know everything that goes on, like the *dueños de cerro?* They send information to God just like a telegram, the same way a *chimán* sends his messages to the *dueño*. They tell him this and that and they arrange everything with God, and he reads the messages sent to him. Is that so?"

"I have not heard of them," I said.

By this time it was after midnight, and I said good night and went home. As I went to sleep I could hear the guitar and Patrona's wailing, and when I awoke in the morning I could hear guitar and wailing still.

All morning the mourners drank coffee and *aguardiente* and smoked. Domingo came and borrowed money from me to buy more *aguardiente*. Patrona continued her lovely, lonely wail. At about eleven the coffin, painted blue, arrived at Domingo's house. Nowadays, all the Indian families that can afford it bury their dead in coffins. The child, wrapped in my blue and red material, was laid on top of the *petate*, which had been put on the bottom of the coffin. Domingo had bought a new straw hat for the child and he put it on top of the coffin; it would never fit inside, I could see. The party left for the cemetery at about half past one. It was pouring rain. I did not go but sent Basilia in my place. She told me afterward that when the coffin was put in the earth, Tata Julián said prayers over it and sprinkled *aguardiente* on it. When Patrona returned home she continued her wailing. I noticed that the youngest child had the new hat on its head.

Throughout the specified nine days Patrona kept up her wailing and went every day to the cemetery with her candle. On the night of the ninth day the family held another ceremony. Candles were kept burning all night to the sound of Patrona's haunting wail.

• • •

Several Indians told me that it used to be the custom to leave the body of the dead person all night on the pyramid at Cumanchúm, the one that

9 When I asked Tata Julián about *mojas* later, he could give no further information.

stands on the west side of the crosses, where the *chimanes* have *cos-tumbre;* but I suspect that this applied only to *chimanes*. Nowadays, when a *chimán* dies, one of his pupils who is also a *chimán* takes all the dead man's equipment, including his table, stool, guitar, *mixes,* crystals, fetishes, *jicaritas,* and gourds, and lays it all on the top of the pyramid; or he may take these articles to the *cerro* of T'ui K'oy, where they also do *costumbre.*[10] On one occasion I went to the top of the pyramid. It was covered with high coarse grass, and everywhere I saw the *chimanes'* equipment. Halfway down, lying on its face, was an idol made of stucco. Both Indians and *ladinos* alike say that to touch those objects belonging to the *chimanes* brings death.

In December, 1946, Chimán Rafael Calmo told Don Pancho:

"When a *chimán* dies no prayers are said over him. They just watch over his body all night. No prayers are said over him for he is a person apart. Sometimes he is good, sometimes bad. It matters little, for he has his contract with the *dueño de cerro.* His body is not placed with the ordinary people who die. He is buried in the cemetery, it *is* true; not under the earth, however, but on top of the earth, in a box. He is a person apart, for he has his pact. His house, when he dies, is in another place from that of other people.

"Many people are dying today[11] because people are bad. They are lacking in respect. Jesucristo is punishing them so that they will acquire a little fear. The people say that the spirits of those who are dying today are carried away by the *gringa.*[12] The children, the little ones, they are not bad. They go directly to the sky. But the grown ones who are evil are tossed about, first to one side, then to the other, no one knows for how long. When they have paid for their sins, then they go to the sky.

"You ask where Jesucristo is. I will tell you. He is in the sky with

---

[10] About burial practices Friar Diego de Landa says (p. 57): ". . . they buried them in their houses or the vicinity, throwing some of the idols into the grave; if he was a priest they threw in some of his books; if a sorcerer his divining stones and other instruments of his office."

[11] This was during the measles epidemic.

[12] This referred to me, during the period when I was being accused of being a *dueña de cerro* and a *bruja*

Tata Grande [Great Father]. When a man dies he dies; he does not return; all is ended. When money has been buried or hidden, then the spirit returns to tell the people where it is, so they can dig it up. An uncle of mine, a brother of my father, died, and afterwards there was a good deal of noise in the house. It was like the crackling of the skin of a sheep or a person walking within the house. My father talked with a *chimán* about this and the *chimán* said to look around well on the day *k'mané* at midday, to be prepared to see a large fly enter the house, to make certain that the fly was green and large. The place where the fly seemed to be scratching would be the place where the money was hidden. Without a doubt the money would be just there. My father found the money, much money, and dug it out, so said my father's other brother.

"You ask why we bury with the dead all their belongings, like sandals, money, and their *mecapales* [leather headbands]. Well, that is because it is the custom of the ancients. When they were here they taught us this, and that is why the people do it today."

# 4

## Religion and Religious Organization

1

BEFORE I DESCRIBE the native religion, let me speak briefly of the type of Roman Catholicism existing in Todos Santos today.

The pueblo has a beautiful little sixteenth-century adobe church (*see plate 11*) but no resident priest. I find that the village never did have one. In the past, the priests who visited Todos Santos were of the Mercedarian Order. They used to carry on their work from various community establishments at Malacatancito, Chiantla, Cuilco, Soloma, and Jacaltenango. At each of these centres there would be three to six priests, who would, in turn, make their sorties—they cannot be called anything else—to the villages. They would stay only a few days at most in each village, and during their visit the local Indians were obliged to feed them.

At present the Maryknoll Father in Chiantla is the appointed priest for Todos Santos. He visits the pueblo a few times a year to officiate at masses and baptisms. The Alcalde Rezador told me that he liked this priest, for he was a kind man and he did not ask to be fed as the other priests had done.

Aside from the visits of the Maryknoll Father and of other itinerant priests who sometimes break their journey by spending the night in the *convento,* Todos Santos today has no contact with the Catholic Church. The village church and the *convento* are used by the Indians to worship at in their own way, and so is the shrine, El Calvario, outside the village.

There are no Catholic altars or saints' images in the houses of Todos

53

Santos Indians as there are at Jacaltenango and Santa Eulalia.[1] The statues of saints in the church seem to mean little to them, except for Santo Todos Santos, patron saint of the pueblo, who has been identified with San Francisco, and perhaps also Santa Lucía and San Isidro, who are prayed to for rain.

Tata Abelino Ramírez was the only Indian who could chant in Catholic fashion, and this he did at all wakes and burials. His chants were a mixture of Catholic names, Mayan day-names, and names of various Guatemalan cities and volcanoes. Tata Julián knew parts of the catechism, and so also did the interpreter who assisted the Catholic priest when he came.

The Indians have great respect for old age. They consider that age brings with it the wisdom which is bound up with the religious tradition they have inherited from their ancestors, the Ancient Ones. This wisdom, this tradition, is part and parcel of their being. They reverence it and guard it, for it is all that is left to them from the past.

As Chimán Pascual Pablo told me, "The customs of the Ancient Ones have never been changed. If a man changes these customs he dies. That is what we *chimanes* have been taught. We do not play with the things of God."

When I asked the age of the pueblo, another *chimán*, Domingo Calmo, said: "My grandparents told me that the pueblo is as old as the world. They said, 'In the beginning there were no *ladinos*, just *naturales*. Tata Dios placed Todos Santos in the middle of the sky.'" Domingo Calmo pointed to the spot where he was standing, and continued: "God said, 'This pueblo is in the centre of the world; it is the heart of the world.'" Domingo Calmo spread his arms out like a cross and turned halfway around so that he covered the four directions. "God said, 'Everything in the world is going to be destroyed, but not the pueblo of Todos Santos.' So this has been a sign to us. Who knows how long a time?"

[1] La Farge and Byers, p. 190; La Farge, *S. E.*, p. 70.

2

For the administration of religion in Todos Santos there are four groups of selected individuals. These four groups, which overlap and even extend into the civic organization, are the Guardians of the Royal Coffer (the *Caja Real*), the church officials, the *principales*, and the *chimanes*.[2]

The first group, the Guardians of the Royal Coffer (*rezadores del Soch, ninzuk,* or *ninzuk t'uit nax*), consists of thirteen *rezadores* or Prayermakers (*see plate 10*), the Chimán Nam, the interpreter, and four *mayores*. For 1947, they were the following men:

| | |
|---|---|
| Alcalde Rezador *(nel gat)* . . | Ponciano Ramírez (Tata Julián) |
| First Rezador *(nel stol)* . . . | Roque Matías |
| Second Rezador . . . . . . | Esteban Mendoza |
| Third Rezador . . . . . . | Marcelino Pablo |
| Fourth Rezador . . . . . . | Félix Bautista |
| Fifth Rezador . . . . . . | Fermín Mendoza |
| Sixth Rezador . . . . . . | Juan Mendoza |
| Seventh Rezador . . . . . | Fernando Jerónimo |
| Eighth Rezador . . . . . . | Pedro Cruz |
| Ninth Rezador . . . . . . | Victoriano Ramírez |
| Tenth Rezador . . . . . . | Mateo Mendoza |
| Eleventh Rezador . . . . . | Manuel Ramírez |
| Twelfth Rezador . . . . . | (not noted) |
| Chimán Nam, "El Rey" . . . | Macario Bautista |
| *Intérprete* . . . . . . . . | Estanislaos Pablo |
| Four *mayores* . . . . . . | (not noted) |

Forty individuals are designated as church officials: two *fiscales*, six *mayores*, thirty *escuelix*, one drummer, and one flutist. The *fiscales* attend to the needs of visiting priests, supervise the care of the church, and ring the bell. The *mayores* and the *escuelix* are, respectively, young men and boys who are assigned various useful duties, such as cleaning. (*See plates 12 and 21.*)

[2] Details of the *chimanes* are given on pp. 90 ff.

There are six *principales*[3] and three officials who, although not called *principales*, serve as such. During my stay in Todos Santos, these were Abelino Ramírez, brother of Tata Julián, and Ireneo Pablo, Raimundo Cruz, Tomás Mendoza, José Pablo, Viviano Matías, Chimán Nam Macario Bautista, Chimán Domingo Calmo, and Chimán Rafael Calmo. The *rezadores* and the church officials are elected each year by the Chimán Nam, the *principales*, and the retiring *rezadores*.

Macario Bautista, Chimán Nam or calendar priest, also called "El Rey," is the unofficial head of Todos Santos and has the final word in all matters, religious and civil. On him and to a lesser degree on the Prayer-makers or *rezadores* rests the fate of the pueblo, the people, the animals, the crops, the weather.[4] If epidemics threaten it is up to the Chimán Nam, along with the Prayermakers, to avert them. He designates the time of all fiestas and *costumbres*, and he gives the final word in all important matters, determining everything by divination with his *mixes*. He warns the pueblo of an approaching eclipse.[5] Together with the

---

[3] The Mam word is *t'oj;* a *principal* who takes part in a ceremony is *t'oj lama*. (Details of the *principales'* function are given below.) I inferred that the *chimanes* who serve as *principales* are never called by the title *principal*, possibly because the title *chimán* is more exalted in rank.

[4] Cf. Landa, pp. 12f.: "The people of Yucatan were as attentive to matters of religion as of government, and had a High Priest whom they called *Ahkin May*. . . . He was held in great reverence by the chiefs, and had no allotment of Indians for himself, the chiefs making presents to him in addition to the offerings, and all the local priests sending him contributions. He was succeeded in office by his sons or nearest kin. In him lay the key to their sciences, to which they most devoted themselves, giving counsel to the chiefs and answering their inquiries. . . . The sciences which they taught were the reckoning of the years, months, and days, the festivals and ceremonies, the administration of their sacraments, the omens of the days, their methods of divination and prophecies, events, remedies for sickness, antiquities, and the art of reading and writing by their letters and the characters with which they wrote, and by pictures that illustrated the writings."

[5] An eclipse of the sun occurred in December, 1945. I was unaware of this until it suddenly grew dark and I heard much clamour in the village. Margarita, my neighbour, warned me to stay in my house and to make a great deal of noise or harm would come to me. Following her directions I stayed inside for two hours or more, listening to the church bells, the beating of pans, and other noises. The next day Margarita told me that it had been a very delicate period as the sun was eating the moon. I asked Margarita and Patrona how they knew ahead of time, and they both told me that the Chimán Nam Macario Bautista had notified the whole village of what was about to occur.

56

Chief Prayermaker, he watches over the *Caja Real,* or Royal Coffer.[6]

Macario Bautista, El Rey, was a fine-looking old man. (*See plate 11.*) He was tall, although he stooped when he walked, and his strong face was aristocratic, intelligent, kindly, and definitely spiritual. His hair and his ample beard were snow-white. The Indians believed him to be one hundred and ten years old. Macario Bautista himself said that he had been a young married man when the first *ladinos,* Clara Herrera and her father Don Celestín, had come to the village. Clara, Don Raimundo's mother, had been twelve at the time, and she had died recently at the age of one hundred and five. These facts were the basis for reckoning El Rey's age.

The importance of El Rey to the Indians was of the gravest. The midwife Rosa Bautista, a sister of Macario, was warm in her praise of him: "There are many *chimanes* in this pueblo over fifty but the most respected is Macario Bautista. This is so because, first, he is the Chimán Nam, and then because his ancestors told him how they made the world. His grandfather, Desiderio Bautista, gave this information to Macario's father, Simón Bautista, and he in turn told it to Macario. Macario is a very old man; he can hardly see. He will pass on all he knows to his son Francisco Bautista before he dies.[7] When he was young, Macario's wife ran away with another man. She ran away because she wanted a man for a husband, not a Chimán Nam."

"What do you mean?" I asked.

"The Chimán Nam can never touch a woman during *costumbre* time and five to twenty days before.[8] Now Macario performs much *costumbre* through the year, though not much during the rainy season. Because of

---

[6] Cf. Morley, p. 172: "The great temple establishments in the ceremonial centers of the Old and New Empires, with their manifold activities of ritual, sacrifice, divination, astronomical observations, chronological calculations, hieroglyphic writings, religious instruction, management of the monasteries, where the many priests lived, was almost as big business for those days as directing the ship of state. The high priests of the different states must have been not only extremely able administrators, but also outstanding scholars, astronomers, and mathematicians, and all this in addition to their purely religious duties."

[7] Cf. Landa, p. 12: "He [a priest] was succeeded in office by his sons or nearest of kin."

[8] Cf. ibid., p. 46: "In some of the fasts observed for their fiestas they neither ate meat nor knew their wives. . . ."

57

all this his wife ran away and he never took another woman."

Every Indian I questioned gave the same report about him: "Yes, he is called 'El Rey' for he is *el rey,* just as his father and grandfather had been before him." I observed that they all treated him with the greatest respect. They kissed his hand or bowed when they met him, and he in turn made a motion with his hand as if to bless them.

Domingo told me: "The pueblo gives money and food to El Rey because he knows about everything. When the new year comes around all the people, young and old, go together, each with his five, ten, or fifteen cents, to give it to the Chimán Nam for his food, clothing, and *costumbre.*[9] They have indeed much respect for him who is El Rey. The other *chimanes* are not *chimanes* of the whole pueblo. The Chimán Nam is a man apart."

All of this, I feel, suggests that the dignitary called El Rey might be the descendant of an ancient line of ruling priest-kings.

In February, 1947, Tata Julián told me that Macario Bautista had just offered the *principales* his resignation as Chimán Nam, because he had lost his sight and could not do his *costumbres* the way he should. "Señorita," Tata Julián told me at the time, "the *principales* are discussing whether they should accept his resignation. As Macario Bautista's father and grandfather were Chimanes Nam before him, it would be proper that his son Francisco should take his father's place. Francisco has been trained by his father, but he is not yet a *chimán.* He would have to become one first, and one can only do that of one's own will. If he accepts and becomes a *chimán* he knows that the secrets of his office must remain only with him; they must remain secret even from his wife." A few days later Tata Julián told me that the *principales* would not accept Macario's resignation.

3

As for the *principales,* let me quote what Tata Julián told me: "The *principales* of the pueblo are selected from those who have served at one

9 Cf. ibid., p. 32: "The priests live upon their [the chiefs'] benefices and offerings."

time or another as Alcalde Municipal. They know the laws and everything that has to do with the administration of justice in the pueblo.
They meet at the *juzgado* whenever they have to decide upon civil
matters, but if the question has to do with the religious side of the
pueblo, they meet at the house of the Alcalde Rezador. There are six
*principales,* but at one time there used to be more. When they die only
those who have been Alcalde can become the new *principales;* that is
why there are now only six."

"Then how can Chimán Domingo Calmo be a *principal?*" I asked.

"As I have just said, the six who become *principales* must have served
as Alcalde Municipal before. Nevertheless there are also certain individuals who are *chimanes* of the pueblo. They are the oldest and wisest
people in the community. These also act as *principales.* Their names
are Domingo Calmo, Rafael Calmo, and he who is Chimán Nam. They
go to the meetings and give their opinions just like the rest."

"The *principales,* are they *principales* for life?" I asked.

"Naturally, for they have all been Alcalde and the community consequently respects them for the rest of their lives. Whatever they decide
in civil or religious matters is approved by the pueblo. No one can say
anything evil of them."

## 4

The most important of the officials connected with religion are the
Prayermakers, the *rezadores.* (*See plate 10.*) They are installed annually
during a ceremony on January 1, at dawn. Their function is to pray
that good may come to the pueblo and the people in general, and that
the animals and the crops may be protected from harm and the weather
be propitious. They alone are allowed to sacrifice turkeys; the *chimanes*
must sacrifice roosters.[10] Strictly speaking, the *rezadores* and the Chimán

---

[10] I found exceptions to this rule. Two turkeys were sacrificed at the house of the *chimán*
at the first Year Bearer Ceremony that I attended; see p. 111. Don Pancho told me he had
witnessed the same thing.

Nam are the only ones who pray, for the *chimanes* do not really pray; they plead and beg.

At the head of the Prayermakers stands the Alcalde Rezador. He is guardian of the *Caja Real*, which is kept in his house. He is likewise chief for all the *costumbre*, though it is under the direction of the Chimán Nam. When he and the First Rezador take office they swear to practise celibacy for the year.

Concerning the nature and functions of the *rezadores*, let me record what some of the Indians themselves had to say, beginning with Chimán Domingo Calmo:

"The function and the obligation of the Alcalde Rezador is to pray and make offerings at the *cerros* to ask that good may come to the pueblo. He sends the *rezadores* and *mayores* to the *cerros* and goes there himself only on the first of the year.[11] Other people always accompany him then. The Chimán of the Pueblo, Macario Bautista, tells the Alcalde Rezador on what days to make *costumbre* and to pray. The Chimán knows the duties of his office well, for he is always very old. Young men know nothing. What have they to gain from this office? The Alcalde Rezador, in his turn, tells the *rezadores* at what time to go to the *cerro* and to which one.

"When the corn is dry they pray that some rain may fall. They beg God to give them just a little water. When there is sickness they pray God to give them counsel.

"I am a *fiscal*. There are two of us. We look after the church; we ring the bells. When the *padre* from Chiantla comes, we see that he has what he wants. The *padres* from your country,[12] let me say, do not ask for all the food that those other *padres* are accustomed to ask for. When the Chimán Nam tells us what the day for *costumbre* is to be, we summon the *rezadores* and *mayores* and tell them what the Chimán has said. The *mayores* obey the *rezadores*. They sweep the church on the day called *k'mané* and also light the four candles on fiesta days."

[11] Cf. Landa, p. 12: "With the matter of sacrifices he rarely took part, except on great festivals or business of much moment."
[12] The Maryknoll Fathers.

On December 3, 1946, Tata Julián came to call on me. We had been old friends since the time I had cured him of an eye infection. He loved to come in the evening to get drops for his eyes and talk, smoke, and look at my copies of *Life*.

"Señorita Matilda," he began, "I have come to talk to you about a very important matter. I want your advice and maybe your help."

"Sit down by the fire, Tata Julián," I said, "and have a cigarette. What do you wish to talk to me about?"

"Señorita, on last Sunday, the day of San Andrés [December 1, the day after *k'mané*], I was elected Alcalde Rezador for the year to come. I said to them at the time that I would like to accept the honour but that I was not able to do so physically. Look at my hands, Señorita, crippled with rheumatism. Look at my knees, they too are in bad shape. Indeed, I am not in good health. But the Chimán Nam said, 'It is the voice of the pueblo that calls you, and if you accept this office, God may cure your hands.' Now, Señorita, I feel that the people of the pueblo know that I am not strong, that I am old and crippled. You cannot know, Señorita, what a responsibility I have to assume. The *Caja Real* will pass into my hands and will be lodged in my house on the first day of the year. I shall be guardian of the coffer, which is so ancient that I do not know how old it is. If harm comes to the coffer when I am carrying it or when it is in my house, death will come to me and my family, and harm to the pueblo. Candles must be kept burning day and night in front of the coffer. They must never go out. I must arise each night and light new candles, and during the daytime I must do the same. I can never leave the pueblo for I am guardian of the coffer. In addition, Señorita, there is the great expense entailed. On the night of the first day when the *Caja Real* passes into my hands, I must entertain the whole religious body as well as the *principales*. I must give them food, coffee, *aguardiente*, and cigarettes. I must buy many candles, quantities of copal, turkeys, and roosters, for before dawn we must go to the four *cerros* to practise *costumbre*. There will be a *rezador* on each *cerro*, and the *rezadores* will kill a turkey, burn copal, and pray to the gods for a good year for the pueblo, for the people, the animals, and the corn—pray that

61

no bad storms will come and that rain will fall when we need it. During the course of the year the Chimán Nam will tell me the days for *costumbre* and he will help me pray.

"Señorita, when I think of all this I worry. The people in the pueblo know I am not well. Look again at my hands, Señorita. Remember also that I am poor and do not have the money now to pay for the necessary expenses. I might send my son to Huehuetenango to sell corn, but they do not want corn now in Huehuetenango and they will not give him a good price. What do you think I should do, Señorita?"

"Tata Julián," I answered, "it is the voice of the pueblo that asks you to be Alcalde Rezador; it is the Chimán Nam; it is God. You have been chosen not for your crippled hands, but for your wisdom and your heart, and because you are an honest and a just man. I feel that in your heart you have already accepted. You are my friend and my neighbour. I have the greatest respect for you and your family. So if now you need money, I shall be glad to lend it to you. Tell me, how much do you need?"

"Thank you, Señorita, I need ten dollars, and may God thank you. Maybe my hands will after all be cured and maybe I shall become strong again. As you know, Señorita, my house is small and full of members of my family, full of things. I do not know where I can put the *Caja Real*."

"Tata Julián, are you being given money by the *rezadores* for candles, copal, and turkeys?"

"Yes, Señorita, I will be given my candles. Each *rezador* and *mayor* will give what he can, but still I shall have to carry the burden of most of the expenses. Thanks to your kindness I shall now be able to go to Huehuetenango to buy the necessary things for the ceremonies of the first of the year."


5

I myself witnessed the processions and other outdoor ceremonies connected with the election of the *rezadores* for the new year. The indoor rites were described to me by Tata Julián. On the night of November 29, 1946 (day *batz,* according to the Mam calendar), there was a meeting of the Alcalde Rezador, the twelve *rezadores,* the four *mayores,* the interpreter (who could read and write Spanish), and the Chimán Nam. They had come together to discuss and vote for the men who would be installed in office in the year to come. They began at once to talk of what man could fill each particular office best. After the interpreter had made a list of the candidates, they voted. The men elected were ranked by the number of votes each had received. When thirteen names had been written down, the list of *rezadores* for the new year was complete. By that time it was early morning of the Mam day *k'mané,* our November 30.

On Sunday, December 1, a dough of corn, cacao, and sugar was prepared in the house of the Alcalde Rezador. This was fashioned into thirteen balls weighing about a pound apiece. These were placed in a pile in front of the *Caja Real.* The First Rezador then took a *pichacha,* a clay censer (*see plate 10*), put copal in it, and swung the smoke over the balls and the *Caja Real,* which constituted the altar. Immediately after, each ball was put in a corn leaf and carried by the *mayores* to the houses of those who had been elected to serve as *rezadores* for the year 1947. Not a single man was permitted to have an excuse for not accepting the ball. Each one would take it and put it into hot water, thus making the ceremonial drink called *bebida.* By drinking the *bebida,* he formally accepted his appointment. If he had not accepted it he would have incurred the contempt of his fellow townsmen.

During the first days of December, the Alcalde Rezador went to see the Alcalde Municipal, so that the *secretario* could make a list showing the men appointed and the nature of their work and duties. The list was then sent in rotation to each one.

A few days later, the Alcalde Rezador sent four *mayores* and two *rezadores* to the mountains to cut five-foot cypress poles as staffs (*see plate 10*) for the new *rezadores.* The bark was removed, leaving the staffs white. The staffs were then carried to the house of the Alcalde and laid in a pile in front of the *Caja Real*, and copal was burned over them.

On December 31 (the Mam day *akbal*), the *rezadores* who had been guardians of the *Caja Real* during 1946 gathered together. When the first rooster crowed, the First Rezador sacrificed a turkey and the Chimán Nam prayed, rubbed turkey blood over the staffs, making them bright red, and, as he did so, evoked the four Alcaldes, the *dueños de cerro*, and the spirit of the *Caja Real*, which is called "Soch." Thus the staffs were blessed and baptized with the blood of the sacrificed turkey, and one was given to each new *rezador* as the emblem of his office. All this took place in front of the *Caja Real*, which served as an altar.

The fiesta the night the *rezadores* took office was not only for the religious body but for the whole village. It was ordinarily also the occasion on which the new Alcalde Municipal and the men who served with him assumed their offices. In 1947, however, because the Alcalde Municipal had been deposed by the Huehuetenango authorities, a new one was not to be elected until March. The whole pueblo went to the house of Tata Julián, who was to be the new Alcalde Rezador, to pay their respects. They beat the *tambor*, played the flute called *chirimía*, and drank liberally of *aguardiente*.

At four in the morning, the procession formed to accompany the *Caja Real* on the way to its new home. The marimba players led, followed by the Alcalde Rezador. After him came the *chirimía* and *tambor* players and then the First Rezador, carrying the *Caja Real* suspended by straps over his shoulders. If it was dropped it was believed great misfortune would come to the pueblo. The other *rezadores* came next, then the *mayores*, one of whom carried in his arms the bloody staffs, then the interpreter, and, last of all, the Chimán Nam. The procession went first to the church, where the Chimán Nam offered up his candles and burned copal, while skyrockets were shot off. Next they went to the boys' school, where the *Caja Real* was put on a table on the porch, against the wall of the schoolhouse, decorated with four branches of cypress, one at each corner.

Then, as the *tambor* beat incessantly, four of the retiring *rezadores* went to the house of the incoming Alcalde Rezador and said, "The Alcalde has sent me to bring you to the *Caja Real* for you to be installed." The incoming Alcalde Rezador then accompanied them back to the school, and this same ceremonial procedure was repeated at the houses of all the men who were to take office for the new year, until all were gathered at the boys' school in front of the *Caja Real.*

In front of the *Caja Real* were the blood-covered poles, and on each side of it was a bench, each facing the other. The men who had served in 1946 sat in order of rank, the Alcalde Rezador being nearest the coffer. Opposite sat the functionaries who were to take over their offices. The Chimán Nam walked between the two rows of men with his *pichacha* in his hand and, as he threw the smoke in their faces, blessed them and the *Caja Real.* The retiring Alcalde Rezador rose, picked up one of the poles, handed it to his successor, and said, "Tata Alcalde, you who are about to enter on this office, this is your place. Do you do your best during the coming year, just as I have tried to do. If the money the pueblo gives you to carry out the duties of your office is not enough, it will be for you to make up the difference. That is your obligation. Take care of and guard well Tata Soch so that he will bestow health upon the pueblo."

Thereupon the new Alcalde accepted the pole and the two men exchanged seats. This procedure was repeated until each man had accepted his pole and all had exchanged seats. Then skyrockets were shot off, the marimba was played, and great quantities of *aguardiente* were drunk.

Later in the morning, the *Caja Real,* still reposing on its table, was moved outside a short distance from the school. Here the new Alcalde Rezador, the First Rezador, and the Chimán Nam prayed, using large candles and copal. Then all the other *rezadores* and *mayores* did the same.

All the people of the pueblo then came to pay homage to the *Caja Real.* By this time the new Alcalde Rezador and the Chimán Nam were so drunk they could hardly stand up. Not so the First Rezador, for his task was to carry the *Caja Real;* he had to stay sober. Later, as they all went to the church, in the same order as in the early morning, the Alcalde Rezador and the Chimán Nam had to be supported. After the Chimán had burned his candles and copal and prayed in the church, everyone went to Cumanchúm (*see plate 15*), then returned and proceeded to the house of the new Alcalde Rezador, sending off skyrockets from time to time along the way. From Cumanchúm back, the Chimán Nam led the procession, for he had to bless the house of the Alcalde Rezador before the *Caja Real* could be placed within. Inside the house he sacrificed a turkey and burned its blood with copal before the *Caja Real.* That night the new Alcalde Rezador formally received all the religious body and the *principales* in his house and served them food, coffee, and *aguardiente.*

6

The *Caja Real* is all that remains to the Mam Indian of the religion of his ancestors. All reverence and worship it, not only the *Caja Real* itself but more particularly the spirit of the *Caja Real,* which is called Soch. Often the spirit of the *Caja Real* is called upon to pass judgment in a dispute or to determine the innocence or guilt of some accused person.

The *Caja* itself is a crudely made coffer about three feet long, eighteen inches wide, and two feet high, so thickly encrusted with the soot of untold years of ceremonial smoke that it is impossible to tell what wood it is made of.

One time, many years ago, I am told, when the Intendente was a *ladino,* the Indians were carrying the *Caja Real* in a procession. Some drunk *ladinos* attacked the procession and broke open the *Caja Real.* I am told that in it they found some old deeds and other papers and a long roll of skin with coloured figures on it. The Indians were so angered by this attack on their holy coffer that the Intendente had to send to Huehuetenango for soldiers for protection.

Tata Julián and Chimán Domingo Calmo told me that in it there are only deeds to the pueblo of Todos Santos, a pair of old-fashioned handcuffs (which, the story goes, the Spaniards had once used to chain a defiant Indian leader), and a broken hoe.

According to Abelino Ramírez, one of the *principales:* "Long ago, when the *padres* first came here and built the church, the people liked it but they also wanted a special place where they could keep the objects belonging to their ancestors. So a coffer was made and named the *Caja Real.* In this were put the objects belonging to our Ancient Ones. This was kept in what was called the 'First House,' a building which stood where the boys' school now stands. Later it was moved to the house of the Alcalde Rezador and candles were kept burning day and night."

Later in 1947, Tata Julián invited me to come to his house and burn my candle in front of the *Caja Real* on the Mam day *k'mané*, March 10, which was the first day of the new year according to the calendar of the *chimanes.* Just before dawn I was awakened by the noise of skyrockets which the *chimanes* were sending off from their houses to greet the Alcalde of the new year. About half past six, I went to Tata Julián's house carrying presents of a litre of *aguardiente*, cigarettes, ten packages of copal, four medium-sized candles for the four Alcaldes del Mundo, and one large one for the spirit of the *Caja Real.* The house was full of people. Tata Julián at once came forward to greet me and to tell me how delighted he was that I had come. Then each of the *rezadores* and their wives welcomed me.

Women may use any one of four gestures for greeting: a mere nod, a pat on the shoulder, a handshake, or a step forward with the right hand raised as if to be kissed but held higher. The last greeting is used towards a superior like a *chimán.* As far as I was concerned, some of the women treated me like a superior while others shook hands.

I presented the gifts to Tata Julián, and he thanked me and told me

67

to sit on the bench at one side of the *Caja Real*. The *Caja* stood on a table in a corner opposite the door. It was decorated with pine branches, and in front of it on the floor stood a huge clay pot from which rose clouds of incense. All about on the floor lay corn husks in which the copal had been wrapped. The floor was covered with pine needles, and on it lay several dead turkeys that had been sacrificed before dawn that very morning. On the table in front of the *Caja* stood a lighted candle.

Tata Julián and the First Rezador opened five packages of the copal I had brought and put them in the clay pot. They put coals on top, and more clouds of incense rose. The two men then prayed for me, addressing the spirit of the *Caja Real*, the twenty places where *costumbre* was practised, all the Catholic saints they could think of, and the various volcanoes, cities, and pueblos of Guatemala. Tata Julián told the *Caja Real* that I had come from a country north of Mexico, that I had come by plane to Guatemala, by bus to Huehuetenango, and by horse to Todos Santos. He asked the *Caja Real* to give me and my family health, wealth, and happiness and to protect me from robbers or other harm on any of my trips.

The atmosphere of the whole room was saturated with reverence and faith.

The four candles were then laid next to the *Caja*, the one large candle being held by the First Rezador. The wife of Tata Julián now came forward, took the candle, prayed for me, and then lit it before the *Caja Real*. She gave me a cup of coffee, and I passed cigarettes to everyone. Then Tata Julián spoke to me, repeating what I had already heard in part from someone else: "Matilde, the *Caja* is so old we do not know its age. In ancient times there was a special house for this *Caja*. When the first *ladino* who ever became Alcalde took office he did not treat the coffer with respect. He tried to break it open and sent soldiers against us. That was long ago. The house where it was then lodged no longer exists. It stood where the school for boys now stands. It was called 'First House.' The *Caja* is all that remains to us from our ancestors. The spirit of the *Caja* is stronger than any spirit that a *chimán* can summon. Nowadays

68

most *chimanes* work for material gain for themselves. But I and all of us here work for the *Caja Real*, and its spirit works for the pueblo. A grave responsibility is ours, for if we do not take proper care of the *Caja* harm will come to the pueblo, to our crops, our animals, all the people of the pueblo. Now the priest from Chiantla says, '*Chimanes* are all *brujos*.' But what do you say, Señorita?"

"Some *chimanes* are *brujos*," I answered, "others are not, just as in the world there are some good and some bad people." Then I added, "Tata Julián, the *Caja Real* gives off great force, a good force, and my heart feels good since I have come here."

"That is why I asked you to come, Matilde. Thank you for coming," responded Tata Julián.

Thereupon I rose and made a silent prayer in front of this *Caja*, black with the soot of countless candles and offerings of copal. I folded my hands and crossed myself four times, as the Indians did.[13] Finally I turned to the others, who were watching me, and said, "Thank you for letting me come. Your *Caja Real* has given me a great deal. Thank you."

They all said, "Thank you, Señorita, for coming."

Then Tata Julián said, "Don't you want a drink before you go?"

I thanked him and refused. I said my thanks was for all of them. I left with a good feeling inside. The *Caja Real* had really given me something.

Late that afternoon a *rezador* came bearing a gift from Tata Julián, a bowlful of *masa*, turkey cooked with freshly ground corn. It was made from one of the ceremonial turkeys, and I felt it to be a great honour. I gave Basilia some, she told the neighbours, and soon the whole village knew about it.

A few days later, Tata Julián told me that no one could tell a lie in front of the *Caja Real*, and gave me an example. That day a man had come to his house with his wife. He told Tata Julián that his wife was unfaithful and named the man. She insisted she was innocent. Tata

---

[13] Forehead, solar plexus, left breast, right breast. It was a custom among the old people and those who held office to make the sign of the cross if they received a personal gift or if they offered gifts, sacrifices, or prayers to the gods.

Julián made her light a candle and place it in front of the *Caja Real*. The candle sputtered and burned down quickly with a great deal of flame. Thus she was guilty, and so she was put in jail. If the candle had burned steadily and quietly it would have meant she was innocent. Many matters are settled in this way. People bring copal and the Alcalde prays as he swings his *pichacha* in front of the *Caja Real* and calls on Tata Soch, the Spirit, to be judge.

# 5

## *The Cerros*

### 1

LIVING IN TODOS SANTOS, one is always aware of the mountains that, on three sides, tower formidably above the pueblo. During the day they often stand out in great clarity and beauty of line, though as often they are hidden by clouds and mist. Sometimes storms gather around the summits, and their zigzag bolts of lightning seem to flash from the very mountaintops. At night the star-filled sky rests on top of their dark outline. The stars give the impression of being the lights of another plane, of a higher world, of the abode of the gods. No wonder that the Indians' most sacred places for communion with their gods are the *cerros*, the summits of these mountains.

The highest peaks, those believed to be nearest to God, are four in number, three on the northeast side and one on the south. They are named T'ui K'oy, T'ui Xolik, Cilbilchax, and T'ui Bach. These four are not the only *cerros* where the Indians worship, but they represent the most important days of the ancient Mam calendar, the four *alcaldes del mundo*. The Indians accord these *cerros* the greatest respect and awe, for they are the domiciles of the gods, the *dueños de cerro*, or, in Mam, *t'au witz*.

### 2

Having been accused (in November, 1946) of being a *dueña de cerro* myself, I decided that I had better visit my supposed home. So that

71

there would be no mystery about it, I told my neighbours that I was going to climb T'ui Bach to see the view and take photographs from it.

Riding my horse, and accompanied by my *mozo*, Domingo, and his two young sons on foot, and my two dogs, I started off for T'ui Bach early one morning toward the end of January, 1947. The sky was clear, for the sun had not yet entered our valley. I rode for about twenty minutes and then, as the rocks were bad and the going almost perpendicular, I dismounted and led my horse. In a short time we came out onto a flat place overgrown with coarse grass, of the kind used for thatching roofs. Here we left Andrés, my *mozo*'s elder son, as custodian of the horse and of our picnic lunch.

We toiled upward, through pine, cypress, and fir. The birds sang and happiness filled our hearts, and evidently those of the dogs too, for they romped all around us. An Indian joined us for a while. He was looking for his sister, who had lost two young sheep the day before, and had gone out before dawn to search for them. We all hoped that the coyotes had not found them first. As we climbed, we could catch glimpses of Todos Santos, very small, far below. The mountains on the other side of the valley did not seem to tower above us so formidably, for we were gradually climbing as high as their summits.

Domingo was a wonderful guide, full of nature lore. "Señorita," he said, "notice the *caca* [droppings] of the coyote—it is white, for it is full of the hair of the sheep." It was true; the *caca*, which was on the ground all about us, looked like gray-white cocoons. "This tree," he said, "the one with the light green leaves, is used in the dry season when there is no grass. We cut the branches, and the sheep and goats like it and they eat the leaves. Now these rocks that are light-coloured, if you build a fire next to them the *cal* [lime] will come out." Thus his conversation went on all day.

Looking up the steep slope, we saw the Indian's sister—she had found her two sheep, and we were delighted. As soon as we reached her we said hello and goodbye and went on climbing. The altitude was now extreme, and I had to rest now and then to catch my breath. Finally we came out on a ridge that looked south and north. Never have I seen such a superb view. As far as the eye could see, one mountain range rose after another, an ocean of them. Some fifty miles southward, the huge volcano of Tajumulco reared up in the landscape in a most dignified and important manner. Northwestward, toward *tierra caliente,* the "hot land," and Mexico, towered a range of mountains whose existence I had not previously known of. T'ui Bach, our destination, seemed as distant as ever, and I began to wonder whether it was real and whether we would actually reach it. Often I doubted that I could make the grade.

The climbing now became really difficult. There were no trees, only rocks. I had to rest quite often, and I noticed that Domingo's breathing too had become somewhat laboured and that the dogs had stopped romping. My *mozo's* ten-year-old son, however, seemed quite unaffected by such a thing as altitude. Domingo told me that he had never been to T'ui Bach or any other high *cerro* of *costumbre.* "No *natural* goes there, Señorita, only *chimanes* and *rezadores.* If you have no fear, I have no fear; I will go where you go." He was pleased to find very good *ocote,* splinters of resinous wood, all over the ground. "Now I know where the *chimanes* get their *ocote,*" he said to me.

The heat of the sun and the rarefied air were nearly unbearable, but on we struggled. The tiny path wound in and out among rocks covered in places with gray moss that was still frosty. We passed steep inclines and sheer drops and I thought of the *rezadores,* making their way in darkness along these perilous trails. Finally we came to the summit of what I thought at first was our destination. But not at all: T'ui Bach still towered above us. The view was even more beautiful and awe-inspiring. I took coloured pictures all along the way.

Domingo encouraged me and helped me along the dangerous spots. At last we reached the summit of T'ui Bach, and I stretched myself flat on my back and struggled for breath. We were certainly 12,000 feet up, for far below I could see the pass of La Ventosa, which I knew has an altitude of 11,200 feet. The view from the place for *costumbre* here, as from all the *costumbre* sites I have visited, was indescribably beautiful.

73

To the east, south, and west the earth was spread out beneath us. We could see five volcanoes clearly, as well as the *cerro* of Xepaxá, legendary birthplace of corn, where the Indians go to pray for rain.[1] My thoughts were of the *rezadores* and *chimanes* who make this climb in all kinds of weather, of the fires they build when they reach their destination, of the sacrifice of the turkeys. To the *dueño* of this mountain, named also T'ui Bach, the *rezador* prays first, and then to the other *dueños*. He knows that other *rezadores* are doing at the other *cerros* just what he is doing here. He swings his *pichacha* as he prays. The smoke of the burning blood and the copal winds up into the sky as dawn lights the world below. No wonder the *rezador* has faith; he is apart from the world, he is at one with his God. At that moment, *he* is the Mountain.

There was on T'ui Bach a main altar that the Indians call "Soch."[1a] It was waist-high and made of four flat slabs of rock, arranged like a little house, three on the sides and one on top, and open at the front. Around this were numerous smaller altars, also called "Soch." At the very front lay ashes, and everywhere there were candle drippings. Some of these altars had inside rocks naturally shaped like birds or animals. Inside the large altar I found a crudely carved little stone idol and fragments of broken pots. The idol was about six inches tall, with hands meeting on the chest and feet meeting below.

Luck was certainly with me, for I had just finished taking pictures of the various views when the clouds rose and engulfed us. Then we started homeward.

## 3

I had seen my mountain[2] and could now understand why the Indians believed that every mountain must have a *dueño*. That is what ninety-

---

[1] See the legend on the origin of corn, Appendix, p. 244.

[1a] The spirit of the *Caja Real* is called "Soch," or "Aj Walal Soch"; see pp. 64 ff.

[2] In April, 1947, I also went to the *cerro* of T'ui K'oy. The many altars of all sizes were in a grove of trees, through which one had a superb view of the pueblo of Todos Santos and the valley. On walking to the *costumbre*, we passed a large rock, about the height of a man, of no significant form so far as I could tell. The Indian who was our guide, a friend of Domingo's, told us that many Indians prayed to this rock.

year-old Pascual Carillo told me in March, 1947, soon after my ascent: "Have the mountains a *dueño*? Ah, *malaya*,[3] where is there a mountain that has no *dueño*? Nowhere. Every mountain has its *dueño*, this one, that one, even the small mountains and hills. Even large rocks, the springs of water, they all have their *dueños*. Look at the spring next to Manuel the butcher. It has a *dueño*. The *dueño* of the water at Manuel's is the *dueño* in the big *pila* in the plaza.

"One day Juan Pablo the son of Marcelino Pablo saw the *dueño* right here where the water is born in the spring. He spoke with him and the *dueño* said, 'Do you want money? I am *dueño* of the water; I have much money. If you want money, bring me the head of a man, and I shall give you money, much money. You will see then how much money I shall give you, but keep your mouth shut and don't speak of this to anyone.' 'Good,' said Juan Pablo, 'but where shall I meet you?' 'Follow this *barranco* [ravine] till you come to a pine tree where there is a hollow,' answered the *dueño*. 'When you bring the head, call out to me. I shall soon see you then.' 'Good, Tata,' said Juan. He went to his house and told his brother, his father, all his family about it. Then he went out to find a wicked man to cut off his head, but he met no one.

"After a while he again met the *dueño de pozo* [spring master], who asked, 'Why don't you bring me the head of a man? I shall give you much money if you do.' 'I have been searching,' he answered, 'but I have not found anyone. Soon, however, I shall bring you a head.' 'This time if you want money,' said the *dueño*, 'I shall give it to you only if you bring *five* heads.' 'Ah, wicked one,' said Juan, 'where can I find five heads?' 'Why don't you go and take the heads of sheep-herders in the mountains?' said the *dueño*. 'Ah, wicked Tata, now you want five heads. Where can I find them?' Then Juan Pablo went to La Ventosa with his brother and waited for a man to come along the trail alone. When Juan saw a man he stepped out, full of wickedness and anger, with his machete in his hand.

---

[3] A sort of interjection that occurs over and over in Mam prayers and religious talk. *Malaya* is probably akin to the Spanish *mal haya*, "alas" or "confound it," but it has overtones of deep reverence.

The traveller was a *canteco* [inhabitant of Chiantla]. 'Stop, *canteco!*' said Juan. The man said, 'Why are you in such a rage? Before you used to be a good man, now you are in a rage, and what a face! If you want money, work for it.' Juan waited, for he knew this man and the *canteco* knew him, and for this reason he did not cut off his head.

"After a while he again met the *dueño*, who asked him, 'Where is the head you promised me?' 'There is none, Señor,' said Juan. 'Well,' said the *dueño*, 'if you want money, I shall give you plenty of it. But now you must bring me twenty heads.' 'Ah, *malaya*, nowhere could I find one head, nowhere could I find five heads, where could I possibly find twenty heads?'[4]

"All *cerros* have great quantities of money," Pascual Carillo continued. "There are many rich bad people. The *dueño* gave them this money. Ah, *malaya*, what kind of work do they do for the money? What value has twenty-five cents? Ah, that wicked *dueño de cerro*, he knows the mountains are full of money."

A month before, Chimán Pascual Pablo had given Don Pancho further details, depicting the *dueños* in a more favourable light.

"Each *cerro*," he said, "has its own *dueño*, and all are good. When a *todosantero* wants corn or wishes to increase his flock, he carries a rooster and a little copal to T'ui Bach. He sacrifices the rooster and prays to the *dueño*, who is the ruler of corn and of the sheep. T'ui Xolik is also one that gives money as well as corn. If you have a pact with him it is then a simple matter; he gives you money. T'ui K'oy is a very good man, he bestows water, corn, and health upon the pueblo. Money also he gives and all that is good. Walk with your *chinchin* [gourd rattle], make a noise when you walk to attract his attention, but never do evil. When a *chimán* calls on T'ui K'oy to do a favour, to defend him, yes, T'ui K'oy will hear him from afar. All the *dueños de cerro* give you something of all the various things they possess. There is not one who gives just *one* thing, and another just *one* thing. No, all give something of everything.

[4] Though this may seem to the reader an abrupt ending of the story, it is characteristic of the Indian.

The best of all the *dueños* are T'ui K'oy and T'ui Bach. Ah, *malaya,* these two are good!

"You ask me if the *dueño de cerro* will die. Never, not a *dueño de cerro.* Why should he die? He is a spirit. Maybe when the end comes, the end of Santo Mundo,[5] then the *dueño* will be finished.

"You ask me if the *dueño* has a pact with the God of the Sky. Has he a pact? Don't you realize he is his son, that he arrived when God made Santo Mundo? The *dueño de cerro,* why should he die? No, never, he will not end.

"You ask me if the *dueño de cerro* came before man. Yes, certainly. When the world was born the *dueño de cerro* was born. With Santo Mundo the *dueño* came. When Santo Mundo dies, the *dueño de cerro* will end. Only God knows when that will be.

"You ask if each of the *cerros* is a day like *k'mané.* Only four *cerros* are days. They are *alcaldes. Alcalde primero,* T'ui Bach, is K'mané;[6] *alcalde segundo,* T'ui K'oy, is Noj; *alcalde tercero,* T'ui Xolik, is Ik; and *alcalde cuarto,* Cilbilchax, is Cum T'ce. This last *cerro* has also another name, Sakabech. The other *cerros* have no day names; only the four mentioned, the four *alcaldes,* have day names, no others."[7]

[5] "Holy world," personified in prayer. Other personifications—or, perhaps better, deifications—may be noted in prayers further along, such as Justicia (justice), Mesa (table), Vara (staff), Tierra (land), etc.

[6] This and the following Mam days are personified, or deified, in prayer. (In the present work the Mam day names are printed in italic, uncapitalized, when they refer to a day, as in Spanish usage; and in roman, capitalized, when the name is personified as a god. The word *alcalde* and phrase *alcaldes del mundo* are treated similarly. It should be added that often the line is not clearly drawn. A civil official of the pueblo is, of course, also called "Alcalde.")

[7] For a detailed list of sacred places where *costumbres* are performed, see the Appendix, p. 245.

# PART TWO

# 1

## *Suspicions and Accusations*

WHEN I ARRIVED at Todos Santos, in November, 1945, my first objective was to gain the confidence of the Indians. That was not easy, but by October, 1946, I felt certain that most of the Indians had accepted me. By this time I had begun to acquire the reputation of being a *chimán*. This had its good side, as will be seen, but it had its bad side as well, for it soon brought on a crisis that almost destroyed all prospects of my obtaining what I was there for.

The Indians knew that my house was always open to them and that I treated them as equals and as friends, offering them food, coffee, and cigarettes. By means of this hospitality I found it easy, in the course of our ordinary conversation and without arousing suspicion, to bring up matters which I wished to check.

Since I was considered to be a *chimán*, Indians not only from Todos Santos but from other pueblos as well came to ask me to perform services such as finding their lost sheep. When I told them I did not have this power, they would say, "Señorita, the *gente* [people] say that you have this power." Most of my reputation for being a *chimán* came, I knew, from all the medical treatment I had given. I had, for instance, treated the wife of Chimán Domingo Calmo for skin trouble and cured her. I had treated a great number of important individuals, including several *principales*, for malaria, eye infections, wounds, and other ailments. Naturally in their eyes I became a *chimán*.

But other things helped along my reputation. Everyone learned that I disliked the *ladinos* and that I had no altar or saints' pictures in my house. They noticed that I went to the church with my candle on their

81

holy day *k'mané*—to them the most important day of the twenty days of their ceremonial calendar, a day which is also equivalent to one of their most important gods. They knew that I was well acquainted with their calendar as I always made it a point to indicate which day it was and whether, according to the native calendar, it was a good or a bad day.

From daily conversation I soon found out that there was a decided distinction between good and bad *chimanes*, the latter being called *brujos*. Nevertheless I had great difficulty in getting information on this subject until I myself was accused of being a *bruja*. That was in November of 1946.

My first introduction to the subject of good and bad *chimanes* came from Basilia. She told me one day, shortly after her child had died, that a woman who lived on the hillside above had accused her of killing *her* child a couple of years before.

"Yesterday, Señorita," said Basilia, "this woman came to me and said, 'You killed my child and that is why your son Carlos died.' "

"But, Basilia, how could you kill her child?"

"Señorita, she thought I had gone to a *chimán* to have him cast an evil spell."

"But I thought a *chimán* would not do anything evil."

"There are good and there are bad *chimanes* here," replied Basilia.

In May, 1946, a fine old man by the name of Feliciano came to see me about his daughter, aged twenty-eight, who had been having palpitations of the heart ever since she had been struck by lightning a month before. I said that it was very difficult for me to give medicine without seeing his daughter, and he told me she lived about four hours away by horse. I questioned him a great deal and discovered that actually the lightning had struck outside the house where she was, and that she had become so frightened that ever since she had been sick and unable to sleep. I asked him into the house while I got some medicine, and gave him a cigarette. He looked around to be sure that Basilia was not near and then said, in a low voice, "Señorita, a neighbour and great friend of my daughter's died yesterday, leaving a husband and two children. The

82

neighbours say my daughter caused her death because she was struck by lightning and has been sick since. They say my daughter caused her friend's death for that reason. When my daughter heard this she had great beatings of her heart. She is very sick."

In a strong voice I said, "Tell your daughter she did not kill her friend. Tell your daughter that if she follows the directions I shall give you, she will be cured."

I gave him five vermilion-coloured sleeping pills and ten black iron pills. Then I said, "She is to take one red pill each night for five nights before she goes to bed. Each day she is to take one of the black pills at dawn and one when the sun sinks. Tell her to look at her stool and if it turns black [which, of course, I knew it would], it is the evil that entered her body when the lightning struck her, and it will pass out of her in her stool. During the five nights she will sleep well and after five days she will be cured."

About three weeks later the old man came to me with a present of eggs, saying that his daughter was cured and that she wondered what kind of medicine the black pills were.

In October, 1946, I had suggested to Don Pancho, who had started working for me as an informant, that he should offer free drinks to Chimán Rafael Calmo and Chimán Pascual Pablo whenever they stopped by the liquor *tienda* he ran off and on. Though I knew they already liked him and considered him also a *chimán*, because of his treating the sick, I thought it might help to cement that friendship if he gave them as many free drinks as they wanted, for there is no *chimán* who does not have a weakness for *aguardiente*. When he felt the time was right to ask questions from the list that I gave him, he would do so. This worked out very well. By the end of October both *chimanes* had accepted Don Pancho as a friend. Pascual Pablo had offered to teach him how to read the *mixes* in exchange for instructions in the use of a few medicines, and in March he agreed to teach him to be a *chimán*.

All went well for me until November, exactly one year after I had come to Todos Santos. An epidemic of measles struck the pueblo, and the children died like flies, mainly because the Indians put their sick children in the sweat-baths, and most of them caught pneumonia when they came out. On top of this epidemic came whooping cough and a few cases of typhoid. None of my neighbours' children died, for I was able to arrest the illnesses in time. But I could do little for those who were more than half dead before I was called in. By December, the deaths averaged five a day, and I had so many patients that I was kept busy from seven in the morning to seven at night. I sent to the departmental Bureau of Sanitation in Huehuetenango for help, but none came; they had too much sickness there themselves. Yet I was able to carry on, thanks to my friends Julio and Maria Matheu, who kept me supplied with medicine from their clinic in Chichicastenango.

The *rezadores* and the Chimán Nam went to the *cerros* to pray and sacrifice turkeys. They performed daily *costumbre* to stop the epidemic, all to no effect.

One day during this period, Chimán Rafael Calmo came to call upon me and asked me to treat an infected sore on his knee. This was the first time that he had ever asked me to treat him. When I had dressed his leg, he told me that his grandchild had been ill many days with measles. Would I come to see her? I knew that she must be very ill or he would never have turned to me for help, for, I felt, he did not trust me any more than I trusted him.

When I entered the *chimán's* house an hour later, I found a former pupil of Rafael, Chimán Elón, performing *costumbre* in front of the *chimán's* table. Rafael Calmo was sitting in a chair with his grandchild in his arms.

"Señorita," the old man said, "I love this child. It is all I have in the world that I care about."

The poor child was in the last stages of pneumonia; I administered sulfa pills and did what else I could, though I knew there was little chance of recovery. I told Rafael Calmo that she was in the hands of God and advised him to pray and to perform *costumbre*. He said, "That is being done." As I walked out of the door I saw two lighted candles burn-

84

ing on a flat stone in front of the house, and Chimán Elón swinging his *pichacha* over them. I wondered if it was to protect the child against the sickness or against me. In two days the child died, and the old *chimán* turned against me. He said I was a *dueña de cerro* and a *bruja*. His antagonism to me, I felt, was due to a number of causes; the death of the child was only one of them. There was the fact that I had taken many of his patients away from him, and one day when he was drunk I had not let him enter my house.

And then a number of other Indians turned against me, saying that I was the cause of all the children's deaths, that I had a list of them and had sent out my evil spirits to carry them away. The idea of a list came from the fact that I had made one when I vaccinated and inoculated the children of the school. The accusations, I am sure, were instigated by old Chimán Rafael Calmo; he had a great deal of influence in the village.

After a very uncomfortable week—during which some Indians I met on the path actually ran off when they saw me approaching and I was told by my neighbours that an Indian called Marcelino Pablo had threatened, when drunk, to kill me—I decided that I must take some action. Thereupon I called on three of the six *principales,* Indians whom at one time or another I had treated and cured and who I felt were still my friends, and to each of them I said, "I have given free medicine and care to your people because I like them and want to help them. With all the money I have paid for medicine I could have bought a good mule [I knew this would impress them]. And what do I get in return? Just evil words: that I am a *dueña de cerro,* a *bruja*. My heart is sad, and so I have decided that, as long as you people think this way about me, I shall not distribute any more medicine or treat anyone except my own friends. I am going away for two weeks to the fiesta at Chichicastenango, and when I return, if I hear any more evil words about me, I shall do what I just said: no more medicines, no more treatments."

"Señorita," one of the *principales* replied, "it is not we who think this way, but only the uneducated *gente,* only they think thus. Don't pay any

85

attention to words of that kind. Remember they are uneducated people."

Then Abelino Ramírez, *principal,* addressed me. "Pay no attention to what these people say," he said. "In the old days, people had hearts and love for each other. Today they have little love for each other and they speak evil of people. You must know that there are good people and bad people. In the old days the *chimanes* were real *chimanes* and very wise. They did only good. Money was not important to them. If someone was sick they were able to say immediately if he would live or die. Now the *chimanes* think only of money and do not perform their *costumbre* as correctly as in the past. They do not tell you when a man will die; they just wonder how they can get more money."

I asked him if Rafael Calmo was a *brujo,* and he said, "Yes," that Domingo Calmo was one also, that even the Chimán Nam was not all he should be, although he was not a *brujo.*

Domingo, my *mozo,* came in the evening, and I told him of my decision to give medicine to nobody except my friends. He too said, "Señorita, don't pay attention to what people say. They just have big mouths. The most important people here are your friends. Of those who are talking against you, many do not even know you. Chimán Rafael has caused all this. He is an evil man. Señorita, the other day a man came to me and said, 'You are selling people to the Señorita; you give her their names and she summons her evil spirits from the *cerros* to kill them. Then she eats them. When she leaves for good she will go back and live in the volcano Tajumulco[1] and you will go with her, you seller of the souls of the people.' Señorita, this is what I said to him: 'Willingly will I go to the country of the Señorita or even to Tajumulco, for I know that she is good and has a heart. She is one of our own; she eats *tortillas* and lives as we do. Indeed she is not a *dueña de cerro.* What harm has the Señorita done to you? Go speak to Adrián the carpenter and find out about her; she saved six of his sons. Go speak to the other people who are her friends. If you do not know a good person from a bad one, you know

---

[1] Which, it may be recalled, has a *dueña,* a female spirit. See p. 17, footnote 6.

nothing. Señorita, these people who speak against you are ignorant people. They said the same things against the *gringo*[2] who lived in this same house before you came. He collected snakes and put them in bottles. The people said he was a *brujo* because he ate snakes. They also accused him of killing people."

From all sides I now heard what suspicions were entertained about me and about what I was doing. Don Pancho told me that Marcelino Pablo[3] had replied when he had asked him if I was a *dueña de cerro:*

"The *gente* say that *la gringa* is a *dueña de cerro.* Look, when she gazes through that machine of hers [my camera] she pulls out a paper and there is the face of a person, that very person! These people that she sees are alive; they have on the same hats and *capixaijes.* The people of this pueblo are gentle people, but when she comes with that machine they run away from fear of what she will do. When she takes a *matrata*[4] of the people of the pueblo she carries away their spirits. This is the reason so many people die; she carries away their spirits on paper. They tell me that in Jacaltenango and Concepción the people ran away in fear when she was there because she took *matratas* of the pueblo, of the people, and of the church. It is for this reason that people die; she points her machine at them the way one kills a deer. Look, once she showed us the papers [photographs]. They were people here and the pueblo. Who knows what her ways are? At Concepción they said to me: 'Why don't you throw her out of the pueblo? Why do you stand for her? Who knows the source of her power?' You know very well that she carries away the spirit of the *gente.* I have seen them, the faces of the people were the same. They looked exactly as if they would speak. I have also seen papers she has given my friends. There they are, the same faces. How does she do this? Probably it is evil. She gives these papers away as presents. What is her work? Where does her money come from? Ah, who knows! She distributes medicine, gives it away free, now to one person, now to an-

---

[2] Raymond (to the Indians, Raimundo) Stadelman, who was collecting data on corn. For his study, see the Bibliography.

[3] Who when drunk had threatened to kill me.

[4] Instead of using a noun formed on *retratar,* "to photograph," he used one formed on *matar,* "to kill."

other, and they pay nothing. Ah, where is there nowadays a person who gives away presents for nothing in return? She carries off many dead people to another pueblo. Maybe it is to the *cerro*."

Even though all this talk made me uncomfortable, the material that I was after came profusely now, of course. My neighbours couldn't wait to tell me what was being said against me, and it gave me an ideal chance to ask questions. It also gave me a fine feeling to know that almost all the people I had treated were sticking by me.

At times, the tales about me were amusing. Patrona, the wife of my *mozo*, told me that one day an old woman came to her and said that the Señorita must be a *dueña de cerro;* she had looked in my window and seen me eating wood. Patrona questioned her and she said, "I saw the Señorita pick up some flat pieces of wood and eat them as if she enjoyed them. Only a *dueña de cerro* could do this." After much pondering I realized that she must have seen me eating some "Ry-Krisp" that had been sent me from home.

After a two-week Christmas vacation at Chichicastenango, I returned to Todos Santos on December 31, to see Tata Julián receive the *Caja Real*. I found few people talking against me, and the epidemic was over.

Many things had helped to allay the suspicions against me. One in particular was important, I feel. It was concerned with a story told by the schoolmistress, the wife of Don Pancho, to whom it had in turn been told by a pupil, Feliciana Pablo, an Indian girl about ten years old. The story spread throughout the pueblo and freed me from suspicion by casting suspicion on somebody else. This was Feliciana's story as Don Pancho's wife repeated it to me:

"About six months ago my brother Francisco Pablo, accompanied by a friend, went to see a rehearsal of the *baile de moros*[5] at the house of the Dance Captain who had organized the *cuadrilla* [group]. It was night and there was a full moon. As the boys walked along the road they smoked and talked. They confided in each other that, not being alone this night, they were afraid of nothing.

[5] "Dance of the Moors," one of the fiesta dances. See pp. 215 ff.

88

"The rehearsal of the dance was being held in the *aldea* Tuit Nam. For this reason they took a path that led over the Bridge of the Bells,[6] on the outskirts of the town a little below El Calvario.[7] As they came near the bridge they saw approaching from the other side two *ladino* men talking loudly. They talked as if they were quarrelling. The two boys hid themselves beneath the bridge to hear what they were discussing. Arriving at the bridge, the two men walked to the middle of it and carried on the discussion there. Immediately Francisco and his friend smelled an odour like that of a dead animal. It was so nauseous they could hardly bear it, but they were too full of fear and curiosity to leave their hiding place, and they wondered what the men were arguing about.

"One of the men was unusually tall and large, the other just of ordinary size. The boys heard the small one say, 'How many children shall we carry away?' The other replied, 'One hundred and fifty children and two hundred women.' 'How many men?' 'About two hundred and fifty.'

"Then the men started on their way, but it was in the direction the boys wanted to go so they decided they would not follow, for they could not stand the odour. Besides, they were frightened, so they decided to return to their homes.

"The next day Francisco did not rise early and search for work as was his custom. His friend came to the house and asked for him. Our mother answered, 'Francisco is still sleeping. He has never slept so late and I am worried that something must have happened to him during the night.' "

Then the friend told her what had happened and what they had overheard—that a pestilence would come and carry to the grave one hundred and fifty children, two hundred women, and two hundred and fifty men of all ages. And that was the cause of the epidemic that had swept through the village. Thus was I absolved from blame.

---

[6] So-called because nearby are bushes with white, bell-like flowers that give off a heavy perfume.

[7] A small, very plain chapel near or on the outskirts of a village, usually used for only occasional observances. See La Farge, *S. E.*, pp. 83, 92–93.

# 2

## The Chimanes and Their Organization

1

EXCEPT FOR MACARIO BAUTISTA, whose responsibilities as Chimán Nam are primarily to the community, the *chimanes* carry on private practice. But they too have work to do for the pueblo. There are times, for instance, when the Chimán Nam or the Chief Prayermaker may call on the *chimanes* to help avert a catastrophe or an epidemic by performing mass *costumbre*, though I have been told this seldom happens. *Chimanes* may be divided into three groups:

1. Those who practise "white" magic—*chimanes baj*, ones "who know."
2. Those who practise black magic—*brujos;* in Mam, such a *chimán* is called *aj qia*.
3. Novice *chimanes*—*zajorines;* in Mam, one is called *aj ij*, "young sun."

All three can be either healers, soothsayers, or magicians or can exercise all of these functions. Their ritual activity is called *costumbre;* in Mam, *salal* or *ix xwox* (the word for copal is *xwox*). Ritual for one in trouble is *costumbre delito.*

When a man becomes a *chimán*, he is given his table of *costumbre*.[1] The night he "graduates" he conducts his first mass at the table and summons the Spirit, or *dueño de cerro.* On his table is a wooden cross, never a crucifix.[2] Later he goes to the *cerros* many times with his teacher and

---

[1] The teacher of a *zajorín* designates when he is ready to receive it.
[2] A Catholic crucifix is considered *ladino*. A *chimán* always has a wooden cross on his table of *costumbre* though it is usually hidden. I have seen only one which was somewhat similar to the one Don Pancho saw. See fig. 3, p. 148.

establishes contact with the *dueño*. Then he is given his chain of office.[3]
But the *chimanes* may best speak for themselves, as they did to Don
Pancho.[4]

2

Chimán Pascual Pablo to Don Pancho (November, 1946)

### DON PANCHO

Tata Pascual, how did you become a *chimán?*

### PASCUAL PABLO

It was a long time ago, before the cinders from the eruption of Santa
María Quezaltenango [about 1902] had fallen, that I learned to be a
*chimán*. There was a time when I had a bad pain in my head, and the
one who knows, he cured me. I took many herbs and I cried from suffering. We sought for a *chimán* to cure me. This *chimán* said, "Your
grandfather was a *chimán* and he did not teach anyone his work and that
is very necessary to do before one dies." For that reason I had to become
a *chimán* myself and I sought for someone to teach me. Otherwise I
would have died. I already had a wife and a child. What else could I do?
I found a *chimán* and I learned immediately. My pain vanished the day
the *chimán* commenced to teach me. Eh, indeed, it seemed as if it was
just pulled out. My pain vanished and I was cured.

Some men become *chimanes* if their fathers or grandfathers had been
*chimanes,* some because of illness or dreams. They do not all become
*chimanes* for the same reason.

[3] This is of metal, similar to a dog chain, with links and a metal ring at the end. See pp.
150 ff. A similar chain was worn about the waist by a Jacaltecan shaman-priest whom I
visited in Jacaltenango in 1946, called Juan Nantejo.

[4] For the rest of this chapter and further in this book, instead of giving a running account of my own, I present the material as the Indians gave it in answer to Don Pancho's
questions, suggested by me. Though perhaps unorthodox, this method has the merit of
best revealing the character of the Indian informants.

## Don Pancho

Tata Pascual, what is the difference between a *chimán* who has a chain and one who has not?

## Pascual Pablo

A *chimán* who has a chain does evil.[5] He who has no chain does good. He prays to God for all that is helpful for the people, the animals, and the pueblo. He asks for very little money or corn or any other things. There is no difference between a *chimán* who cures and one who prays or does the *mixes*. They are the same. A *chimán* who has a chain has a pact with other gods, maybe bad ones. Who knows? It is not like that with me.

*Brujos, chimanes, zajorines,* what is the difference, who knows? *Brujos* are bad, evil. They know how to harm, to do evil to people, to cast spells on animals or people, to make one's body or stomach sick.

A *chimán* knows his profession. Now a *zajorín* is a young man learning to be a *chimán*. A *chimán* does only good; he is never a young man. Young men do not know much, so first they have to be *zajorines*. Only afterwards do they become mature and old *chimanes*. It is better that this is so, for with age one learns many things. There used to be women *chimanes* in Todos Santos once but now they have all died. Today there are none.

The customs of the ancients have never been changed. If one changes the customs one dies. That is what we *chimanes* have been taught. A *chimán* does not play with the things of God. No, a *chimán* is good. If he does not do as he has been taught he becomes crazy in his head.

When a *chimán* dies his spirit goes to work for the *dueño de cerro*, for the *dueño* will still give him work. There has not been a time when the *dueño* has not owned a *finca*. He is very rich, I am telling you, the *dueño*. Below Mocá[6] there is a *finca* of one of the *dueños de cerro*. At

---

[5] This statement later proved to be false. See pp. 150 ff.
[6] A place south of Quezaltenango.

THE CHIMANES' ORGANIZATION

Antigua, near Guatemala [City], there is another, and yet another in the mountains near Olintepeque.[7] Near Martalo there is another *finca*. There are no *fincas* near here, but there are many Todos Santos people who work in these *fincas*. They cannot leave, for it is impossible for them to leave a wicked *dueño*. Look, a brother of Domingo Calmo called Dionisio Calmo was carried away by a *dueño de cerro*. He vanished and no one in his family has ever seen him since, but afterwards his brother Domingo claimed he was working for the *dueño* on his *finca* near Santiago Chimaltenango.

My *dueño de cerro* calls himself Juan. He has shoes and beautiful clothes, I tell you. He is rich; like a warehouse is his house. His *finca* is a pueblo. I do not know him, but I speak to him when I burn copal at the *cerro* or at my table. Then he is contented. I am not afraid when I talk to him, for we just talk. When I die I know that I shall go to the *finca* to work for him. For a *chimán* is a man apart from the people of the pueblo.

### 3

Chimán Rafael Calmo to Don Pancho (November, 1946)

#### Don Pancho

Tata Rafael, who taught you to be a *chimán?*

#### Rafael Calmo

No one. When I was born from my mother, a man saw me with the umbilical cord around my neck. He exclaimed, "He who carries a lasso around his neck will be a *chimán*." As I grew up, little by little, I learned to be a *chimán*. I am an old man and I know much about the world, good and bad. I was Alcalde in 1902 and also in 1911. During that period food and *aguardiente* were cheap. The holy earth did not punish people,

---

[7] Where the great battle between the Indians and Alvarado, the Spanish conqueror, took place, and where the Quiché chief Tecum Umán was killed, five miles north of Quezaltenango. I cannot locate Martalo.

people were good. Now a man steals another man's woman. This happens often. It is an unusual occurrence today if a woman looks after her husband and sons.

### DON PANCHO

Tata Rafael, when a *chimán* dies, where does he go?

### RAFAEL CALMO

He goes to the *cerro,* for that is where he has made his pact. The *dueño de cerro* carries him to his house and from there he will never leave.

### DON PANCHO

Do you know the *dueño de cerro,* Tata Rafael? Have you talked to him?

### RAFAEL CALMO

I do not know him but I have talked to him just as the man in the telegraph office talks. That is how I talk to him. I do not see his face, I only hear him. Yet that is how he talks to me. If someone is with me at the time, he hears nothing, for he has no pact with the *dueño de cerro.*

### DON PANCHO

When are the times that a *chimán* talks to the *dueño de cerro?*

### RAFAEL CALMO

Every twenty days or whenever it is necessary.

4

Chimán Rafael Calmo to Don Pancho (January, 1947)

### DON PANCHO

Tata Rafael, are the *dueños de los cerros* good or bad?

94

### RAFAEL CALMO

All the *dueños* are good, on one side or the other.[8] They are always good.

### DON PANCHO

What pact has the *chimán* with the *dueño?*

### RAFAEL CALMO

When he receives his table, every *chimán* makes a contract with the *dueño de cerro*. First he goes with his teacher from one *cerro* to another. He burns copal for one entire month of twenty days. The teacher prays and talks with the *dueño* and tells him, "This young man wants his table. Give him a little of your perception; he is a good friend." The *chimán* listens when the *dueño* speaks. Maybe then all at once, the young man will hear what the *dueño* is saying. This then is the pact. The *dueño* knows everything. He gives all. He speaks with one and he gives counsel on anything, such as making money, entering an agreement, or changing one's work. In short he gives advice on whatever one wants to know.

### DON PANCHO

Tata Rafael, is the *dueño* well dressed?

### RAFAEL CALMO

I shall tell you, but you will have to keep your mouth shut about it. One day, the tenth of March, many people were at my house hoping the *dueño de cerro* would come to answer their questions and to make forecasts for the year to come. I had taken many drinks with the *dueño*. He does not actually drink, he just breathes the drink in. The people were sitting outside my *corral*, in darkness, with the fire extinguished. I slept in my little chair with a rug about me. My first wife, and a good woman

---

[8] I.e., the mountains on either side of the pueblo.

she was, waited outside with the people. When she heard no sound from me she asked if I would like a cup of coffee. I drank some. Then I remembered hearing a voice say to her, "Another drink, but a small one." I asked for *ocote* to light a candle. My wife entered the room and lit the candle. On the other side of the table, which was the altar, sat the *dueño de cerro*. He was not tall, just of medium height. His clothes were like pure gold. My wife asked me, "Who is the dead person sitting here?" I said, "Shut your mouth, he is my *patrón* and he is drunk." Poor woman, she had looked on the face of the *dueño de cerro* and that brought death, death for her, my wife. In a short time, a very short time, she was not here; she had gone away. The *dueño de cerro* is like the *gringa* [i.e., the author], very rich.

### DON PANCHO

Tata Rafael, is it true that the *gringa* is a *dueña de cerro?*

### RAFAEL CALMO

Yes, certainly, the *gente,* the people, say so. Who is it gives her all the money she has? She has been curing people, yet all the time she was making a list of the names of the children—and after this they died. Why does she give medicine for nothing? Who pays her? She has a *mozo* who lives in the house next to her—I can't remember what the good-for-nothing is called. Before she came he was very poor, his clothes were ragged as were those of his wife, and the children were in rags. Now he has a new hat, a new coat, and his wife is fat, has a new skirt and *huipil.*

Without doubt she is his *patrona* and gives him money. She gives away much medicine. Look, one day she sent her *mozo* to Huehuetenango to go to a *tienda*. "Go," she said, "here is a letter for 145 quetzales for medicines. Go and bring them back. Here is the money to pay for them." She gave him only a piece of paper [a check], no money. He went to Huehuetenango and received the medicines for only a piece of paper. Yes, she has her magical power. She is a *dueña de cerro,* no question about it.

96

Look, before she came here a *gringo* lived in the same house, a man.[9] He was my friend, yet that I did not die is a miracle. He also gave medicine for nothing. Once I went to his house and he had a can that was closed. He said to me, "How much does this can weigh?" I lifted it and said, "Four, perhaps six pounds." Then he opened the can and drew out of it, by its neck, a huge snake. He allowed it to wind itself around his neck and arms and had no fear. Why didn't it try to kill him? Without a doubt he had his magic just like the *gringa's*. These *gringo* people are probably no good. They must have a pact with the devil or a *dueño de cerro*.

## DON PANCHO

Where do you think the *gringa* will go when she leaves here, Tata Rafael?

## RAFAEL CALMO

I don't know but probably to the *cerros*. Look, she does not eat *tortillas* or meat like the rest of us, just bread. She is very rich, she has much money.

Once I went to Mazatenango to sell a few potatoes. On the road I met a man from Momostenango and we walked along together. We smoked and talked and he told me the following story:

"I was going to the coast one day to make a little money. When I had gone a little way, at a turn in the road I saw a man about to hold his horse with a lasso. He saw me and asked where I was going. 'To the coast to make money,' I told him. Then the man asked whether I was going to make money or to pay off a contract. 'No,' I answered, 'I am the gainer, I am in debt to no one.' Then the man, who was well dressed and had a mule with large ears, said, 'Come to my *finca* and work for me. I will pay you more than the others.' 'Where is your *finca*?' I asked. 'Which one is it?' 'It is here nearby,' he said. 'If you care to you can work a month or less or leave when you wish to and take your money with you.' 'Good,' I said,

[9] Raymond Stadelman.

'if I need not make a pact to remain forever.' 'No,' said the man, 'when you don't want to work any longer you can go home to your house. Only remember you are not to say anything of this to anyone. If you do I will not give you work another time.' 'Good,' I said, 'I will try working for fifteen days.' The man then said, 'Shut your eyes.' I shut my eyes and when I opened them I was on a *finca*. Ah, what a large pueblo! What quantities of sugar cane, sheep, and goats! What quantities of fruit! There were many people there. It was a wonderful pueblo. The *finca* was divided by a high wall that kept people from passing from one side to the other. The ones who were there to make money and to work were on one side. On the other side there were people of a different kind, probably those who had died, *chimanes* like me. For this reason I did not see them. After working for fifteen days I thought of my home and told the man I must go. The man said, 'Good,' and gave me a roll of bills, much money."

This is just like the *gringa*, who does not count her money. She must have much money and she is probably rather wicked too.

# 3

## *The Year Bearer Ceremony*[1]

THE ANNUAL EVENT of greatest esoteric significance for the *chimanes*—indeed, for the pueblo as a whole—is *Xoj K'au,* the ceremony held at the houses of the *chimanes* from dusk till dawn on their Mam New Year's Eve.[2]

The Mam year is based on the calendar of the *chimanes,* which is a survival of the Mayan ceremonial calendar (*guaxakláj xau*).[3] The calendar

[1] See La Farge and Byers, ch. 19, and La Farge, *S. E.,* pp. 123–25. For the Year Bearer Ceremony as depicted by the Maya in the Dresden Codex, see plate 14 of the present work; as depicted in the Codex Troano, see fig. 1. Further details on the Mam calendar are given in ch. 9, pp. 188 ff.

As Morley explains (p. 295), only three of the Mayan codices, or manuscript books, have come down to us: the Codex Dresdensis, the Codex Tro-Cortesianus, and the Codex Peresianus. It is known that the Maya had many "books" treating of history, chronology, astronomy, and the various aspects of religion—ritual, divination, prophecy, medicine—which, had they survived, would have cleared up many mysteries. The Dresden is essentially a treatise on astronomy, the Tro-Cortesian a priests' text-book of horoscopes, and the Perez a ritualistic work. The codices were made of the bark of a tree called in Maya *copó (Ficus cotonifolia;* though some scholars say of maguey fibre), pounded into pulp and held together with gum of some sort, treated to produce a smooth, glossy surface, produced in long strips, folded like a screen, and painted in many colours. They depict glyphs and pictures of gods and ceremonies. These ancestors of the Mames were, says Morley (p. 452), "the greatest painters in ancient America." He numbers the codices among the finest of their paintings that have survived and considers the Dresden the best. "The brushwork is of the highest quality, the lines are sure, bold, and fluid, indicating the hand ol a master" (p. 420). As McGhee says (pp. 7–8), such religious documents of the Maya "fell under the ban of the missionaries and most of them were destroyed [as by Landa; see p. 39, footnote 11] or secreted and lost. . . . The few that reached Europe seem to have been conveyed surreptitiously in private hands and to have found their way, accidentally and unnoted, into libraries and museums."

[2] According to Lincoln (pp. 105–6, 109), the Ixil Indians, who live around Chajul, east of Todos Santos, call the Year Bearer *"ij yab"*; in Mam, this means "year."

[3] Cf. Landa, p. 70: "The first day of *Popp,* which is the first month of the Indians, was its New Year, a festival much celebrated among them, because it was general, and of all; thus the whole people together celebrated the festival for all their idols. . . . When all were

99

as used in Todos Santos has a year of 360 days with five days added on at the end, making a total of 365 days. The 360-day period is divided into eighteen months of twenty days each. These twenty days are not only days but gods. Every fifth day of the twenty is called an *alcalde*, making a total of four *alcaldes del mundo*. These are powerful gods; the most powerful of the four is the day *k'mané* (also called *ee*), while the others—*noj, ik,* and *t'ce*—are co-equals. The Mam year is always ushered in by one of the annually rotating *alcaldes*, and this *alcalde* is chief *alcalde* for the year and reappears every twenty days.

After I had been in Todos Santos two months, I knew the Mam calendar. It was familiar to the Indians, who made no attempt to keep it secret. I made it a point to let the Indians know that I knew, and this they seemed to take for granted. When March came, they talked to me of the ceremony of the *chimanes*[4] and of the New Year, but no *chimán* invited me to his house, so I decided to take a chance in another pueblo.

I chose the Mam village of Santiago Chimaltenango,[5] for I had heard that the Indians there were friendly and practised their ancient customs. It was my first expedition, so I decided to take Don Pancho along to help me. Besides, he knew one of the few *ladino* families in Santiago Chimaltenango. This family had lived there many years and spoke Mam fluently.

At 6:30 A.M. on March 9, 1946, my friend Don Pancho, my *mozo* Do-

---

congregated, with the many presents of food and drink they had brought, and much wine they had made, the priest purified the temple, seated in pontifical garments in the middle of the court, at his side a brazier and the tablets of incense."

[4] Domingo told me that there would be a big fiesta of the *chimanes*. In his father's time, he said, the whole village went first to the house of El Rey bearing him gifts. They either stayed there or went on to their *chimán's* house to hear the prognostication for the year. Behind a blanket, the *chimán* answered questions or foretold events. When the ceremony was over everything such as candle drippings, ashes, or pine needles had to be swept out of the house or harm would come to the pueblo. This may be a continuation of the Mayan customs mentioned by Landa (p. 70): "They swept their houses and threw the sweepings and all their old utensils outside the city on the rubbish heap where no one dared touch them, whatever his need."

[5] About seven miles southwest as the crow flies, but somewhat more as we travelled.

mingo, his son Andrés, and I started for Santiago Chimaltenango. The next day would be the New Year's Day. I had no plans but hoped that in some way I could participate in the ceremony which would usher in the "Year Bearer" or *alcalde del mundo*.

Don Pancho and I rode and the two Indians walked, carrying their loads slung from leather straps across their foreheads. Andrés carried my army cot and Domingo a blanket, tinned food, medicines, and the like.

The sun shone as we climbed through the clouds back of my house. We passed through beautiful country. We dipped into deep valleys, thick with ferns and strange flowering bushes, and we crossed rushing brooks, where we watered our horses. We climbed steep trails through forests of oaks, their trunks covered with moss and parasitic flowering plants. We rode along the tops of the mountain range, in the teeth of a strong, cold wind that blew away the clouds and revealed to us another world. As far as the eye could see, one mountain range rose after another. To the west lay the distant lowlands of Chiapas, in Mexico.

During the six-hour journey we saw only one pueblo, and it was in the distance—San Juan Atitán, which we were going to visit on our return. Now and then we passed a few Indians going to the market at Todos Santos. During the last hour we saw no one. We were not surprised, for we knew that the Indians were worshipping in their houses or off in the mountains, for this day was the last of the five "bad days" that preceded the New Year. The Indians consider these five days evil, as the Mayans did long ago.[6] Those Indians who still live by this calendar do not work, overeat, eat meat, or have sexual relations on these days. The *chimanes*, further, on those days cannot prognosticate, tell their *mixes*, or in other ways lead normal everyday lives, nor practise the many customs to be described later on.

We descended to Santiago Chimaltenango, situated half way down a steep mountain, a vertical patchwork of thatched roofs, each house on

---

[6] Cf. Landa, p. 81: "During these days [the five evil] they neither combed nor washed, nor otherwise cared for themselves, neither men nor women; neither did they perform any servile or heavy work, fearing lest evil fall on them."

(23)                                    (22)

Fig. 1. The Year Bearer Ceremony, from the Codex Troano.

These four pages (20–23, displayed in reverse order) are believed to correspond to the four from the Dresden Codex depicted in plate 14, though
they have not been explained as fully as the latter. The Mayan days
signified by the Year Bearers here differ from those in the Dresden, and
it is thought that this codex represents a much later stage in calendar
development. (The following notes, much simplified, are based on
Thomas, I, pp. 67–92.) The glyphs in the horizontal strip stand for the
last two days of each year; the cross appearing in the Dresden is also
here. Occurring in each picture, at bottom, is the symbol for a heap of
stones, each time surmounted by a god, including in No. 23 the god of
death shown in the Dresden. In No. 21, upper left, is a figure dancing
on stilts and carrying a dog. (Morley, p. 246, says that in the event of
drought or of over-sprouting of the corn, old women were made to
perform a dance on high stilts, carrying pottery dogs containing food.)
In upper right of each picture, a priest or god is depicted either casting
corn grains in divination or (Morley, p. 147) planting corn with a plant-

102

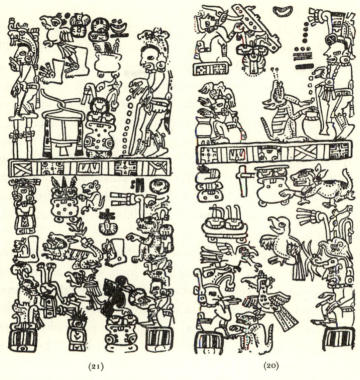

(21)                                    (20)

ing stick. At bottom, the serpents coiled under vessels are said to denote
each a period of 52 years; the vessels are cinerary urns, "symbolic repre-
sentation of the idea that the years have closed—are dead—and . . . the
ashes of the years may be said to rest in these vessels." In the urns are
hieroglyphs for the *uayab*, the last five days of the year. In No. 22, upper
left, are two figures falling head-downward, the lower one being dashed
to pieces on a pyramid, over which streams blood: these likewise represent expiring periods of time. (Reproduced from Seler, I, pp. 382–83,
after the Codex Troano. Morley says [p. 299]: "The Codex Tro-
Cortesianus, divided into two unequal sections, was discovered during
the sixties of the last century in Spain. Although each section was found
in a different place, students have been able to prove that both pieces
are parts of the same manuscript. The larger section [Codex Troano]
was owned by a Señor Juan de Tró y Ortolano, of Madrid; the smaller
section belonged to a Señor Jose Ignacio Miro, who . . . called it the
Codex Cortesianus, believing it had been brought [to Spain] by Cortes.
. . . Both sections rejoined and called the Codex Tro-Cortesianus are
now in the Museum of Archaeology and History at Madrid." See also
plate 14 and p. 99, footnote 1.)

103

its own terrace. The pueblo showed no sign of life, not even smoke. As we passed down the steep, narrow path to the plaza, a few curious Indians poked their heads out of their houses to take a look at us. The Santiago Chimaltenango Indians wear striking costumes. The women of that pueblo wear *huipiles* of bright red cotton run through with fine lines of yellow or white. In front, above the breasts, there are six symbols, embroidered in silk, of different colours. They have wide, stiff woolen belts of black, white, and red, lovely in design, and blue skirts. Their hair is worn high and held in place by a red woven band. The men wear white cotton trousers and white blouses sometimes striped in blue. Over the blouses they wear dark brown or black woolen *capixaijes*. They wear red scarves thrown around their shoulders or wrapped turban-like around their heads.

On one side of the small plaza stood the church, simple and charming. On an adjoining side was the *juzgado*, which served as meeting-place, court, and jail, and in which we were to spend the night. It consisted of one large room with a large table, a bench, and a Government telephone. A few friendly Indians watched us unload. With particular interest they watched me wash at the *pila* in the centre of the plaza. Then we went to call on Don Pancho's *ladino* friends. The husband was away, but the wife, seven children, two pigs, two ducks, and several chickens and dogs were much in evidence. The wife, Maroka, had a long Spanish face, full of character, weary and worn. Not only did she cook, wash, clean, and look after the children, but, to help eke out the family's living, she baked bread to sell in the pueblo—*pan dulce*, the sweet corn bread that Indians love. She had lived in Santiago Chimaltenango most of her life, except for a short time in Todos Santos, and she spoke Mam like an Indian. I could see she was very much respected by the local *naturales*.

Maroka told us that all the Indians were in the mountains or in their homes. That night, she said, the *chimanes* would receive in their houses those Indians who had questions to ask or who wished to hear the prognostications for the coming year—that is, if the Spirit should come. She informed us that roosters and turkeys would be sacrificed that night and the next day in front of the church and the cross.

I asked if it would be possible for us to go that night to the house of one of the *chimanes*. Maroka said she would ask but doubted it very much, as the Indians allowed no outsiders, including *ladinos,* at any of their religious rites. Nevertheless she sent one of her children to the house of a woman *chimán,* only to discover that she had already gone to the mountains. By chance, however, an Indian woman whose son was learning to be a *chimán* passed by. Maroka told her (in Mam) that Don Pancho and I wanted very much to go to the house of a *chimán;* that I had come from a distant country and that, in my country, I was used to visiting *chimanes*, especially for the New Year ceremony. She told her that I had come all the way from Todos Santos to see a *chimán* on this special night and to burn my candles. We were her friends, Maroka said, and were like members of her family. The woman asked why I had not gone to the ceremony at Todos Santos. Maroka passed this on to me, and I told her to tell the woman that the *chimanes* in Todos Santos did not have sufficient power. The woman thereupon said that she would speak to her son, who was going that night to the house of his teacher, and perhaps he in turn would speak to the *chimán* who was doing *costumbre.* In half an hour she returned and said that the *chimán*-teacher did not like the idea, for he felt that we would not have sufficient respect and might think their customs ludicrous, and that the Spirit might not enter the house if we were there. We tried to convince her of our sincerity and of our respect for Indian *costumbre.* I told her that we would bring the *chimán* the customary presents, besides paying him, and I gave her twenty-five cents by way of additional persuasion.

In an hour and a half, she returned and said, "If you are willing to walk [six miles] up into the mountains to the house of the *chimán* in order to be looked over, and if he then approves, you can stay through the night and return at dawn. If he does not approve, you will have to return immediately to the pueblo."

If we agreed to this, she said, she would take us there herself, leaving at six in the afternoon. We accepted. I was tired, for I had risen early, and besides had a cold, but I knew this was an opportunity for an invaluable experience. I had ready four bottles of *aguardiente*—it is always used in Indian ceremonies and is a customary gift to the *chimán;* six packages of cigarettes; and eight candles, which I wrapped in a red cloth. Andrés was left behind to watch our baggage, and at six we were on our way. Our guide was about sixty years old, with shining eyes and a pleasant smile, though I could tell she was not sure she was doing the right thing. She carried herself well, padding along on her bare feet. She reminded me of a bright little bird as she now and then looked back over her shoulder to see if we were following. Up and up we went until breathing became somewhat difficult. We were stopped by numerous Indians returning from the coast to celebrate the New Year. They questioned both Domingo and our guide, and I could see by their faces that they did not like the idea of our journey.

When we reached the top of the ridge the sun was setting, and a glorious sight spread for miles before us: range after mountain range of all colours, deep mysterious valleys, and far to the south, like a mighty king, the huge volcano Tajumulco keeping watch over his kingdom. For a long time we went along the crest, then down into a small valley, then up again, until we came to a section, called Florida, on the other side. In the darkness we could see several fires burning, and our guide pointed out a distant fire half-way down in the valley. We turned off the main trail and then followed a tortuous one through brush and trees. Suddenly I remembered that both Don Pancho and I had left our flashlights behind. We laughed over our carelessness, for this was the night we were going to need them most.

We passed one house, full of people, where the guide said another *chimán* lived, and then, a little further on, arrived at our destination. The house was surrounded by trees and in front of it was a fire. There was great excitement as we were led into the firelight so that the *chimán* could look us over. He was rather dark in complexion, with a strong face, large penetrating eyes, a short beard, and a powerful build. I noticed another man, much older, watching us from the other side of the fire; he had a long face, penetrating grey eyes, a beautiful Mayan nose, and two deep lines that ran down the side of his face from nose to mouth. One sensed great strength, dignity, and also sadness in him. He and the *chimán* talked together and then to Domingo, who finally told us we would be allowed to stay.

The house was decorated with pine branches and, around the door, the shiny, dark-green, elongated leaves of the *pacaya* plant. Inside was a large rectangular room. The thatched roof was very high and steep, and from it a storage platform was swung about seven feet above the earth floor and about four feet from the walls. On the dirt floor several fires were burning, and many clay vessels of all sizes and shapes, containing food, were steaming, while women were busy about them. We sat to the left of the door, on a narrow bench against the wall. Opposite us, built into the corner, was the *corral,* the so-called room of the *chimán* (in Mam, *pach jaimes*).[7] It was a topless enclosure formed by screens of bamboo poles, with an entrance over which a blanket was draped when the *chimán* was summoning and communing with the Spirit. It was not unlike a voter's booth, and around its doorless entrance was a garland of *pacaya* leaves. Within was an altar. The floor was covered with pine needles. This was the room from which the *chimán* would answer questions if the Spirit or *dueño de cerro* came.[8]

A small fire was built at our feet, and by its light the faces were revealed. The *chimán,* who did not speak Spanish, asked us through the older man (whom I shall call "Mayan Nose") why we had come. He also questioned Domingo. I was deeply impressed by their sincerity and friendliness. First passing around cigarettes, I answered, "I have come tonight with my candles and questions for I am far away from my own

[7] Cf. Landa, p. 66: ". . . in this festival they also built a new oratorio for the demon, or else renewed the old, and gathered there for sacrifice and offerings to him, all going through a solemn revel; for this festival was general and obligatory."

[8] I found out later that it was the *chimanes'* code to construct their houses of four poles, one in each corner. This might possibly signify the four *alcaldes del mundo*. See fig. 2, p. 108; also, p. 203.

land, my family, and my friends. In my country there are also *chimanes,* and since I am unable to go to them I come to you. This night is an important night. We are leaving *ik* and entering into *t'ce,* a good year. My thoughts turn to my country and my family and so my question is, 'How are my mother, sister, and brother?' "

Domingo translated this to the *chimán,* who seemed impressed, as also was "Mayan Nose," he of the sad face, of whom I was more acutely aware

According to Förstemann (p. 173), we see here a god sitting in a tent, on the roof of which there is a vessel containing food of some kind. The square tent is perhaps an antecedent of the *corral* of the Mam *chimán,* with its four poles. (From the Gates edition of the Dresden Codex, p. 36, lower right. See also plate 14 and p. 99, footnote 1.)

Fig. 2. Mayan priest or god sitting in his house (?), from the Dresden Codex.

than of the *chimán.* Don Pancho, for his part, said that he had come because of a strange buzzing in his left ear which he had now had for over a year and which no doctor could cure.

The *chimán* asked if we had brought our candles and *aguardiente,* and as I handed him the candles I said, "Here they are for the four Alcaldes del Mundo, two for each." He put the candles and the two bottles (I had given him only two of the four) on the altar with the other offerings.

To the left, in the shadows, two musicians played constantly, on a home-made violin and a guitar. One was the brother of the *chimán.* I feel that they improvised as they went along; their music was good. All night they played, seldom the same tune and never anything gay or violent. Their music, I thought, expressed nature, the sad side of nature.

The men all crowded around us, those who spoke Spanish questioning and then translating. Domingo gave a long oration, and though I could not understand it I felt it was about me, how I had cured people and paid off his contract. I watched the faces of the men and boys around me: strong, good faces, well modelled, aristocratic, the contours standing out boldly when touched by the firelight, then melting into the mysterious darkness that filled the room. These were pure Maya, I reflected, and probably only a few of them ever realized what a great civilization they had sprung from.

The *chimán* told us that it was the custom for all to eat together on this night before the Spirit came. We ate *tortillas* and drank coffee and smoked cigarettes given us by the *chimán*. I noticed that "Mayan Nose" had gone into the *corral* of the *chimán* and was keeping a fire of *ocote* sticks going. He had a beautiful profile, very much like one of the priests on the carvings of Palenque.[9] I wondered who he was, and had Domingo ask someone. Domingo told me:

"He is the teacher of the *chimán,* and the *chimán* is the teacher of the son of the woman who guided us here."

About ten-thirty, the *chimán* spread pine needles all over the floor of the house, and then he joined "Mayan Nose" within the *corral.* Shortly afterward, I was called in, and I knelt before the altar on the pine needles between the two old men. The *chimán* was on my left in front of the altar, the teacher on my right. The room was tiny, and we were crowded close together. The altar, which was the table of the *chimán,* was covered with a cloth of white banded with red, and around it was a garland of *pacaya* leaves and some bananas. On the altar were two carved gourd bowls, in each a small gourd cup.

(Rosa Bautista explained to me later: "The gourd cup or *guacalito* is used by the *chimán* to put *aguardiente* in; he can drink the spirit of God which presents itself during the hours of prayer. The gourd bowls or *jicaritas* are used for drinking *batido.* When one drinks it, it signifies the union of all the participants, that all are one.")

Between the two bowls lay the candles and the gifts of *aguardiente* from the people. At the back of the table were four skyrockets, and on

[9] Mayan ruins in the state of Chiapas, Mexico, about 150 miles north of Todos Santos.

the floor in front, six clay candleholders. "Mayan Nose," who could speak Spanish, asked me the names of the members of my family and then gave them to the *chimán*. He then took the candles in both hands and, speaking in a quick, strong voice, pressed them against my shoulder. He held them there as he prayed. The only words I could understand were "Santiago" (St. James), who is patron saint of the pueblo, the names of the four Alcaldes del Mundo, and the names of the members of my family. He then went to the altar and prayed for a long time, then lighted the candles and put them in the six holders. The two extra ones he stood on the floor. As he sat to the left of the altar, I noticed a heavy metal chain lying on the floor at his feet, and wondered what it was.

(Rosa Bautista subsequently told me: "The chain is the pact between the *chimán* and the Spirit, the *dueño de cerro*. Every *chimán* is given one a short time after he has given his first mass. The *chimán* holds the Spirit by the chain so that he will fulfil the requests the *chimán* has made in his supplications. The large ring at one end is used by the *chimán* when he evokes and when he receives the Spirit. The body of the chain is passed through the ring which he holds in his hands. If the Spirit does not come, the *chimán* pulls the chain back through the ring. There are times when a Spirit does not respond and come to a *chimán*. When this happens over a long period of time, the *chimán* can go to the mountains and break his chain and his connection with the Spirit.")

The *chimán* now opened one of the bottles, took from the altar a crystal wine glass with a broken stem, filled it with *aguardiente*, and passed it first to his teacher, then to me, then to himself, and finally to his pupil. I drank a toast to the three of them and to the four *alcaldes* and drained the glass in one gulp, that being the custom.[10] They asked me to put ten cents on the altar, and were more than pleased when I put twenty-five cents there instead. Thereupon, I left, and Don Pancho

---

[10] Cf. Landa, p. 45: "Then they brought a fine chalice of wine and quickly offered it to the gods, invoking them with devout prayers to receive this small gift from the children; this chalice they then gave to another officiant called *cayom*, that he might empty it at a single draught; for him to stop to take breath in this was regarded as something sinful."

entered. When they were finished with him they called me back again, along with the *chimán's* young pupil and the *chimán's* wife. We drank again and again and the *chimán* became very much agitated. His hands trembled and the force from his voice was awe-inspiring. All this time the old teacher stood there, serene and yet sad. Again I was offered a drink, but I passed it to the *chimán's* wife, who seemed grateful for it. We went back to our bench, the *chimán* with us. The teacher remained praying while we drank coffee and smoked.

About twenty minutes past eleven, the wife of the *chimán* carried into the *corral* a beautiful, big white rooster and the three *chimanes*— that is, old teacher, *chimán,* and pupil—sacrificed it. Of this I caught only a glimpse, because a man standing in the doorway obstructed my view. A *pichacha* containing copal stood on the floor in front of the altar. Two *chimanes*—"Mayan Nose" and the pupil—held the rooster head down while the other cut its throat. The rooster flapped its wings as the blood flowed onto the copal in the *pichacha*. A few minutes later the woman came out carrying the limp body of the fowl. Then two turkeys were sacrificed. By that time it was nearly midnight. A boy sitting next to me told me that since sunset many birds had been sacrificed, twenty in all, possibly for the twenty days of the year. A blanket was hung over the entrance of the *corral,* leaving the three *chimanes* inside. The fires in the outer room were put out, and we sat in darkness.[11]

The *chimán*[12] now, in a strong voice, began to pray, and as he spoke

[11] The Mayans also had purifying rites during the Year Bearer Ceremony. Cf. Landa, pp. 70–71: "The *chacs* [officials for helping the priests] seated themselves in the four corners, and stretched from one to the other a new rope, inside of which all who had fasted had to enter, in order to drive out the evil spirit. . . . When the evil one had been driven out, all began their devout prayers, and the *chacs* made new fire and lit the brazier; because in the festivals celebrated by the whole community new fire was made wherewith to light the brazier. The priest began to throw in incense, and all came in their order, commencing with the chiefs, to receive incense from the hands of the priest, which he gave them with as much gravity as if he were giving them relics; . . . After this burning of the incense, all ate the gifts and presents, and the wine went about until they became very drunk. Such was the festival of the New Year, a ceremony very acceptable to their idols."

[12] Cf. ibid., p. 47: "The most idolatrous of them were the priests, the *chilanes*. . . . The *chilanes* were charged with giving to all those in the locality the oracles of the demon, and the respect given them was so great that they did not ordinarily leave their houses except borne upon litters carried on the shoulders."

one could smell blood mixed with the burning copal. He pronounced the names of the Alcaldes del Mundo and of Santiago and, I assumed, called on the Spirit to come. He must have stood there supplicating for a good half hour when suddenly his voice changed. It was as if it had been spurred on to a double tempo. He spoke so fast and with such force that he sounded to me like a machine-gun. His voice never stopped for a breath until he began to make what seemed to be statements and to answer questions. He would call "Chucia Chuán!"[13] and his wife, who was in the outer room with us, would answer. What she said sounded like "Yes, Father, we are here. Do not leave us."

(Rosa Bautista told me afterwards: "The wife of the *chimán* who conducts the mass is called Chucia Chuán, and she is the servant of the Spirit. When the Spirit says, 'Are you there, Chucia Chuán?' she says, 'Yes, my Tata, I am here.' She does everything the Spirit asks of her. Sometimes it is for *aguardiente* he asks, or water, other times he commands her to dance with him. If she does not execute his commands correctly and is not obedient he beats her with a whip, and severely.")

This all went on for about an hour and a half. Among other things, I heard the *chimán* say "Estados Unidos," and I knew he was answering my question. The bench I was sitting on was so uncomfortable that I could scarcely bear it. I had to close my eyes to keep the smoke out of them, and moreover it was all I could do to keep awake. Suddenly I felt something touch my head. I looked up. It was "Mayan Nose" passing me on his way to send off a skyrocket, for the Spirit had gone.

When the *chimán* came out of his *corral* I noticed that he was bathed in sweat. Then we all had coffee and a smoke, and we were told what had been said. The Spirit had accepted us and said that we were all right, that my family was well but that my mother was sad because I was so far away, that the Spirit said I must come three years in succession, then I would be well for the rest of my life. Don Pancho's ear trouble could be

---

[13] But Chimán Pascual Pablo told Don Pancho that every wife of a *chimán* is called "Chucia Bank," for that was the name of the wife of Ambrosio, called Ténom, the first *chimán* of the world. See pp. 122, 135, 138, 143.

Pl. 2. Todos Santos. On the right stands the *juzgado*, in the centre the two *pilas* or fountains.

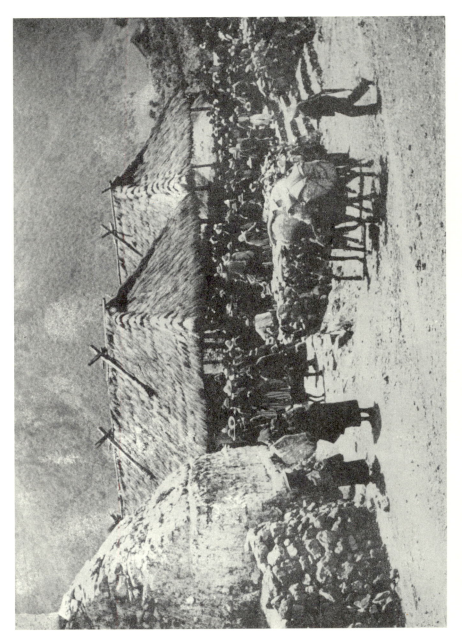

Pl. 3. The market place at Todos Santos.

Pl. 4. A typical house.

Pl. 5. The author lived in the whitewashed house; her *mozo* and his family in the house in the foreground. Margarita Elón lived in the one to the rear. Fruit trees and

Pl. 6. Domingo, the author's *mozo*.

Plate Pac: Luis, wife of Patron, ——— laid in L'Huerez, we cent for the eldest son, Andrés ———

Pl. 8. Basilia, the author's servant.

Pl. 9. Rosa Bautista, midwife and *pulsera*, sister of "El Rey," the calendar priest.

cured, but he had on him the sin of his father or grandfather who had shot and killed a man. I told Don Pancho to give the *chimán* another bottle, which he did, and we were then called again into his *corral* for another drink. The *chimán*, through "Mayan Nose," told Don Pancho that because of the sin he had on him he would have to make an offering to the church next morning of two turkey eggs, some copal, and ten candles. Don Pancho got out of it by giving the *chimán* thirty-five cents so that he might perform the *costumbre* for him.

As I returned to the large room I saw the women putting the plucked and cleaned birds in a huge pot. The musician, brother of the *chimán*, came over to me and asked me if I could cure him, that he was very sick: he could not eat and when he did he lost his meal, he had no strength, he had chills all the time. I questioned him a little more. It was evident he had malaria.

"Yes, I can help you," I told him, "if you take two pills a day of the twenty yellow pills I shall give you. Then you will be relieved." I smiled to myself at the thought that the brother of the *chimán* would come to me to be cured, and at such a time.

The fires were now put out again and the *chimán* went into another trance behind the blanketed doorway, as before. Then another sky-rocket was sent off. When he came out he carried in a red cloth the bananas that had decorated his altar. One of the group cut the bananas, on the red cloth, into as many pieces as there were people—about thirty-five or forty—and the pieces were put into hats and passed around. Whatever was left, such as the skin, was collected and put into the red cloth and burned.

(In explanation Rosa Bautista subsequently made this comment: "After the Spirit leaves and the fruit has received his blessing, it is cut into as many pieces as there are people present. When they eat it their sins will leave them.[14] The left-over parts must be collected and burned,

---

[14] This is a form of communion, as are the partaking of the *aguardiente* in the house of the *chimán* and the eating of the flesh of the turkeys sacrificed by the *rezadores* or the Chimán Nam.

for if a child should eat or touch this it would receive the sins of all who have eaten the fruit. If a woman has had intercourse with any man during the five evil days, she cannot eat or touch the fruit, for it would bring sickness or possibly death to her.")

I invited the *chimanes* to visit me if they came to Todos Santos, and they all seemed pleased. We left about four, though they begged us to wait and eat of the sacrificed birds and see the last skyrocket be sent off at dawn. I thanked them for their kindness in letting me come and said I would be back in a year. (The following year, in April, 1947, I visited this same *chimán* again, and only then would he give me his name, Manuel Andrés. He told me that while General Ubico was President of Guatemala[15] all *chimanes* had been persecuted, and that was the reason he would not give his name the first time.)

The moon had vanished and we were without flashlights so Domingo carried *ocote* to light our way. Though I was exhausted, I enjoyed the long walk back. The strange night smells, the sounds of animals rustling in the bushes, the light of the flickering torch on the trees and on my companions, these were all well worth the fatigue. We could see a faint glow to the east when we came out on top of the ridge, and a few lights below in the pueblo. From time to time a streak of light appeared, a sky message to the Alcaldes del Mundo.

The next morning the families of Santiago Chimaltenango sacrificed roosters in front of the church and the cross. In the afternoon, the woman *chimán*, Catalina Aguilar, a great friend of Maroka's, gave me the names of the twenty days of the month and their four *alcaldes*. She informed me that I was more fortunate than she—the Spirit had not come to the *chimán's* house she had visited.[16]

---

[15] Jorge Ubico Castañeda was President—more accurately, dictator—of Guatemala from 1931 to 1944. He died in 1946, and perhaps the *chimán* thought he had been President right up to his death.

[16] On the Mam New Year's Eve of the following year, I was invited to attend the ceremony at the house of a *chimán* of Todos Santos. See pp. 204 ff.

# 4

## How to Become a Chimán

ONE YEAR AFTER this Year Bearer Ceremony, Chimán Pascual Pablo
agreed to teach Don Pancho to be a *chimán*. The *chimán* allowed Don
Pancho to write down all the prayers, the names of the holy mountains,
the list of the days, the chart for casting the *mixes*, and the chart of the
*costumbres* of a *chimán*.[1] He consented to this when Don Pancho explained that it was the custom of *ladinos* to write down what they wished
to memorize. I shall begin with Don Pancho's account of his conversations with the *chimán* and of his initiation.

1

Chimán Pascual Pablo to Don Pancho (March 20, 1947: *ik*)

### DON PANCHO
When will you teach me to be a *chimán*, Tata Pascual?

### PASCUAL PABLO
Some other day I shall teach you. When your table is ready bring it
directly here, and see that it is carried in a sack, for no one must see the
table. Do not take it to your house. Bring your materials, your candles
and copal here and then I will teach you. Put your house in order for this
is a very delicate matter. I will teach you prayers you do not know; put
them down well [on paper]. Every five days you will have to come to me,
every five days you will have to come to me. I shall teach you how to op-
erate with the table, I shall teach you what your office is. Every day of an

---

[1] Some of this material is given in the Appendix, pp. 245 ff.

115

*alcalde* once, every day of an *alcalde* once. On *k'mané* we will carry the table to your house. Two roosters must be ready for they will be needed.

## 2

### The Birth of the Table

Given by Don Pancho (March 29, 1947: *batz*)

I arrived at the house of Pascual Pablo, where he was to teach me to be a *chimán,* about five in the afternoon. I carried in a sack a small table made of white cypress without a nail in it, as ordered to do by Pascual. I also carried four balls of copal and four candles of *cera.*[2]

He received me with pleasure and asked me to put the things on the floor. He took the table from the sack, turning it around several times to examine it. He said it was good and placed it next to his black table, black from many years of practice of *costumbre.* He told me to put coals into the *pichacha* which stood in front of my table and to take the four candles that I had brought.

"Look, do it like this," he said. "Santa Silla Bank, Santo Mundo, Santa Justicia, Santo Jesucristo, Dios del Mundo." He then took the four candles in his hand and said, "Touch your table and mine with the candles, repeating, 'Dios del Chimán Baj K'mané, give permission to Don Pancho to receive his table in the ancient manner.'

"Ah, *malaya,* Santo Mundo, Santa Silla Bank: ah, *malaya,* Santa Justicia, ah, *malaya,* Dios del Cielo, be with Don Pancho, hear his words, his pain. Receive his gift with love. Ah, four Alcaldes del Mundo, K'mané, Cuman T'ce, Ik, Noj, Santa Casalera del Mundo, Batz, hear Don Pancho, Caballero K'oy, Caballero Xolik, Caballero Bach, Caballero Cilbilchax, aid this man, Santo Mundo, Santa Silla Bank, Santa Justicia, Dios del Cielo, give to Don Pancho the *costumbres* of the *naturales* of the pueblo."

He turned and faced me and then said, "Take a match and light the

[2] The *cera* is beeswax; candles are also made of *sebo,* animal fat, tallow.

wick of one candle, for only in this way can you give light to the others."

When the candles were burning brightly, he put them in a clay candelabrum, all coated with candlewax and with soot. Taking the four balls of copal, he gave me two and told me to kneel in front of my table with the balls in my hand and to say the following, which I did: "With permission, Santa Mesa, Santo Mundo, Santa Justicia, Dios del Cielo, with all my heart I receive you. Ah, *malaya,* Santa Mesa, give me health, money, and animals and pleasure to live in this world. Give me understanding in my head so that I can work well, for the good of the people. Ah, *malaya,* Santa Mesa, Santo Mundo, Santa Justicia, Dios del Cielo, give me the good fortune to come upon money. Ah, *malaya,* give health to my wife, children, friends, and keep them from being harmed by evil people. Caballero K'oy, Caballero Bach, Caballero Xolik, Caballero Cilbilchax, hear me, help me to be delivered from suffering. Receive my offering today, Dios Batz."

Throughout all this the *chimán* held two of the balls of copal in his hand and I held the other two. He told me to throw mine in the *pichacha* and he did the same.

While these were burning we talked and he said, "I shall teach you something that no one must know, not even your wife. I will expect you tomorrow, *k'mané,* with copal, candles, and a turkey egg to close the mouths of the *gente.*"

3

*The Birth of Don Pancho*
Given by Dan Pancho (April 1, 1947: *ix*)

I went to Tata Pascual's on the day *k'mané* as he had told me to come, but he was occupied so he told me to come today, the day *ix*.

At 4 P.M., I was received by Pascual Pablo in his house, and after a short talk I gave him the following things: four candles of *sebo,* four balls of copal, and a turkey egg. He told me to start a fire in the *pichacha.*

He took two packages of copal and the candles and he swung the *pichacha* in front of the table, saying the following:

"Ah, *malaya*, Santa Mesa, Santo Mundo, Santa Justicia, Dios del Cielo, here he is, here is Don Pancho. Receive him with love. Now your son has been born, give to him good thought, hear his voice, hear his love, hear his troubles, and defend him a little. Ah, *malaya*, Santo Mundo, Santa Mesa, Santa Justicia, Dios del Cielo, give to Señor Don Pancho, *ladino*, permission to know the *costumbres* of the *naturales* of the pueblo. Make his heart good, his law good, let him not go astray, let him keep a straight course, a little. Dios T'ciik, close the mouths of the people, take away evil thoughts from the *gente*, rid Don Pancho of evil, take away evil from his family. Señor del Cielo, direct his course, his work, give him food and animals, and refresh his head a little. Ah, *malaya*, Caballero K'oy, Caballero Bach, Caballero Cilbilchax, Caballero T'oj Xolik, be with Don Pancho. Señor Todos Santos, receive Señor Don Pancho as a true son of the pueblo."

This he spoke to his table and mine, and ordered me to take the two balls of copal in my hand and place myself between the two tables and make the following invocation:

"Santa Mesa, Santo Mundo, Santa Justicia, Dios, permit me to be able to understand the *costumbres* of the pueblo and to serve your sons in their sufferings. Permit that I may be good. Ah, *malaya*, Mundo, Santa Mesa, Santa Justicia, Dios del Cielo, be with me always. Señor K'oy, Señor Bach, Señor Cilbilchax, Señor T'oj Xolik, aid me to bear my afflictions."

Shortly thereafter I moved to my table with the copal in my hand and spoke as follows, as the *chimán* had asked me to pray alone and ask for what I wished:

"Ah, *malaya*, Santa Mesa, be my comfort. Santo Mundo, Santa Justicia, Dios, I receive you with love in my house, and I will give you your food and you will give me mine. Keep my family from sickness, and for myself give me good luck in finding work; give me money, animals, food, and peace. Ah, *malaya*, Mundo, Señor T'ui K'oy, Señor T'ui Bach,

Señor T'oj Xolik, Señor Cilbilchax, help me in the *costumbres* of the table."

Then I threw the two balls of copal into the *pichacha,* and the *chimán* did likewise. I now lit the candles as he had instructed me and put them in the candelabrum, all four together. Also I put the turkey egg in with the copal. Then I talked with the *chimán* and he said, "To-morrow, come with the same material."

### 4

Given by Don Pancho (April 2, 1947: *tsikin*)

At four o'clock, I went to the house of the *chimán* with the necessary things. We repeated everything that we had done the day before except that he ordered me to fix a place in my house where the table could eventually be put and he told me that we must pray that Santa Tierra would receive the table with love.

### 5

Chimán Pascual Pablo to Don Pancho (April 7, 1947: *najpu*)

DON PANCHO

Tata Pascual, what are the words used in the act of sacrifice or the act of killing a rooster?

PASCUAL PABLO

This is what they say: *"t'chimolal jun k'o"* ["this rooster is your of-fering"].

DON PANCHO

What word does a *chimán* say when he kills a rooster?

PASCUAL PABLO

*Biol ee.*

119

## Don Pancho

Tata Pascual, which candles have most power for *costumbre?*

## Pascual Pablo

*Cera* to ask for a favour, money, or advice; *sebo* to defend oneself when a wicked man casts illness upon one.

## Don Pancho

Who is the *dueño* of the river, Tata Pascual?

## Pascual Pablo

*Mar,* so he is called.

## Don Pancho

Tata Pascual, do you remember when the church was built?

## Pascual Pablo

No. When my father was born it was here and when my grandfather lived it was here. Who knows how long ago?

## Don Pancho

Good, Tata Pascual, you must teach me well. I want to learn to be a *chimán;* I want you to teach me well so that the people will not laugh at me. I want you to teach me the prayers you know, so that I can write them down and learn them.

## Pascual Pablo

I have told you all that my heart wishes to teach you, and with love. Little by little you will learn. Do not worry. I shall teach you how to draw out sickness by means of the river, how to cure one bewitched.

## Don Pancho

What is that about the river, Tata Pascual?

## PASCUAL PABLO

Always there are women, always there are men. Sometimes there are bad men who have one woman, then another and then another. There are also bad women who have many men. This is what must be done. Ask for four turkey eggs, light candles of *cera,* a little copal or still better some incense. Then on either a day *ix* or *imix,* take the transgressor into the river at night and carry your materials with you. Send the transgressor into the river to wash his feet, hands, face, and head. Put copal and a turkey egg in the *pichacha* and pray thus:

"Ah, *malaya,* Señor Patrón Todos Santos, ah, *malaya,* Dios, ah, *malaya,* Santa Justicia, ah, *malaya,* Santo Mundo, drive out the evil from this person [saying the name]. Make him forget his urge to seek another woman. Ah, *malaya,* Santo Mundo, cool his body a little. Ah, *malaya,* Santa Justicia, cleanse this person of his desire. Ah, *malaya,* Santo Mundo, cool his body a little. Ah, *malaya,* Santa Justicia, cleanse this person of his evil. Ah, *malaya,* Caballero K'oy, Caballero Bach, Caballero Cilbilchax, drive the evil out of this man, cool his body, let the water, let the river carry away his evil; carry it away, river; carry it to your house. Wicked is this man."

When this is finished, let him come out of the river for a little. Then enter the river again. Burn another egg and copal and repeat the same prayers. Altogether four times this must be done: to go to the river, to burn the copal, to use four turkey eggs, to repeat the same prayer. No candles are burned on the table with these prayers.

## DON PANCHO

The river, is it used just to cool the body or has it any other purpose?

## PASCUAL PABLO

Yes, indeed it has. There is no time that one does not go to the river to confess one's sins. When people go to the river they confess their sins and say who their worst enemies are, who is the evil one who has cast an evil spell against them, and they pray that the evil may turn back on the one who has sent it. Then there is a burial.[3] I have taught you how to extract a burial. When you do extract it—ah, *malaya*, then the person is well.

DON PANCHO

How do you drive the bewitchment out of one who is bewitched?

PASCUAL PABLO

I shall tell you little by little, we shall bull-fight[4] a little to see how you are. You must have no fear for if you do you are lost. Take care you do not run; a *chimán* must have no fear. I was a young man when I learned to be a *chimán*. I shall teach you how to become one, because the Word has been changed. When the world was born only one man knew how to cast the *mixes*. Ambrosio, this one was called. But later he changed and for that reason the Word was changed. There are things I shall teach you. But only your heart and my heart must know this. If you tell anyone else you will be lost.

You must look after your table, the little one, as you would a baby. If you do not it will not grow. You must never tell your wife, your sons, or your friends. If you tell you are lost. Only teach others when you have given them their tables. If you tell others before then you are lost. One does not learn everything at once, but only little by little. I must also find a *fiador* [sponsor or guarantor] for one who is learning to be a *chimán*. A *dueño de pozo*, that is a *fiador*. On *k'mané* we shall take the table to your house. When the table is in your house I shall teach you your obligations.

DON PANCHO

Tata Pascual, one owes the table much respect, does one not?

---

[3] A "burial" of such personal things as hair, clothing, or nail parings, or of an effigy, is made by a *chimán* for the purpose of casting a spell or of defending his patient against the effects of a *brujo*. See pp. 160 f.

[4] Don Pancho asked the old *chimán* many times what he meant by "bull-fight," without receiving an answer.

PASCUAL PABLO

Yes, very much, like the respect for a saint, for a saint in the church. When you make *costumbre* you must not touch a woman. If you do, Santo Mundo will not hear you. Do not fight, and do not be *bravo* [bullying] in your house. Patience, always have patience, and then Santo Mundo will hear you.

[*After this I gave Chimán Pascual my materials, and he told me to make a fire in the* pichacha. *He took two balls of copal and gave me two, and then—*]

PASCUAL PABLO

In the name of God, Santa Justicia, Santa Mesa, Santo Mundo, receive with favour the offering of this poor man. Permit it that he learn the *costumbres* of the *naturales* of the pueblo. Give permission, Santo Mundo, to Señor Don Pancho, a true son of the pueblo and of yours, Santa Mesa. Hear his troubles, hear his complaints, aid him in caring for the sick, give him work, give him money, give him comfort, give him food, and give him a little chain. Ah, Dios Najpu, receive Señor Don Pancho as you would a *natural*. Ah, *malaya*, Caballero K'oy, Caballero Bach, Caballero T'oj Xolik, Caballero Cilbilchax, take care of Señor Don Pancho and give him good judgment that he may not stray from the path.

[*During all this, Chimán Pascual stood with my table on his left and with me on his right. Finishing the prayer,—*]

PASCUAL PABLO

I shall speak Spanish to you so that you may learn well.[4a]

[*I then threw the copal in the fire and so did he. He took the candles and ordered me to light them and place them in the candelabrum.*]

PASCUAL PABLO

I shall teach you everything well because you gave me a present of

[4a] Don Pancho spoke some Mam, but not fluently.

trousers and a jacket.[5] God will pay you. The people of this pueblo give nothing. They give food, a drink, cigarettes, only such things, and for this reason we are poor. Ah, *malaya*, never trousers, a jacket; other things, no. They give nothing.

6

### The Fiador

Chimán Pascual Pablo to Don Pancho (April 8, 1947: *imix*)

DON PANCHO

Tata Pascual, what is a *fiador?*

PASCUAL PABLO

A *fiador* is a man who knows one's indebtedness to another man and says, "I shall pay for you, but you must pay me."

DON PANCHO

That is all right, but what is a *fiador* in the *costumbres* of a *chimán?*

PASCUAL PABLO

It means the same. There is never a time when someone is sick, very sick, that we do not look for a *fiador*. This is how it is done. On the day *akbal*, the sick one brings eight candles of *sebo,* eight candles of *cera,* and eight balls of copal. If he is very poor, a quarter of a litre of *aguardiente;* if he has a little money, half of a litre; and if he is rich, a litre. We carry the sick one to the *cerro,* one *cerro* after another, whichever one you want. There we implore the *dueño de cerro* to serve as *fiador* and in this way the sick one will not die. We speak as follows when we are on the mountain top with the sick one:

"Nombre de Dios, Santa Justicia, Santo Mundo, Santo Cerro."

In your two hands you must hold copal, a *trago* of *aguardiente,* and

---

[5] In January, Don Pancho had given these to cement their friendship.

candles. Then move your hands about, touch the head of the sick one with the candles and say:

"This sick man wants you to be his *fiador* so that he will not die. Ah, *malaya*, Cuman Dios [God who is good], defend this poor man, drive out his sickness. Ah, *malaya*, Santa Justicia, remove the debt of the poor man so that he will not die. Ah, *malaya*, Santo Mundo, drive out the pain of this poor man. Ah, *malaya*, Santo Cerro, you must be his *fiador* so that the poor man will not die. Cuman Ik, Cuman T'ce, Cuman Noj, Cuman Ee, come, Señores, pardon us; come, protect this sick one. Caballero K'oy, Caballero Bach, Caballero Xolik, come, Señores, here I am waiting, give me your help, help for this man, to drive out his sufferings. Ah, Dios, Señor Todos Santos, Santa Tierra, Santo Mundo, Santo Jesucristo, Santa Justicia, Dios del Cielo, give to this patient your *t'chimolal*. Here is this poor one. Ah, *malaya*, Santo Mundo, Santa Tierra, Santa Justicia, Cuman Dios!"

Now burn four balls of copal, four candles of *sebo*, and four of *cera*. Burn the four others of each on the *costumbre* table at night. The sick one will then be cured. There is never a time that Cuman Dios does not hear whatever you want to ask him. Ah, he is very good.

### Don Pancho

Tata Pascual, you haven't taught me the days on which the *chimán* must go to pray at the *cerros* and for what he must pray.

### Pascual Pablo

A *chimán* does not pray at the *cerros*, only the *rezadores* do that. A *chimán* begs or implores at the *cerros*, but he does not pray. He goes to the *cerros* to ask for what he wishes. I do not know all the *cerros*. No, I know only T'ui Bach, and I know only how to ask for sheep for a poor person. I do know Cilbilchax, however, and how to ask for a little money from him, for he will give it. These I know, other *cerros* I do not know.

When you go to the *cerro* to ask for something, carry your material along with you. There should be eight candles of *cera*, eight of *sebo*, eight balls of copal. You ask them with the candles and copal in your hands, at the following times: when the sun rises and when the sun sets; and you must ask of T'ui K'oy and of T'ui Bach. Yes indeed, you must put copal in the fire and light the candles. And you must implore them powerfully as follows:

"Ah, *malaya,* Santo Mundo, Santo Cerro, Santo Jesucristo, Dios del Cielo; ah, *malaya,* Señor Todos Santos, grant me a favour, work or money, for I am poor. Do not lie, I beg of you."

Ah, *malaya,* most certainly they will grant it to you. There never was a time when the *dueños* were *mala gente,* the *dueño de cerro* is rich, he has a great deal of money.

7

*Transferring the Table*

Given by Don Pancho (April 9, 1947: *ik*)

At 11 A.M., I went to the house of Pascual Pablo. He had invited me to come as he was to transfer his table to the new house which was being constructed for him by most of the inhabitants of the *aldea* El Rancho, where he lived, because his old house had become dilapidated. This work they did for nothing, out of gratitude to their *chimán.*

The old house had half of its thatched roof gone. The sun filtered in and shone on the two tables, on which candles, copal, and a bottle of *aguardiente* were standing. In front of the tables burned two candles, each in a candelabrum.

At the new house, nearby, nine men were at work putting on a roof of straw. I saluted them and deposited copal, candles, and a turkey egg on the tables in the old house. The *chimán* moved to a place in the shade and asked me to sit by him.

We talked and smoked and at the end he said, "This day we must move the table to the other house. The new house is not yet completed, but we must nevertheless go ahead as today is *ik.* Midday is a good time because there is more force then. You will carry your table and I shall carry mine. And half of your copal you should burn here and the other half in the new house. Do it now."

I put the copal in the *pichacha* and lighted a candle and, a minute later, another. The hour had come, and the *chimán* said, "Let us go and see where the best place is."

We went to see the new house in the process of construction. We entered and walked about and a mass of straw fell on us, for people were working on the roof. When the *chimán* found the appropriate place he took a hoe and smoothed the earth. We then returned to the old house and he told his wife to walk ahead of us and carry the *pichacha* with the copal. With the burning candles in one hand and the copal in the other, walking backwards, she slowly led the march. The *chimán* took his table and ordered me to carry mine in the same manner that he carried his. With all the candles and copal that were on top of the tables, we commenced to walk backwards very slowly, just as the *chimán's* wife was doing. When we had arrived halfway between the two houses we turned around and walked straight ahead until the tables were in the place chosen for them.

On the table of the *chimán* there was a large candle. He ordered me to make more fire in the *pichacha* and to put more copal into it to make smoke. As soon as I had done what the *chimán* ordered, he took the large candle and said to his wife and to me, "Come here!" There in front of the two tables the three of us knelt. He ordered the woman to grasp the candle in her right hand above his right hand and he told me to grasp the candle above her hand with my right hand, so that it was held by the three of us. Then he prayed:

"Ah, *malaya*, Santo Mundo, Santa Mesa, Santo Dios, Santa Justicia! Do me a favour; do not punish me because I have taken you out of your house. Ah, *malaya*, Santa Mesa, have love for me, do not quarrel with me because I brought you to the other house. Have patience with me and with my family. I brought you with me because my house is now old, not because I wished to. Pardon me. Ah, *malaya*, Santo Mundo, Santa Mesa, Santa Justicia, Dios del Cielo, take care of my family, of me and of my friends. Ah, *malaya,* Santo Mundo, Santa Mesa, Santo Alcalde Ik, Santo Dios, give me health, food, and good fortune, give me patience in this life. Ah, *malaya,* Caballero K'oy, Caballero Xolik, Caballero Bach, Caballero Cilbilchax, help me."

Soon the candle went out and he lighted another and gave it to me to put in the ground in front of the tables.

"Today there is a mass," said Tata Pascual, "we will bull-fight, so return at four or five in the afternoon. Bring *aguardiente* with you, for I have none to give to my people who work on the house. When they finish the house we will give them a drink and a cigarette. Who knows how I can arrange to pay for the *tragos?* However, little by little I shall pay. We are poor; my people have no *tragos.* I am ashamed." I told him I was poor also, and left.

At five in the afternoon of the same day I arrived again at the house of Pascual. I carried copal, candles, a turkey egg, and a litre bottle of *aguardiente.* The men were completing the work on the roof of the house, but carefully, for the *chimán* was sitting in front of the tables on an old stool of wood and hide. He was praying and twenty candles[6] were burning on the tables, as was copal in the *pichacha.*

"Come in," said the *chimán.* "Have you your material?"

"Yes," I said, as I drew it out of the sack.

"Put it on your table for it comes from you. The Dios Ik and Dios del Cielo will receive you with love.

"Ah, *malaya,* Dios, ah, *malaya,* Santo Mundo, receive Señor Don Pancho. Ah, *malaya,* reward him with health, money, food, and love. Ah, *malaya,* Silla Bank, Santo Mundo, take the hand of Don Pancho that he may not go astray on his course."

After a few minutes he said to me, "When the men come down from the roof, give them all a drink. Make smoke now."

I opened four packages of copal, broke the copal into small pieces, and put them in the *pichacha.* The men had finished their work and that was

6 Probably signifying the gods of the twenty days.

good, for not only had night come but also rain. They went to one side of the fire. In front of the tables were many large candles.

We were sixteen in all, for the members of the *chimán's* family were there, some of them women. I started to give them all a drink as the *chimán* had told me, but he stopped me and said, "Wait, I want to give a blessing."

He took the bottle and cup in his hands and began:

"Ah, *malaya*, Dios, Santa Justicia, Santa Mesa, Santo Mundo, throw out your light with this *trago* that your son will take, for his comfort, for his health. Dios Ik, come to me; Dios Noj, come, man; Dios Cuman T'ce, Dios K'mané, pour out *t'chimolal* with this *santo trago.*"

"Give them all another drink," he said to me then, "but commence with those who have beards."

I obeyed his orders and gave each of them one of my cigarettes too. We all talked of different things until nine-thirty. By that time it was raining hard and there was lightning. The *chimán* told us we must eat something and ordered a young man of eighteen years to serve us. This boy without doubt had done this before for he did it well. He took a *jícara* of sweet *batido* from the hands of one of the women, and with a special intonation and in Mam said, "With your permission, Tata Chimán."

The *chimán* answered with a grunt and then to each one the young man said, "With your permission, Señor."

Thereupon he gave it to the oldest man, with a cane and a beard, then to the *chimán* and then to me. The *jícara* was so large I knew I could never finish it. When we had all finished, the *chimán* asked what the time was.

"Ten o'clock," I said.

"Now, it is the hour. Throw the copal in," he told me as he drew out an appropriate altar-cloth and ordered me to do likewise. There was much wind and it kept putting out the candles. Finally the *chimán* commenced his invocation:

"Ah, *malaya*, Dios, Santo Mundo, Santa Mesa, Santa Justicia, receive Santa Mesa so that the family may hear. Come, Señor, come to me. Ah,

129

*malaya,* Mundo, come to me. The family wishes to hear your voice. Ah, *malaya,* Santa Justicia, ah, *malaya,* Santo Jesucristo, ah, *malaya,* Dios del Cielo, come to me. Caballero Comitancillo, Caballero San Pedro Necta, Caballero Chajul, Caballero Ayutla, Caballero Santa Ana Huista, Caballero Quezaltenango, Caballero Santa María de Jesús;[7] ah, *malaya,* Dios, Santo Mundo, Caballero Antigua Guatemala, Caballero Tacaná, Caballero Tajumulco, Caballero K'oy, Caballero Bach, Caballero Xolik, Caballero Cilbilchax; ah, *malaya,* Santa Justicia, come to me."

During the invocation to the gods the copal burst into flame in the *pichacha.* The *chimán* stood at one end of the table and I stood at the other. He ordered me to put out the light. We were sitting in darkness a short time when I felt the table tremble, and realized it came from the *chimán's* body. In a pleading voice he said:

"Good evening! Many thanks for coming here to visit me, and for not forgetting me. You should all behave properly. I don't know why the others did not come, why they don't visit me properly. Maybe they have no need of me and that is why they are not here. Help one another and I shall help everyone, even this Señor Ladino here. If you look for me I shall help you. The table will grow at my command."

Continuing, he said to me: "Do not put a cross on the table, except one with a Christ on it, for one without a Christ is the cross of a *natural.* [*See fig. 3, p. 138.*] If you have an obligation do not burn copal but burn *estoraque.*[8] Do not be ashamed to make *costumbre,* for if you are you will be lost. On the day *batz* carry the table to your house with music, with rockets and *trago.* The people who brought copal, these I receive. Burn the copal. The man who is now playing the guitar must play when the table is carried to the house of the Señor Ladino. Have great respect, for respect is what the world wants. Men must respect one another. If they don't they are like dogs that have no shame. Love, love, love everyone. Yes, this is the house of the *chimán.* Thank you and little by little you will be paid."

---

[7] Pueblos and towns of Guatemala, as are Antigua and Tacaná a little further on.
[8] Incense made from storax gum.

Thus ended the session. Then we made light again and everyone said good night, but we could not leave on account of the rain.

As we sat there the *chimán* and I talked of the day when I would receive my table. The *chimán* told me to throw some copal in and to light the candles that lay on the table.

"When you light the smallest ones of *sebo*," he said, "throw them into the fire in the *pichacha* in a bunch like wood."

When the candles were all burned he again spoke, saying, "That was the food for the table."

We spoke of the lack of respect of people, their lack of morals and education. We spoke of the place to be given the table in my house and of the matter of engaging the boy who plays the guitar to come on the night *batz*.

"Burn all the copal," the *chimán* cautioned as the candles were reaching their end. So I unwrapped the packages of copal and put them all in the *pichacha*.

On the table stood a package of candles wrapped in paper and some candles of *sebo*. The *chimán* took a handful of them and exclaimed, "To end the mass, pray like this always. Ask for anything."

Then standing in front of the tables, I held the candles and made this invocation: "In the name of Dios, Santa Justicia, Santa Mesa, Santo Mundo! Ah, *malaya*, Dios del Cielo, let there be justice for these people here who care for and respect you. Ah, *malaya*, Santa Mesa, look after your family who are here before you. Ah, *malaya*, Santa Justicia, you are in the heart of each one of your family here. Ah, *malaya*, T'ui K'oy, T'ui Bach, T'ui Xolik, Cilbilchax, help your family, God of the Sky and of the Earth. Give your blessings to all of us."

After this I touched the heads of all of the people present, who were awaiting my gesture with great respect. When this was finished, the *chimán* said, "You know how to pray well, *padre nuestro*."

Standing to one side of the tables with the candles in his hands, he said in a very strong voice, in front of everyone, *"Padre nuestro."* This he repeated three times.

It was one in the morning when I made ready to leave. The *chimán* ordered me to come another day, when he would commence to train me to bull-fight. The candles he put in the *pichacha* and they all went up in one flame.

8

*The Blessing*

Given by Don Pancho (April 11, 1947: *kets*)

At five in the afternoon, I arrived at the house of Chimán Pascual. He was sitting in his chair, as always. He received me with affection and asked me if I was ready for work. I drew from a sack copal, candles, and a turkey egg. He took the things and said, "Kneel down here." He stood over me with his hands raised and uttered the invocation:

"Nombre de Dios, Santa Justicia, Santa Mesa, Santo Mundo! Ah, *malaya*, Dios, Santo Mundo, give courage to Don Pancho that he may receive his table, as the *naturales* of the pueblo receive their tables. Ah, *malaya*, Dios Kets, give courage to Don Pancho that his soul may receive a table. Ah, *malaya*, Caballero K'oy, Caballero Bach, Caballero Xolik, Caballero Cilbilchax, give courage to Don Pancho, he is ready to receive his table. Ah, Dios, ah, *malaya*, Mundo, ah, *malaya*, Dios, receive what the man has brought; receive it, Cuman, with love."

When this was said he touched me several times with his hands, which had copal, candles, and the egg in them. Shortly he said, "Make a fire."

I rose and executed his orders. As we stood in front of the tables he offered up a prayer in Mam. A moment later he threw copal in the fire and he gave me the candles to light and put together in the candelabrum. When the fire was burning well he threw the turkey egg into the *pichacha*, exclaiming, "Ah, *malaya*, Dios, close the mouths of the people!"

We then sat down together and he said to me, *"Kets, kan, kimex,* and *cuman t'ce.* You have three days to think. If you are afraid, say so on the

132

day *cuman t'ce*. There is still time; this is no joking matter. If you think so, God will punish and you will go crazy. Think well, you are old enough. Talk with your family, do not decide alone."

"Don't worry," I answered, "I have talked with my family and they are contented. But tell me, what did you say in the prayer you just made in Mam, at the table?"

Pascual answered, "That is the same as the prayer in your head. I pleaded for permission from the table, from Dios, from the *cerros* and the four Alcaldes, for you. I am *fiador*. On *cuman t'ce* you must say either yes or no. If you receive the table there will be no recourse for you. If you do not, good, there will be no trouble. If you wish to receive it, make your house orderly. Make a *corral* for the table. From the day *cuman t'ce* to the day *aj*, you must not touch a woman. Think carefully about it if you decide to receive the table. Then on the day *cuman t'ce*, come. You will have to perform a mass alone and see how it goes."

9

*Baptism*

Given by Don Pancho (April 14, 1947: *t'ce*)

It was ten o'clock in the morning when I arrived at the house of the *chimán*. After a short talk he asked me what I had decided upon.

"I want to receive the table," I answered.

"Have you talked to your wife about this?"

"Yes, my family are contented."

"Good. Did you bring the materials?"

I gave him the copal, candles, and the turkey egg. He put them into a bag that was hanging from a pole in the house and said, "Let us now go to see the *fiador*."

We left the house. I did not know where we were going. About a quarter of a mile from the house, in a northeasterly direction, we came to a spring. Here he stopped, put the *pichacha* on the ground and the bag in the shade.

133

"Awaken the fire," he told me, and I blew into the *pichacha* so that it would burn. Then the *chimán* drew the copal out of his sack and commenced his prayer:

"Santo Pozo, San Juan, I bring to you this man who will receive his table. You will be his *fiador*. Nombre de Dios, Santa Justicia, Santo Mundo, ah, *malaya*, Cuman T'ce, ah, *malaya*, Cuman Ik, ah, *malaya*, Cuman Noj, ah, *malaya*, Cuman Ee, witness this pact. Santo Pozo, San Juan, look well, he is a poor man; always shall you command him. Ah, *malaya*, Santo Mundo."

After he had said this he took the copal in his right hand and, making sure that the fire in the *pichacha* was burning brightly, threw in the copal. He then went to the spring, took a handful of water, and returned to where I was kneeling and blowing on the coals in the *pichacha*. As I knelt, with his hand he wet my head and prayed in Mam. Four times he again touched my head with his wet hand but only the first time with actual water, making five times in all. We waited a few minutes until the copal burned brightly and then returned to his house.

He put the *pichacha*, which was still sending off clouds of smoke, in front of the two tables. He took the candles and egg out of the bag and, holding them in his hands, said:

"Ah, *malaya*, Santa Mesa, Santo Mundo, Santa Justicia, Dios, receive Don Pancho who is here. Give him health, food, business, and good fortune. Receive, Señor, receive Santa Mesa, a little food for yourself, a little for your daughter."

Then he touched his table and my table with his candles. He now gave me the candles to light and put in the candelabrum. Then he dropped the turkey egg into the *pichacha*, saying, "Ah, *malaya*, Dios, close the mouths of the people."

After the candles and egg had burned he turned to me and said, "It is necessary for us to have the testimony of two old people on the night you receive the table, the day *batz*."

I answered, "Bring them but seek people who are old and honourable."

Then we spoke of other things, and he dismissed me.

10

## The Mass

Chimán Pascual Pablo to Don Pancho (April 15, 1947: *k'nel*)

[*At four I arrived at the house of the* chimán. *I had made many visits only to burn copal in front of our tables. He now informed me that the next day* t'coj, *at noon, I must come so that he could teach me how to perform a mass, how to call the Spirit, and he made an invocation.*]

### PASCUAL PABLO

Nombre de Dios, Santa Justicia, Santa Mesa, Santo Mundo, Jesucristo, *nuestro padre* Dios. Ah, *malaya,* Mundo, come. This man desires to hear your voice, to hear your counsels, to follow your paths. Ah, *malaya,* Santo Patrón of the pueblo of Todos Santos, come to me. This man desires your blessings, your counsels, your comfortings. He desires to hear your advice, that of a father for his sons, like that of a hen for her chicks. Ah, *malaya,* Batz, Mayor Casalera del Mundo, come to my house today to aid me for at least one or one half hour. Cuman Noj, Cuman Ik, Cuman T'ce, Cuman Ee, come, Señores, here is my heart and it awaits you with love. Ah, *malaya,* Mundo, be with me. Ah, *malaya,* Cuman Dios, give us your blessing. Señor Ambrosio, creator of the *chimanes* since the creation of the world, do you come also to instruct us well in your profession. We want to hear your counsels, to hear your voice, we want you to teach us well so that we shall not err in our course. Caballero K'oy, Caballero Cilbilchax, Caballero Bach, Caballero T'ui Lan, Caballero Xolik, Caballero T'ui T'suts, Caballero T'ui Yembel, Caballero Punliak, Caballero Chan Chuyé, Caballero T'ui Tal T'ce, Caballero T'ui Soch, Caballero Xétajo, Caballero T'sipego, Caballero Tiqnak, Caballero Xemolak, Caballero Xemina Cruz, Caballero Xepaxá, Caballero T'ui Cumanchúm, Caballero Chalajuitz, Caballero Xinakabiok! Ah, *malaya,* Santo Mundo, come for a little while; here are your sons who await you. Caballero México, Caballero Comitancillo, Caballero Tacaná,

135

Caballero Tajumulco, Caballero T'ui Xak, Caballero Santa María de Jesús, Caballero Baul, Caballero San Pedro Atitlán, Caballero Antigua Guatemala, Caballero Acatenango, Caballero Chingo, Caballero Cayón, Caballero Caviok, Caballero Omak, Caballero Impasoják. Ah, *malaya,* Santo Mundo, come for a little while, here are your sons who need your help, your advice, your comfortings, who wish to hear your voice, who wish you to serve them as guide on the path of life. Caballero Chajul, Caballero Santa Ana Huista, Caballero Ayutla, Caballero San Pedro Necta, Caballero Conxak! Ah, *malaya,* Patrón del Pueblo, Señor Todos Santos, come, come!

[*I wrote the invocation down so I could learn it by heart for the following day. Then we conversed a little.*]

### DON PANCHO

What is the proper use of the chain, Tata Pascual?

### PASCUAL PABLO

The chain is used for one to feel during a mass or when one delivers a burial to the patient. The chain clinks or rings. That is a sign that the work is finished and the patient cured. Some day you will receive your chain but it takes time. One day will pass and then another and then suddenly you will come across your chain in the mountains. The *dueño de cerro* will give you your chain.

### DON PANCHO

What significance has the day of the cross?

### PASCUAL PABLO

The same as Santo Mundo.

### DON PANCHO

What does Corpus Santo Cristo mean?

PASCUAL PABLO

The same as Christ himself.

DON PANCHO

Tata Pascual, I do not quite understand this Batz.

PASCUAL PABLO

The Casalera of the World is Batz. Look, there has never been a time that the Casalera has not held the world in his hand.

DON PANCHO

How many *casaleras* are there?

PASCUAL PABLO

Only one. Where are there more? There is only one.

DON PANCHO

Are there not more, like the four pillars to a house?

PASCUAL PABLO

No, Señor, one calls on him for work, corn, whatever one wants to ask, and Batz, this god, hears you.

DON PANCHO

Then who is Batz?

PASCUAL PABLO

The same god but only one. There are not four; of the Alcaldes del Mundo there are four.

DON PANCHO

The cross on the table of the *chimán,* what does it signify?

137

PASCUAL PABLO

The same as the Santo del Mundo.[9]

DON PANCHO

Do all *chimanes* have crosses on their tables?

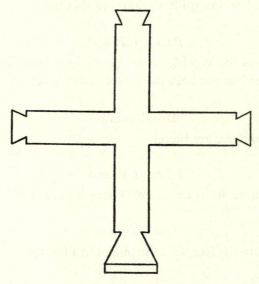

Fig. 3. *Chimán's* cross of *costumbre*.

PASCUAL PABLO

Where is there a table of a *chimán* that has not a cross? All have it because it is Santo Mundo.

DON PANCHO

What is he named in Mam?

PASCUAL PABLO

Ténom, First Chimán of the World.

[9] The cross is, of course, found all over the world from prehistoric times on. Without
doubt the Mayans, the Incas, and other American peoples had the cross long before the
advent of the Spaniards. The foliated cross of Palenque, in Mexico, is a good example.
Cruciform signs for the planets Mars and Venus can be found in the codices. See plate 14.

## DON PANCHO

Tell me, Tata Pascual, when was the world born?

## PASCUAL PABLO

Who knows when the world was born? There was no time when Santo Mundo was not born. He was alone then, there were no *gente*. There were probably many mountains and high trees. Afterwards came the people. Who knows where they came from? No one knows that. There were two men, the first, the very first ones. One was good, the other bad, very bad. The bad one hunted the good one to kill him. The good one played about, one year, two years. Who knows how much time? As the good one passed by he would say to the people and the animals, anybody and anything he met, "If a bad man comes and asks you if I have passed by, do not tell him." "Good," said the animals or the people or whoever was there.

One day the bad man met a tree on the road, a very tall one, and he asked the tree if a good man had passed this way, a clever one. "He is one who accomplishes many things in this world. Is he on this road?" The tree answered, "He passed by last year when I was in flower. Now I am about to bloom again and he is not here." All this time the good man was in the hollow of the tree. And so the bad one passed by without seeing him.

At another time when the good man was so tired, so tired that he was about to fall on the earth with fatigue, he met a man harvesting his corn and said to him, "Señor, hide me, for there is a bad man after me and, if I rest, he will kill me." "Good," this man said, "put yourself in this corn-leaf." In a short time the bad man passed and asked the man who was picking corn if he had seen a clever man pass by, one who was accomplishing many things in the world. "He passed by long ago," answered the man. "I was planting my corn when he passed by. Now I am harvesting my corn." "Good," said the bad man. "If you are lying to me, no one will give you any more corn."

At another time, when he wanted to rest, the good man was in a large open place. There was no place to hide, but he saw a horse which was eating. The good man said to the horse, "Where can I conceal myself? A bad man is about to catch me and kill me." "Have no fear," replied the horse, "just put yourself in my stomach." So the good man hid himself in the stomach of the horse. A short time later the bad man arrived and said to the horse, "Did not a clever man pass by here to visit you, one who is doing evil things in the world?" "No, Señor," said the horse, "I do not know him. Few people come to see me." "Good," said the bad man. "If you have told me a lie, this earth will not give you your food." And then he passed on. Nearby was a vulture, however, who told the bad man where the good man was hiding. Thereupon the bad man turned back and said to the horse, "You wicked one, why did you tell me that lie? The man I am looking for is in your stomach." "No, Señor," said the horse, "I have nothing. Examine me; he is not here." "Ah, you lying vulture," said the bad man, "not until the horse dies will you have anything to eat, not until then." The bad man walked on in pursuit of the good one. In the end he caught him, the tired good man, and said to him, "You shall die by the fire." The good man answered, "Never!" Together they threw wood on the fire, and when it was burning the bad man said to the good one, "You are a good force. I am an evil, evil force. Yet in the world there will be only one force. I shall be that force and you will die by fire." He tried to throw the good man into the fire but twisted his foot and himself fell into the fire. In this way the bad one was burned and God won his dispute.

11

Given by Don Pancho (April 16, 1947: *t'coj*)

At 11 A.M., I arrived at the house of the *chimán*, as he was completing the dismantling of his old house. We saluted each other. He was above and I below. He asked me to look for a ladder so he could come down. Once down, he pointed to his house. There was no one there, not even his wife. I made a fire on a piece of pottery, and when it was burning well I put in the *estoraque*.

The *chimán* ordered me to drink some *aguardiente,* and he did the same. In fact, we took several drinks for the effect it would have. Soon he said, "Good. Now, with your candles in your hand, pray to God for health for yourself, your wife, your sons, and your friends. Beg for what you want."

I took my candles. I was sitting in a small chair. The *chimán* ordered me to move to his chair, and so, sitting in his seat next to the table and behind the curtain, I commenced:

"Nombre de Dios, the highest in the sky and of the earth, our Jesucristo, Father of God, Santa Mesa, Santo Mundo, Señor Dios of the day *t'coj,* ah, *malaya,* Dios! Here am I supplicating before you. Receive me with love, give me health, business, money, and peace for the soul of the world."

Then I threw more incense onto the coals. Soon after I began to invoke the *cerros,* but that was the second part. We first drank more *aguardiente* and it was then that I repeated the invocation to the *cerros.* When I was in the middle of this the second time, I felt as if there was a weight on my shoulders, a pressure on my throat, as if the muscles of my throat were tightening. I could not continue. But the *chimán* spoke to me, saying, "Don't be afraid, speak!" After that I really don't remember what I said for my mind was not functioning. I felt the sweat breaking out on me, I touched my face to see if it was true. I was sweating terribly. I think that I said what I was thinking of and I heard the *chimán* telling me not to be afraid, that the Spirit was here with us. He said the same to the old man and woman, who had arrived and were seated on the other side of the curtain which hung in front of the tables.

"Many thanks, Señor," they both said to me, and I answered: "Do you take care of one another, for in this world no one knows who will take care of one."

"Many thanks, Señor," they answered.

I now waited a moment until I felt normal, and then I heard the *chimán* say, "Yes, you will pass, yes, you are dependable. Come and visit us, we shall look forward to that with pleasure."

I did not feel anything strange any more except for a tightness in my throat. The *chimán* was very well satisfied. He spoke to me and said, "Tomorrow we shall teach you some more."

We had now finished the *aguardiente* and the old man took the curtain away. The old woman occupied herself with the fire and soon we had coffee. We spoke of the rite, and the *chimán* said, "For the first time you were natural [i.e., talked like a *chimán*], but you do not understand much as yet. However, little by little, you will acquire knowledge."

He told me the twenty days of the month and what my duties would be on each day. The names preceded by "Cuman" are *alcaldes:*[10]

| | |
|---|---|
| *CUMAN EE* | Pray at the church for everything concerning yourself. |
| *aj* | Pray at the river, that it may lift the spell from a sick person. |
| *ix* | Pray at the table, that it may calm those who are fighting. |
| *tsikin* | Pray to God in the house of the sick person; or here is a crime. |
| *ajmak* | Pray that the father who has been offended will pardon his son, the offender. |
| *CUMAN NOJ* | Pray at the table that you may be forgiven. |
| *tcij* | Pray to the gods that they may punish those who cause trouble among people. |
| *tciok* | Pray to the gods that he who has done evil will pay for his sins. |
| *najpu* | Pray to the gods that there will be work. |
| *imix* | Pray to the gods that they will give us corn. |
| *CUMAN IK* | Pray to the gods that they will protect the corn against wind. |
| *akbal* | Pray to the gods that they will protect us from sin. |
| *k'ets* | Pray to the gods that they will free us from bad women. |
| *kan* | Pray to the gods for the one who stands in front of you. |
| *kimex* | Pray to the gods to relieve the sufferings of the ones who have died. |
| *CUMAN T'CE* | Pray to the gods for the animals and for the sick. |
| *k'nel* | Pray to the gods for health for the sick ones; they will pay for it. |
| *t'coj* | Pray to the gods to protect prisoners or sick people. |
| *t'ciik* | Pray to the gods to cleanse those who have unclean hearts. |
| *batz* | Pray to the gods for peace in the world. |

[10] Cf. Chimán Pascual Pablo's chart of types of prayer for the twenty days, in the Appendix, pp. 251 ff.

12

*Transporting the Hearts*

Given by Don Pancho (April 17, 1947: *t'ciik*)

At a quarter to twelve in the morning, I arrived at the house of the *chimán*. I carried the same materials with me as on the day before: *aguardiente, estoraque,* and candles. We talked and I asked him to tell me more about Señor Ambrosio, for I did not understand who he was, and he told me the following:

"Ambrosio or Ténom he is called. He was the first male *chimán* when the world was created. He knew all things well, for God had told him this: 'There are many people who will come to your house. They will come from afar for they are sick; cure their sickness and tell them how to live properly.' God told him this in order that he might know and understand everything well. This *chimán* worked well with the *mixes,* but later he entered into a pact with evil. He did good to some, to others evil, and that is why God changed the Word. God directed him and told him which was God's way, that there were only two ways, one good and the other evil, and that a man had to choose one or the other: 'If you choose the good, you will know only the good; if you choose the evil, ah, better change your Word, you will pay.' The master of the *mixes* is this Ambrosio, god of the *mixes,* Cuman Ee."

As we were finishing our conversation, an Indian arrived, a *chimán* called Julio Matías, a former pupil of Pascual's.

"He has come," said Pascual. "When I changed houses, the hearts of all the sons of the table were left where they had been guarded in the place the table occupied in the old house. For that reason Julio Matías could not help in the construction of the new house of the table. We will do his work when you have finished your work."

I made a fire on a piece of pottery and, when it burned brightly, threw on the incense. Then I opened a bottle of *aguardiente* and the three of us had a drink. I moved to the seat of the *chimán* and prayed as I had done the day before, but with much more confidence and with no feeling of pressure in my throat. When I had finished we drank more *aguardiente* and talked a little. Soon the three of us went to the ruins of Pascual's old house. Each *chimán* carried a small chair on which he was to sit. Fire was made in the *pichacha,* and Julio Matías drew out of his sack a litre of *aguardiente,* fifty cents, some copal, and many candles of both *sebo* and *cera,* and laid these on the floor. Pascual then asked for four candles of *cera* and made the following invocation in front of the spot where the table had stood.

"Ah, *malaya,* Dios, Santo Jesucristo, Santo Mundo, receive this copal, receive these candles of Julio Matías. He comes to beg of God that he may carry away his heart and the hearts of his family which are in this spot. Santa Tierra, ah, *malaya,* Mundo, give permission for Julio Matías to carry away his heart."

He then gave me the candles to light and stick in the ground. He asked Julio for a candle of *cera* for each member of his family. Julio mentioned the name of each member as he handed Pascual the candles. There were eleven candles of *cera* and after a while eleven of *sebo.*

Pascual then prayed: "Ah, *malaya,* Dios, Santa Tierra, Santo Lugar [Holy Place], with your permission I shall take out the heart of Julio Matías together with those of his family. Ah, *malaya,* Mundo, I do it not by reason of any dispute or bad intention, but only because he will take them to his own house. Ah, *malaya,* Dios!"

Thereupon he took a cloth and gave it to me to hold, for shortly he was to put into it for each member of Julio's family a little of the earth taken from a hole where the table had stood. As Julio pronounced the names of his family, the *chimán* took a pinch of earth for each one and put it into his cloth. Folding this earth up in the cloth into the form of a tamale, he put it to one side, holding the candles in his right hand all the time. He then asked for a red bandanna and put it on the ground. In this bandanna he arranged the candles, took one or two balls of copal, and exclaimed: "Ah, *malaya,* Dios, Santo Mundo, Santa Tierra, grant permission to Julio Matías to carry away his heart, with love, with pleasure. There is no dispute. Here is his offering." Into another wider piece of cloth he then threw small pieces of copal, broke two turkey eggs on them, and mixed them up together. Then he took a pinch of copal for each member of the family, giving the name with each pinch as he put it in with the rest. All of this he dropped into the *pichacha,* which was burning well. On top of this he put an unbroken turkey egg. He wrapped up the rest of the copal with the earth and the candles, putting them all in one package, and gave it to Julio to burn in his house. Chimán Pascual kept one candle of *cera* and one of *sebo* to burn on his table for each member of Julio's family. When this was all finished we drank three *tragos* of *aguardiente* on the spot where the table had formerly stood. I went home and the two *chimanes* went to the new house.

## 13

### Initiation
Given by Don Pancho (April 18, 1947: *batz*)

At five-thirty in the afternoon, I arrived at the house of the *chimán.* He was awaiting me and with him was his wife, two older women, and a young man who was to play the guitar all night for fifteen cents.

I greeted him and told him I had brought the necessary materials, and that all was ready in my house, ready to receive the table and the expected guests.

The materials for this night consisted of sixteen ordinary candles of *cera,* sixteen of *sebo,* and four large candles of *cera,* as well as turkey eggs, quantities of copal and incense, *aguardiente,* cigarettes, coffee, sugar, bread, two roosters for sacrifice, and four skyrockets. I had brought with me only the candles, copal, incense, one rooster, two skyrockets and one bottle of *aguardiente.* The rest I had left at my house to await our arrival.

The *chimán* took a drink and ordered me to do likewise, and the others did the same. More and more people came until there were twenty adult Indians present. The *chimán* offered the copal and candles in front of the tables to the gods of every *cerro,* and before we drank he did the same with the *aguardiente.*

He then performed a mass for Chimán Juan Pablo. This took place at nine o'clock and was solely for the benefit of Juan Pablo and his family.

At ten o'clock we commenced with the matters concerning me. The *chimán* took the rooster, holding it by the breast, and ordered me to hold it with the feet in my right hand, and my left hand just below its head. The *chimán* then made his invocation:

"Nombre de Dios, Santa Justicia, Santa Mesa, Santo Mundo, here is the offering which Don Pancho has brought you. He will carry your daughter, he will carry your table. Watch over it, it will grow, it will not remain small. He is a good man. Ah, *malaya,* Mundo, receive his gift with love. Receive, Señor, a little for you, a little for Don Pancho, a little drink for health, good business, money, animals, and good luck. Give health, Señor, to his wife, to his family. Ah, *malaya,* Cuman Dios, ah, *malaya,* Mundo, he is here for the table, for love, there is no dispute, Señor, he goes with a good heart. Give Don Pancho understanding that he may know your law well. Ah, *malaya,* Santa Justicia, be with us, receive this man with love. Cuman Noj, Cuman Ik, Cuman T'ce, Cuman Ee, receive him, Señores, give health to Don Pancho, to his wife and to his family. Ah, *malaya,* Caballero K'oy, Caballero Bach, Caballero Cilbilchax, Caballero Xolik, visit Don Pancho with love, there is no dispute here, Señores."

When this was said we both lifted the rooster higher than our heads as far as our arms could reach. Four times we did this while the *chimán* prayed in Mam. We then sat in the two small chairs. The *chimán* asked for my knife to make the sacrifice. He took the rooster by its feet and, with his free hand, made four small balls of copal which he put on a piece of a clay pot. He then plunged the knife into the neck of the rooster. The blood ran out. Some was allowed to run onto the copal, but most of it was to be used to sprinkle on the white legs of my table. He then cut the neck again and out came more blood. This was for the copal in the *pichacha.* The bird began to struggle. I wanted to hold its wings

146

so it would not spatter me with blood, but the *chimán* said, "No, if it jumps about vigorously, that is good luck."

The people all sat in respectful silence. When the rooster was dead the *chimán* laid it on the floor, and half an hour later his wife began preparing to cook it. The guitarist played now and then.

We now took some more drinks, and I moved to the seat of the *chimán*, and he to mine. The curtain had already been pulled shut because of the mass the *chimán* had recited for Juan Pablo. I took one of the large candles in my hand, stepped forward, and faced the people, who all sat with bent heads and with eyes looking at the floor. By this time there were many more Indians present and two *ladinos*, members of my family. I gave the usual invocation and blessed them all with the candle, touching the men on the heads and the women on the shoulders, such being the custom. Then I stepped behind the curtain and all lights were put out. I now gave the mass as I had been taught, and again I felt a tightening in my throat and broke out in a sweat. When it was over I took an aspirin tablet I had with me and stepped out from behind the curtain. At this moment the Alcalde Municipal, Macedonio Pablo, entered. I moved back to my seat and the *chimán* took his. We opened another bottle of *aguardiente* and smoked. I passed the first cup of *aguardiente* to the *chimán* and the second to the Alcalde, and then passed cups of *aguardiente* to the rest of the people. Then I spoke again and prepared to move the table to my house. It was after eleven o'clock at night. I drew out of my bag a dollar and, in the presence of all, addressed the table of the *chimán*. I held up the dollar as high as possible and said: "Santa Mesa, Santo Mundo, here you are, here is your offering. I shall carry your daughter to my house. I shall look after her well. I shall give her food. I shall expect a great deal from her, just as I do from my wife. It is with your permission, Santa Mesa, that your daughter departs, so do not be troubled."

The *chimán* tied his sash to the legs of the table, leaving a loop that went around his neck so that he supported the table by the sash in front of his stomach. All the people then left the house and surrounded the *chimán.* An Indian carried the *pichacha,* and I threw incense on the coals every few minutes, the fragrance constituting an act of recognition and respect. I walked carefully so I would not fall, and after a few yards the *chimán* surrendered the table to me, for in this manner it was to be carried. We came to the road, the main road from Huehuetenango to Todos Santos. There he told me to put the table on the ground, and we offered up the following:

"Dios del Cielo, Dios del Mundo, Santa Justicia, grant me pardon, Señor. Ah, *malaya,* Mundo, be with us at least an hour or half an hour."

The *chimán* then took the table and we walked slowly to my house. The guitarist accompanied us and played, off and on, until dawn.

In the corner of my house I had constructed the *corral* of the *chimán* in the manner that he had told me. It was of bamboo, the size of all the houses of the *chimanes* made for this purpose. The main supports were the four corner posts. It was decorated about the door and around the place where the table or altar would stand with cut crepe paper of all colours and with flowers and fresh pineapples. A white curtain covered the door. The *chimán* put the table in the proper place and set on each side a small chair, one for himself and one for me. On the table he put my cross, a crucifix. In front of the *corral* were benches where the Indians who had come with us could sit. We all took another drink and the *chimán* said, "Let me have your right hand."

He took my right hand in his and we held our hands together as high as possible over the table. Then he said: "We are together now; we are one and the same, in the name of God, Santo Mundo, Santa Mesa, Santa Justicia, only you and only I. Ah, *malaya,* Mundo, Cuman Ee, Cuman Noj, Cuman Ik, Cuman T'ce, be with us!"

I picked up the rooster to sacrifice for my table, and we sacrificed it in the same manner as he had done in the house of the *chimán.* We sprinkled the table with the blood of the rooster and put blood on the copal, to burn the next day. I invoked the spirits in the same way as I had done before, but this time the *chimán* Juan Pablo departed. I don't know why.

One skyrocket was sent off after the mass at the house of the *chimán,* one as we left his house, one when we arrived at my house, and one after I had given the mass there—four in all. After the mass we drank more *aguardiente,* and my wife and family served coffee and bread several times during the night until dawn. Everyone left at five in the morning, drunk and contented.[11]

[11] Pascual Pablo charged Don Pancho twelve dollars for teaching him to be a *chimán.* The expenses of the ceremony, which included *aguardiente,* food, and ceremonial equipment, amounted to twenty-three dollars.

## 5

### The Regalia and Functions of the Chimanes

IN THE preceding chapter I gave an account of how a *chimán* is initiated. Pascual Pablo had agreed as early as January, 1947, to give Don Pancho this instruction but he had not specified the time the instruction should begin. From the very first, the *chimán* had said that if Don Pancho seemed unqualified the lessons would cease, or if Don Pancho wished to withdraw he might do so at any time. During the period of probation, many preliminary conversations took place between the two which gave me an excellent chance to coach Don Pancho in the delicate questions I wished him to put to the *chimán*. These concerned the sacred objects of the *chimanes*, their regalia, and the methods they used in their profession. Again I am presenting the material in the words of the interlocutors.

1

### The Chimán's Chain

Chimán Pascual Pablo to Don Pancho

#### DON PANCHO

Tata Pascual, do you use a chain? If you are my teacher I want to know. I am your friend, why don't you tell me of this?

#### PASCUAL PABLO

Look, Don Pancho, I will teach you well, but do not talk of this thing. Why do you grumble at me? Take care the *dueño de cerro* does not punish you. Yes, I have asked the *dueño* if I could teach you, and he answered me in these words: "Teach him not to do evil, for if he does evil, I shall know it and punish him."

### DON PANCHO

Tata Pascual, I am old, I am not a boy who does not know his mind. When I ask you to teach me well, it is because I desire to learn not to do wrong. Tell me now, what is a chain, what is it used for?

### PASCUAL PABLO

The *dueño de cerro* gives the chain. He it is who gives it. It symbolizes the agreement the *chimán* makes with the *dueño de cerro*. When he receives the chain from the *dueño*, it is his pact. Yes, it is a contract such as one receives when he buys a piece of land. *Malaya*, could one do a wicked thing with the *dueño de cerro*? No, never, there is not a time that the *dueño de cerro* does not see all. Where is there a *chimán* who has not a chain? If there is a *chimán* who has no chain, he is a deceiver, he is not a *chimán*.[1] Such a one wishes only to gain the wicked one for himself. I have a chain. However this is a very delicate and secret subject. No *chimán* states that he has one, for if he tells this the *dueño* will surely punish him.

### DON PANCHO

When the *dueño de cerro* gives the *chimán* the chain, does the *chimán* see the *dueño*?

### PASCUAL PABLO

No, it is this way. When you are in the mountains and pass a pine tree, there will suddenly be a chain hanging in the tree or lying on the path. There will suddenly be the noise of a chain in the mountain. It is the *dueño de cerro* that has carried it there. That means that the time has come for you to obtain it. The *chimán* knows his work for he is appointed *chimán* by God, just as, right here in the pueblo, they appoint a *rezador* or *síndico*. So also is a *chimán* appointed. If he has already

[1] Though he had denied this before; see p. 92.

151

been appointed a *chimán* and he does not care to become one, ah, he will first be sick for a long time and then die.

The chain hears well. When a *chimán* begins his *costumbre* for a sick person or anything else, the *chimán* asks for help from the *dueño de cerro*. He asks for a little health, for a little food, so that the mouths of the *gente* be shut, so they do not talk too much. The Santa Mesa makes a noise [raps]. This means that the *dueño,* my patron, has heard. Then the *chimán* says, "T'ui Dios, my sainted patron." The *chimán* then lifts up his hand with the chain in it and the table raps again. This is the purpose it serves.

2

### Curing the Sick
Given by Chimán Pascual Pablo (November, 1946)

When a *chimán* is called on to help a sick man he makes a note of the day *cuman t'ce*. On the table for *costumbre* he burns copal and candles and begs God to give counsel to the sick man. After this, he goes to the cross in front of the church and to T'ui Cumanchúm, to burn copal. He repeats this the following day and each day thereafter until *k'mané* comes. The night before *batz,* at eight o'clock, at the cross in front of the church, he must sacrifice a rooster. He puts the blood in the *pichacha* and burns copal in it. Then he begins his prayer. He offers the blood and copal at T'ui Cumanchúm, to the *costumbre* table, and last of all in the house of the sick man. Candles should be burning on the day *k'mané,* on the table of *costumbre,* and also in the church in the morning of the day *k'mané.* The rooster is to be eaten by the *chimán* in the name of Santo Dios, Santa Vara, Santa Letra,[2] Santa Justicia, in the house of the sick man and in the presence of all of his family.

Five candles are used, four for the four Alcaldes del Mundo and one larger one for Todos Santos.

2 *Vara,* "staff, pole," no doubt refers to the holy staff of office that the *rezadores* carry. *Letra* means "handwriting"—to the Indians, "knowledge."

The prayer is as follows: "Ah, *malaya*, Dios, give health to this sick one. Ah, *malaya*, draw out his sins, the poor man. Ah, *malaya*, make him a little happy. Ah, *malaya*, give him of your strength that he may work. Ah, *malaya*, Dios, remove the sickness of this poor man. Ah, *malaya*, make him contented with his sons, with his woman. Ah, Dios, see that he can take a drink. Ah, *malaya*, Dios, make him able to eat his *tortilla* and do all that I ask of you. God hear me."

### DON PANCHO

Tata Pascual, do *chimanes* sacrifice birds or animals other than turkeys or roosters?

### PASCUAL PABLO

No, only turkeys and roosters are killed, no other creatures. Long ago when God made the world he taught men that they must kill only turkeys and roosters. They could not have killed other creatures, for they were not taught to do so. There never was a time when the blood was not meant to be smoke for the *dueños* and the body food for the people.

### 3
### *Defending a Person Against Evil Magic*
Chimán Rafael Calmo to Don Pancho (January, 1947)

### DON PANCHO

In what *costumbres* do they burn the wings, feathers, intestines, and feet of the rooster?

### RAFAEL CALMO

This is done for purposes of defence, when someone wishes to molest another, when one is against another, wishes to do him harm or do something evil to him. Then the *chimán* takes to defence. He kills a rooster, puts the blood, the feathers, the gizzard, the intestines, and the feet in the *pichacha*. With great care he then removes the skin and puts it too in the *pichacha* on top of the other things. Copal, likewise, is put in. He

153

burns the copal and appeals to the Gods of the World. Then he names the one who has done harm to the man whom the *chimán* is defending. But first he says, "As I kill this rooster, may the wicked one feel the punishment inflicted! When I skin the rooster, may he feel it!" Then, when the *chimán* has supplicated at all the *cerros,* the *dueño* comes down to defend the man. Some day I shall teach you this.

DON PANCHO

Tata Rafael, what happens to the body of the rooster?

RAFAEL CALMO

You do not eat it, you burn it; for if you ate the meat, harm would come to you.

4

## The Details of a Specific Treatment[3]

In the above conversations between Don Pancho and the two *chimanes,* such questions as how the *chimanes* cure diseases and how they exorcise evil are discussed in somewhat general terms. But to understand such practices properly it is best to study them in terms of concrete cases. I am therefore devoting the rest of this chapter to instances I myself witnessed.

In September, 1946, Carlos, the child of my servant Basilia, became very ill. I sent her with Carlos to the doctor at Huehuetenango, as I suspected that the child had tuberculosis. The doctor said he had only a chronic cough, however, and he gave Basilia some cough medicine and some injections for the boy.

By October, the child was much worse. Margarita, my neighbour, and Basilia came to me, and Basilia said, "Señorita, much medicine has Carlos taken, much medicine, and the time has come when the body of Carlos wants not medicine but *costumbre.* We are *naturales,* Señorita,

---

[3] Given by the author, as are all passages not otherwise attributed.

154

and our doctors are *chimanes,* and we think Carlos should be taken to a *chimán.*"

Margarita then broke in: "The mother of Basilia came to me and said, 'Margarita, we are *naturales,* Basilia is a *natural.* But her ears are turned towards the ways of the *ladinos.* Now Carlos has taken plenty of medicine. I feel he should go to a *chimán.*'"

I said to Basilia, "You know very well that I have great respect for *chimanes* and whenever I have a question to ask I go to one of them. If you now feel that Carlos's body wants no more medicine, but needs *costumbre,* by all means take him to a *chimán.* As I know you have no money, I shall gladly pay for it."

The two women talked it over and decided to go to Chimán Rafael Calmo. Basilia went off with Carlos and returned in about an hour.

"Señorita," she said, "the *chimán* and his assistant talked to me and looked at Carlos. The *chimán* said that Carlos was very ill, but that a *costumbre* would cure him. He cast the *mixes* and then said, 'I shall cure him, but you will have to buy certain things.'"

Basilia and I figured out the cost of what he required:

| | |
|---|---|
| two young turkeys | $1.00 |
| four young roosters | 1.00 |
| five turkey eggs | 0.25 |
| one large bottle of *aguardiente* | 1.10 |
| five candles of *sebo* | 0.15 |
| two candles of *cera* | 0.10 |
| copal | 0.20 |
| TOTAL | $3.80 |
| *chimán's* fee | 0.50 |
| GRAND TOTAL | $4.30 |

Patrona came over after a while, and the three of us talked about the expenses. She said to Basilia, "Rafael is very expensive. His assistant *chimán,* Luis Elón, is my *chimán.* He saved the life of Andrés when he lay ill one month and two years ago and lost two basins of blood from his nose and lay like one dead. Luis Elón performed *costumbre* and then Andrés recovered. He is of your family, Basilia, and if you go to him this evening with Domingo I think he can do a simpler and cheaper *costumbre*."

They went around to visit him at seven o'clock and returned in an hour, Basilia with tears in her eyes. "Señorita," she said, "the *chimán* cast the *mixes* and he said that Carlos was very ill, that he was filled with *ladino* medicine, that his body did not want this. The only thing that could save him, he said, was a *costumbre*. First, a small *costumbre*, and then if Carlos lived twenty days more, a big *costumbre*. I must go now and buy five cents' worth of candles and put them in the church. Tomorrow I must buy and take to him a medium-sized rooster, two turkey eggs, copal, a medium-sized bottle of *aguardiente*, and five candles, three of them of *sebo*."

The following night Basilia went to the *chimán* with everything except the rooster. That would be sacrificed before dawn. She returned in an hour and a half and told me that the *chimán* had cast the *mixes* and said that Carlos might live. They burned the candles and offered *aguardiente* to the Spirit, and they both drank *aguardiente*. The *chimán* went into his *corral* and the Spirit came, but the voice of the Spirit was not clear.

The next morning at four, I woke Basilia, and she went off with Carlos on her back and the rooster in her hands. She returned in an hour and told me that just before dawn the *chimán* sacrificed the rooster before the cross in front of the church. First he cut off its head and let the blood run into the *pichacha* full of copal, and then he cut off the wings and the feet and put them and the head in the *pichacha*, burning them with the copal as he swung the *pichacha* and prayed.

In the afternoon Carlos was worse. Domingo, my *mozo*, said to me, "Señorita, Basilia never should have taken Carlos with her this morning when the *chimán* killed the rooster. It is bad luck, and the *chimán* should have told her not to bring Carlos. Señorita, while Patrona was washing her clothes yesterday a *pelote* [vulture] dropped his *caca* right next to her with a big splash. That means bad luck, I hope it does not mean the death of Carlos."

About a month later, while I was in Guatemala City, Carlos died.

5

## Detecting Buried Objects

Domingo, my *mozo*, came to me one day and said, "Señorita, a friend of mind who has a house above the ruins of T'ui Cumanchúm wants you to visit his house. A great deal of noise goes on in the house day and night and he is concerned about it. When he built the house he found an *olla* [pot] in the earth that belonged to the Ancient Ones. A *chimán* told him there were treasures buried there. Now he wants you to tell him if there are treasures or if there are just the bones of the Ancient Ones. Señorita, he is afraid to dig alone and wants you to tell him what to do."

I said, "Tell him that I don't do things of that kind. I only cure sick people. However, I will get Don Pancho to cast the *mixes* and he will find out if there is money buried in the floor."

The next day Domingo, Don Pancho, and I went to the house. It was late afternoon, and Don Pancho had to cast the *mixes* by the light of *ocote*. The intent faces of Domingo, of the man and the three women, were proof to me of Don Pancho's success as a soothsayer. The man asked, "Is there money or is there an ancient burial under the earth, and what causes the noise in the house?"

Don Pancho told them there was nothing buried in the earth. The noise was made by enemies who practised evil against him. The husband told us that the last time he had gone to the *tierra caliente* his wife was to join him the next day. She did not come for five days, and when she came, her hair was cut off. Her story was that she had spent the first night in the house of a friend and when she awoke in the morning her hair was gone—cut off in the night, she said, by evil spirits. She went to a *chimán,* who cast the *mixes* and told her that Chimán Domingo Calmo had sent the evil spirits to cut off her hair. She had to stay the other four days in the pueblo to burn candles in the church, so that her *chimán* could ward off the evil.

Don Pancho told them, "You have not done your *costumbre* as you should and all the evil has not yet left. You must both do *costumbre* for the next four days and on every *k'mané* day."

The Indians were grateful for all this and gave both Don Pancho and me presents of corn. The husband told me that I could stay in his house in the *tierra caliente* whenever I wanted to.

## 6

And now for two final examples that involved me personally.

Towards the end of January, 1947, most of the Indians had stopped insisting that I was a *dueña de cerro* or *bruja,* except Chimán Rafael Calmo and possibly Chimán Domingo Calmo. I had rebuked the latter that January, and I felt he had been working against me ever since.

The incident I am referring to was in connection with two Americans, one a photographer, who had come up to Todos Santos for a few days. I had warned them about taking photographs of the Indians; nevertheless they did take some, in the market place. At the time, Chimán Domingo Calmo happened to be sitting on the steps of the convent, which faces the market place, and the American photographer went up and asked permission to take his photograph. The *chimán's* answer was to open his trousers and expose himself. All the young Indians sitting around roared with laughter. The Americans told me what had happened, as did my neighbours also. I spoke to two of the *principales* and to Tata Julián, the Alcalde Rezador, of what a disgraceful thing the *chimán* had done; that he, a *chimán* and a *principal,* one of the wise men of the pueblo, had set a bad example in front of the young men, and that he had also insulted both the strangers and me, for they were my countrymen. They agreed and told me they could not understand a *chimán's* doing such a thing.

When Domingo Calmo came to call the next day I said, "Tata Domingo, are you my friend?"

"Señorita, how can you doubt that I am your friend?"

"Well, I doubt very much that I am your friend or that you are my friend after the way you insulted my countrymen yesterday."

He denied the whole story, but from then on the *chimán* seldom came to my house.

But he would often come just to my gate and say, "Señorita, how do you feel?" I would always say, "Never better." After he asked this question many times, I decided that he was trying to cast a spell against me, for he always looked so disappointed when I said I was "never better."

Basilia confirmed me in my suspicions. She told me she felt that Chimán Rafael had made a burial against me.

"Last night, Señorita," Basilia said, "I met Chimán Rafael on the path, and he asked me if it was true that you left the house every night and returned at midnight. I said to him, 'Certainly not; she goes to bed at nine and never goes out at night.' Then he asked me, 'What does she go in search of between the hours of nine and twelve?' 'I just told you she does not go out,' I said. 'Where do you get such ideas?' 'Ah, the *gente* tell me that they have seen her go out and come back,' he said."

As Basilia told me this story I thought of my dog, which always went out when I went to bed and came back around midnight. What the *chimán* suspected, perhaps, was that I went out in the form of a dog.

# 6

## The Chimanes in Defence and Attack

MOST OF THE ENERGY of the *chimanes* is spent either in freeing people from spells or in casting spells upon them. The following accounts will illustrate the techniques involved and the theory behind the techniques.

1

Given by José Miguel del Valle y de Castillo[1]

In the year 1943, when the Intendente of this pueblo was Señor Fortunato Ríos Hidalgo, a *ladino,* an Indian presented himself one day at the *juzgado,* saying that he had just encountered Chimán Rafael Calmo in the cemetery making a burial for the purpose of doing evil against someone, therefore he had come to the authorities to have them intervene. Immediately the Señor Intendente sent the Commissioner of Police, Rigoberto López, to the cemetery to see if it was true. He found Chimán Rafael Calmo there, but he would give no explanation as to why he was in the cemetery and what he was doing. The Commissioner took him to the Intendente, who questioned him in various ways but still received no proper answers. Finally he said that if the *chimán* did not answer his questions he would send him to the judge at Huehuetenango. After these threats the *chimán* could only confess and talk. Yes, it was true he was doing evil, but only because the one against whom he was doing evil had cast a spell on someone else, the man whom he was defending. All this he said in a plaintive voice. Yes, he was making a burial in the cemetery that would kill this evil person. The Intendente sent the

[1] The *ladino* telegraph operator at Todos Santos.

160

*chimán* to the cemetery, accompanied by the police, who were to bring the thing buried. The Commissioner saw the *chimán* open a hole which had been closed by a rock. Inside was half of a snake and also a small figure made of dirty rags so tied that it looked like a human form. The other half of the snake was in another hole at a certain distance.

All of this was put on the table of the Intendente, and he told the *chimán* that he was to be put in prison and could only leave when he had paid his fine.

2

Obtained by Don Pancho from Chimán Rafael Calmo (January, 1947)

To protect someone on whom a spell has been cast, it is necessary to have a piece of old clothing that has been worn close to the skin by the person who has cast the spell, or a piece of his hair, or better yet both hair and cloth; a tin can, a little chili (the strongest possible kind), a little copal, one large candle of *cera,* two candles of *sebo,* and the urine of the sick person.

The rite must be performed in the middle of the night of either of the days *najpu* or *noj.* Inside the house of the *chimán,* in front of the door to the *corral,* stands the *chimán.* He takes the can and pours into it the urine of the man he is protecting. He tears up the chili into small pieces and puts it into the can with the urine. With his *pichacha* in his hand he now commences to pray:

"God who is the greatest of all Gods in the World, there are good people and there are bad people. Abandon this one, this accursed one, who has done evil against this sick man. Proceed against him; do evil to him. This can will be the world, so that it will carry its odour to the wicked one who has done this evil to the sick one. May the evil one's body become rotten, like the rottenness that will come to this cloth. May his body be always cold; may he suffer the same agony that he has caused the sick one."

Immediately afterwards he takes the two candles of *sebo* and puts them upright on the floor. By this light he then makes the sign of the cross. He now puts the dirty piece of cloth and the hair of the one who has cast the spell into the can with the urine and chili. He then searches for the best thing he can find to close the top of the can. He puts the can opposite the two candles burning brightly before the door of the officiating *chimán*. Immediately he bends the large candle double, the two ends pointing up and the portion that is bent fixed as firmly as possible on the floor. He lights the two ends, puts more copal in the *pichacha*, and by the light of the candles begins to perform the rites in a crouching position. Then he stands erect, holding the *pichacha* in his hand, before the improvised altar with the tin can as its centre, the two candles of *sebo* at one end and the candle of *cera*, bent double with its two ends lighted and brightly burning, at the other. He now swings the smoke of the *pichacha* over all this and makes the following invocation:

"Gods of the Mountains, hear me, that my work may be good. My pact is with you. You are my Gods, so assist me that the accursed one will become as rotten as his cloth. May his body be always cold; may he suffer the same agony as he has inflicted on this sick one. Caballero T'ui K'oy, Caballero T'ui Bach, Caballero T'ui Xolik, Caballero Cilbilchax, Caballero T'ui Yembel, Caballero T'ui T'suts, Caballero T'ui Punliak, Caballero Chan Chuyé, Caballero T'ui Tal T'ce, Caballero T'ui Soch, Caballero Xétajo, Caballero T'sipego, Caballero Tincoig, Caballero Tiqnak, Caballero Xemolak, Caballero Xepaxá, Caballero Xemina Cruz, Caballero T'ui Cumanchúm, Caballero Chalajuitz, Caballero Xinakabiok! Eha, God of the World, fearless, you must be against the wicked one that he will become rotten as his cloth. May his body be always cold; may he suffer the same agony as he has inflicted on the sick one. [The list of Caballeros is here repeated.] Do to him as he did to the sick one, and to the sick one give health, as he has committed no wrong."

During all this the *chimán* swings his smoke-filled *pichacha* over the altar. Then he takes the can, and, taking care not to spill any of its contents, carries it out of the house to a spot that is damp with water. Here he buries it in an upright position so that it will not leak, covers the hole with a stone, and then prays again:

"Gods of the *cerros,* give me help, so that the evil one will pay his debt."

He now swings the *pichacha* the same way as in the house. Throughout this time the candles have been burning brightly in the house and they will continue to do so until they burn out. The *chimán* then returns to his house, and for a period of five days abstains from sexual intercourse.

3

Chimán Pascual Pablo to Don Pancho (January, 1947)

DON PANCHO

Tata Pascual, you are my friend, I love you and want you to do me a favour. You know how to cast a spell well. Now there is a *ladino* here called L——. I have nothing against him but I wish him to leave the pueblo because he is bad, very bad. Teach me how to cast a spell on him.

PASCUAL PABLO

Have no anxiety, I shall tell you. You must get four turkey eggs, four candles of *sebo,* three cents' worth of copal and a small bottle of *aguardiente.* On the night of the day *batz* [January 28] I shall pray at my table. Have no fear, I shall close his mouth so that he will have to leave the pueblo. When the dawn of *k'mané* [next day] comes the work will be done. But you are learning to be a *chimán* so you must work with me. Do the *costumbre* on the porch of your house. Put coals in a piece of an old clay jar. Close to the coals heat the four candles, sprinkling salt on each one. Immediately after twist the candles into the form of a rope. Do not light the wicks at the top of the candles but find the wick at the bottom of each candle and light it with *ocote.* Then stick them on the floor, bottom up. These are the Gods. Then make the invocation:

"Are you there, Gods? Master, Señor Jesucristo, Señor Saint of the

163

mountain top T'ui K'oy, pardon me for summoning you. You are the Saint of the highest mountain top of the pueblo. Señor T'ui Bach, I have great respect for you. I have called so that you will hear me. Señor T'ui Xolik, I am calling upon you. Please come to me. Señor Sakabech, Señor T'ui Lom, Señor T'ui Cumanchúm, Señor Nim Cruz, Santo Dios, I am calling you because L—— is biting me. I have done no wrong. For this reason I have called upon all of you so that he will give up his position and leave the pueblo. Are you there, Santo Dios of the mountain? You know my heart, I am not a bad person. Put out this man L—— who is annoying me and my family. Why is his heart bad? Close his eyes, his mouth, and his ears. Here is a little bit of copal smoke. Pardon me, all of you, for summoning you."

Then stir up the fire in the *pichacha* or in the piece of clay, and in a separate place put the copal in leaves and put a turkey egg on top of the copal, then put all these in the fire of coals, saying:

"This smoke will close the mouth of L——. What he does to me, may it return back to him."

When one egg is burned then do the same with the others, until all four have been burned and offered. They should explode with much noise. That will be a good sign. If there is no noise, that is not so good. The next day, *k'mané*, carry four candles to the church and burn them for Señor Todos Santos, who will hear your complaint.

I shall do the same, only you do it on the porch of your house and I shall do it on my table. Burn copal, one egg, and one candle at the wrong end. Do the same at the *santa cruz* at T'ui Cumanchúm, and at the table once more after I return. I shall recite the same prayer. If L—— does not leave the pueblo in twenty days, repeat the same on the day *batz*. If he still does not leave, repeat the same until everything has been accomplished. I don't think he can endure it four times. After this has been done the first time, he will loosen up a bit; after the second time he will probably leave. Few people can endure it four times. He will probably get sick. You and your family will soon see.

# 4

Chimán Pascual Pablo to Don Pancho (February, 1947)

## PASCUAL PABLO

You ask me how a *chimán* casts a spell on a person who has done him no harm? Now where is there a person who does only evil? When one does harm against someone, the man who does it probably does so not because he likes to but because he has to.

The other day I taught you how to cast a spell and draw out evil with candles, copal, and turkey eggs on the porch of your house. There is another way of doing the same, namely by prayer, nothing else, that will both cast a spell and draw out evil.

Buy ten cents' worth of candles of *sebo* and twelve turkey eggs, for there are people who are very strong and do evil. On the day *tcij*, when night comes, make a fire in an *olla*, a large fire, and put it in front of the table of the Master. Put into it a little copal. Light a candle of *cera* and put it on the table at the right hand and then say: "Santo Dios, Santo Mundo!" Now light a candle of *sebo* and put this at the left of the table, saying, "Santo Copal, Santo Humo, give health to this sick one who has a pain in his head [or whatever the sickness is], Santo Dios del Mundo!"

Then take two candles, one of each kind, and put them on each side of the table, and make the following invocation:

"Caballero, Dueño de Cerro, come to me, help me drive out this sickness, this pain in the head of the poor sick one."

Then put a whole turkey egg on the fire and at the same time put candles on the table and say:

"Caballero T'ui Bach, Caballero T'ui K'oy, Caballero T'ui Xolik, Caballero Cilbilchax, Caballero T'ui T'suts, Caballero T'ui Yembel, Caballero Punliak, Caballero Chan Chuyé, Caballero T'ui Tal T'ce, Caballero T'ui Xak, Caballero Xétajo, Caballero Xinakabiok, Caballero Xepaxá, Caballero Xemina Cruz, Caballero Chalajuitz, Caballero Tiqnak, Caballero T'sipego, Caballero T'ui Cumanchúm, Santo Dueño de

Cerro, and Santo Mundo, bestow the favour of health upon this sick one. Receive the smoke. May the sickness leave the sick man."

When the turkey egg explodes, put a hen egg in and repeat the above. Alternate them, first using a turkey egg, afterwards a hen egg. Also use a little copal each time that an egg is put in until all are used up. Do not leave the table, but pour out some *aguardiente,* a drink, for the *dueño de cerro* likes it very much.

Now tomorrow I shall teach you how to do a burial, only with candles, to cast a spell. This is a very good one.

## DON PANCHO

Look, Tata Pascual, what does one do to find out how to dig up a burial that another *chimán* has made?

## PASCUAL PABLO

It can be done only with a table. When you have your table, then I shall teach you, but not before. It is not time yet. When the day for your becoming a *chimán* arrives then will the *costumbre* for your table begin. Then if you in turn are a very good teacher, you will be called Tata Don Pancho, Tata Chimán.

## 5

Given by Chimán Pascual Pablo (March, 1947)

When a native of this pueblo becomes ill he sends for a *chimán,* who says whether it is God's illness or a sickness cast upon him [a spell]. The *chimán* casts his *mixes* and these tell him to whom the sickness can be attributed. The one who is sick knows which of his enemies is the most dangerous and so he can doubtless identify him.

Search with great care for a bit of hair belonging to the one who has done the evil or a bit of his soiled clothing that has been worn next to the skin. Get a bottle and put in some blood [sap] of the pine and some old *ocote.* Make a small figure of a baby out of the blood of the pine and put the hair of the wicked one on the head of this figure. Put the piece of soiled cloth on it for clothing. Make three small crosses out of the old and coloured *ocote* and put everything in the bottle. Make three small crosses of *ruda* [rue, an herb] or of cypress and put them in the bottle. On the day *ix, tcij,* or *t'ciik* put the baby figure with its clothes on into the bottle, and put in also another cross of *ocote* and one of *ruda* [eight in all]. Do this at midday, for that is a powerful hour. Put water in the bottle or, if the evil one is very evil, put in vinegar or *chilmol* [chili]. This is much stronger and the wicked one probably won't live then but will die outright. Put four candles of *sebo* on the floor, bottom up, in front of the table. Stop the bottle up well so that nothing can come out, and then pray:

"Ah, *malaya,* Santa Mesa, Dios Ix, punish this person who has done this harm against [name of patient]. I know the reason that [name of *brujo*] has done this. He is wicked and deceitful. It is true. Put the sickness on him and consult your heart where the burial is to be, for he will die if you do not. Santo Ix, make sick this wicked sly one who has done this evil to [name of patient]. Ah, Dios, Santa Mesa, Santo Mundo, Santa Justicia, Santo Nombre de Dios, four Alcaldes del Mundo, Ee, Cuman T'ce, Ik, Noj. Make the wicked [name of *brujo*] sick that he may pay his debt in the same manner as he has done to [name of patient]. You are here, you are present."

Then light the candles and the copal. When the candles have burned out put the bottle in the corner of your room. Then send word to the wicked one so that he will become ill and die unless he extracts the burial of poor [name of patient]. If he is willing to deliver up the burial, it is good. If not, wait till he gets sick. Then pass by his door and ask if he is well and what is wrong with him. If he pauses to think, say to him, "There is a debt, if you wish to regulate it. If you care to give me the burial that you have made, I will give you mine."

When sickness has been cast on a patient of a *chimán,* the *chimán* always works to force the attacker to surrender his burial. This is done by showing the attacker the bottle and its contents prepared by the *chimán.*

The *chimán* who protects a man does not get sick. He makes the man who has done evil get sick, for the *chimán* called upon by the victim has the figure of the baby in the bottle. If the attacker does not surrender the burial he will die; without doubt he will die.

As I said, a *chimán* does not do this because he likes to do it; he does it only when it is necessary. What I have told you is right. You will not like throwing the sickness back upon the attacker.

## 6

Given by my *mozo*, Domingo (February, 1947)

Yes, Señorita, Chimán Rafael Calmo is a *brujo*, the *gente* know it. Señorita, you remember when you first came here to Todos Santos, how sick Patrona was, how she almost died? It was all caused by that wicked old man Tata Rafael.

Patrona, the children, and I had been in the *tierra caliente* working. I was trying to pay off some of my debts. In front of the shacks at the coffee *finca* where we worked was a huge pool of dirty water. Patrona looked after the children while my son Andrés and I picked coffee. A woman from Todos Santos who was there picking coffee asked Patrona to watch her pig. The pig loved to roll around and soak in the pool of water. One day the pig died and the woman said that Patrona had killed it by letting it sit in the water, that she should have kept it out of the water. Señorita, who ever heard of keeping a pig out of water? One might tell the children not to sit in water but never a pig. The woman called Patrona all kinds of names and said she would pay her back. Within a month after we returned here Patrona got sick and became very ill. She felt someone had cast a spell on her, so I went to see a *chimán* who lives up over the mountains at the hacienda and told him all. The *chimán* cast the *mixes* and suggested that I should stay for the night, for the *mixes* had told him that Tata Rafael was working evil.

"It is he who has cast the spell on Patrona," said the *chimán*. "I shall summon the Spirit up tonight, and I shall ask him to find what Tata Rafael has buried in the cemetery."

That night the *chimán* went into his *corral* with the *aguardiente,* copal, and candles that I had brought. The fire was put out and his wife and I sat in darkness waiting. Suddenly the Spirit came. I could hear him talking.

The wife said, "Are you there, Tata Dueño de Cerro?"

"Yes, I am here," he answered, and with that there was a thump next to me as if someone had thrown a rock. When the fire was lighted I saw a bundle next to me. Wrapped in an old cloth were four candles, copal, a small box with pine sap in it, a piece of Patrona's hair, and a small piece of her *huipil*.

The *chimán* said, "The Spirit found this buried in the cemetery and has brought it here."

Señorita, we smashed the candles with rocks and burned them with the other things in a huge fire. I paid the *chimán* fifty cents, and in a few days Patrona was better. The *chimán* I went to has more power than Tata Rafael. An evil man is Rafael; a *brujo* is Rafael.

# 7

## *The Dueños as Naguales and Sorcerers*

### 1

IN TODOS SANTOS the belief that those called *brujos* (in Mam, *aj qia*) could transform themselves into animals was universal, as was the belief that the *dueños de cerro* could change themselves at will into either human or animal form. All the Indians questioned denied that they believed in *naguales*[1] (animal co-spirits). Most of them, in fact, had never heard the word. In March, 1947, I requested Don Pancho to ask Chimán Pascual Pablo whether a child has a *nagual* when it is born. The *chimán* answered that this was not true for Todos Santos, but that on the coast it was true and that the *nagual* was a snake, a turkey, a horse, or a dog. He stated that in Comitancillo, for instance, everyone had a *nagual*. When Don Pancho asked Chimán Pascual what a *nagual* was, he answered:

"Those who know claim that a child is the same as the animal who is its *nagual* and that when the animal *nagual* dies, then the child dies, on the very same day in fact."

When, again at my instigation, Chimán Pascual was asked whether either a good *chimán* or one who was a *brujo* could change himself into a dog or any other animal, he answered that this was not true for Todos Santos, but that it did hold for the inhabitants of San Juan Atitlán and San Sebastián. In these two pueblos, he claimed, there existed evil people who could do just this.

It was not easy to get Indians to speak about these matters, and

[1] See Brinton's extensive work, *Nagualism*.

consequently many of the specific details I obtained on the subject came from *ladinos*.

The first of these accounts was related by Alberto Herrera, whose grandfather had been the first *ladino* in Todos Santos; the second by his father Raimundo Herrera; and the third by the *ladino* teacher at the boys' school, Gerónimo Villatoro. The fourth one was told by an Indian, the *síndico municipal*, Manuel Mendoza, who could read and write Spanish.

2

Given by Alberto Herrera

A long time ago when my father was a boy, his father adopted an orphan Indian boy named Manuel, from San Juan Atitán. Manuel was brought up to help around the house and he was accustomed to obey my grandfather, Celestín Herrera, in all matters. When my father Raimundo was twelve, he and Manuel were sent as shepherds to watch some flocks of sheep, to inspect the corn, and to see that all was well.

One day when there was no wood in the kitchen my father and Manuel were sent to fetch wood. In those days it was not necessary to go far for that as there was plenty of wood near the pueblo. After they had gathered their wood and had tied it into two loads they started homeward. Manuel put his load down and so did my father. Manuel then asked my father if he would be afraid to see a huge coyote and my father said no, he knew coyotes, he had seen them in the country and had no fear of them. Manuel then stepped back a short distance in a place where he could look around in all directions. My father saw him take off his clothes and, when he was naked, tie the sash that held up his trousers around his waist so that one end hung down in back like a tail of an animal. Then out of his clothing that was on the ground he took a small package. In it were some black powder and three small crosses, each smaller than the other. He laid these on his clothes on the ground and rubbed a little of the powder on his body. He thereupon said a few incoherent words and made three somersaults forwards and three back-

171

wards, and suddenly where he had been there stood a handsome coyote, which let out a howl.

My father, who was just a boy, cried out with fear when he saw the transformation of Manuel and began to run in the direction of his house. Looking back he still saw Manuel in the form of a coyote standing near the wood. When he drew near his house he looked back and saw Manuel as Manuel, with both loads of wood on his shoulders. My father heard him call out to wait for him but he would not do it. On reaching the house he ran to my grandfather and told him everything. When Manuel arrived home my grandfather gave him a good talking to and a sound beating.

Many days then passed, but from that time on my father was always afraid to go into the countryside with Manuel. After a long time and after much insistence from Manuel he regained his self-confidence and went with him to look after the horses which were grazing nearby.

When they were a good distance from the house Manuel said, "Look, Raimundo, if you are not afraid I shall go and bring you a small sheep from the flock that is grazing over there."

"Good," said my father.

Manuel, who had a sack in his hands, told my father to wait where he was and that he would return immediately. Thereupon he walked away. My father noticed a flock of sheep grazing on the other side of the Limón River and he also saw the shepherd and dogs. In a short time he saw a coyote running among the sheep. The dogs barked and the shepherds cried out in fear. In a few seconds the coyote caught a small sheep and carried it away from the flock. The shepherds did not follow, as they saw the coyote was a bold fellow and they feared he might attack them.

Manuel arrived later with a sheep in a sack, not dead, but alive. When they returned to the house, Manuel offered the sheep as a present to my grandfather and told him that he had found it alone in the country and that if he had not taken it someone else would have. My grandfather kept the sheep and fattened it, and when fiesta time came they ate it.

## 3

Given by Raimundo Herrera after an Indian's Account

Not long ago, in the mountains in the direction of San Juan Atitán, many Todos Santos Indians were pasturing their sheep. During that time many sheep were lost and the shepherds could not understand how the sheep were taken.

One day an owner lost five sheep from his flock and five more the next day. He then went personally to inspect the place where the sheep had been stolen. He went with his wife and his eldest son, who was the one who had been looking after the sheep.

They walked in the direction of the mountains and the son showed him where he had been pasturing the sheep when they vanished. After the father had looked the place over he sent his wife and son off to pasture the sheep, while he himself climbed the highest tree near the spot where the sheep had vanished.

He waited a long time before anything happened, and then he saw coming toward him a family of Indians consisting of a large, elderly man, a woman, and three children between the ages of ten and fourteen. The elderly man looked the country over with great care and then led the family to a nearby tree. Standing under the tree, he said something to them, and they all took off their clothes. When they were naked they tied their sashes around their waists so that one end hung down in back like a tail. They all made several somersaults forwards and backwards and then turned into coyotes. The father became a large coyote, the mother a medium-sized one, and the children small coyotes. In this order they marched off. The man in the tree waited until they were out of sight and then descended from the tree. He could not explain to himself how this had happened, but when he saw their clothes he decided on vengeance. He collected *ocote* and wood, of which there was plenty, and made a big fire. Into this he threw the dirty clothes of those who had turned themselves into coyotes. The smoke the fire gave off attracted two Todos Santos Indians who were pasturing their sheep nearby. When they heard of what had happened (for they also had lost sheep and wished to see an end put to this business) they all climbed trees and waited in silence.

Not much time had passed when they saw in the distance five coyotes of different sizes, and when these came nearer the Indians saw that each one carried a sheep about its own size slung over its back. The coyotes walked to where they had left their clothes, and when the old coyote saw no clothes he dropped his sheep, and the others did likewise, and they ran in all directions looking for their clothes. They became frantic, and when the old one saw the fire he realized that their clothes had been burned. He spoke some words to the others and they all went and rolled in the ashes of the fire. When nothing happened, they walked away with sad faces, the oldest leading as before. Without doubt they knew that never again could they regain their human forms and that their lives henceforth would be those of coyotes roaming the country.

The men climbed down from their trees, shocked by what they had witnessed but contented, for they knew that from now on their sheep were safe. The man who had burned the clothes told the others that he had recognized the Indians before they transformed themselves. They were not Todos Santos Indians but some Indians from San Juan Atitán.

## 4

Given by Schoolmaster Gerónimo Villatoro

One of my pupils, a boy called Matías, had been absent from school many days on account of sickness, though his friends told me he was well and working about the house. I sent two Indian boys to find out why he did not come to his classes; one was named Antonio Calmo, second grade, and the other Tiburcio Pérez, first grade. To get to Antonio's house they had to take the path near where one can fetch water from the streamlet that feeds the *pila* of Todos Santos. This place is just before one gets to the ruins. There Antonio Calmo saw ahead of him a man, an Indian, who was very well dressed. His clothes were new and on his hat were beautiful plumes. There was nothing strange about the man except that he was unusually tall and formidable-looking. As Antonio looked he saw the man become smaller and smaller, little by little. Antonio did not move from where he was. He was close enough to see him grow so small that he vanished, and in his place stood a turkey which soon began to dance. Antonio then became filled with great fear, he felt the man was the *dueño* of Cumanchúm, and he was so frightened that he fell like one dead into the ditch next to where he was standing. Tiburcio, who had seen nothing except his friend falling into the ditch, pulled him out and as they started on their way back, Tiburcio ran ahead and informed me and Antonio's father of what had happened. We went together and found Antonio pale, his face drawn with fear. When we suggested visiting the place where he had seen the *dueño*, his body shook with great fear and he clung to my trousers and also to his father's in such fashion that we knew he had seen a strange phenomenon, for such have been seen before in Todos Santos. Since that day the children call Antonio Calmo "El Dueño de T'ui Cumanchúm."

5

Given by Manuel Mendoza

About three years ago, the evening before the fiesta of Corpus Cristi, quite a number of *escuelix,* the boys who clean the church and convent (*see plate 12*), were ordered to go early the next morning to the mountains to bring back pine needles to cover the convent floor. The priest from Chiantla was coming.

The boys slept in the convent. One boy, aged fourteen, happened to wake and saw that it was already daylight, so he rose without waking his companions, as he wished to be the first to bring back the pine needles. When he stepped outside he realized that there was no sun; it was the full moon that made everything so clear, just as if it were daylight. Nevertheless he decided to go on, for he knew well the country

175

where the best pines were. They were in the *aldea* El Rancho about four kilometres away.

When he arrived at the place he cut down many branches of pine. Suddenly he saw a bitch, a black and white one, and she came close to the boy as if she knew him. The boy thought it strange for the bitch to be alone.

"Maybe she is one of Don Raimundo's," he thought. "I shall tell him on my return."

Soon the brave boy noticed that the bitch was running in wide circles, but he saw nothing strange in that. A few minutes later he saw a tall man coming towards him out of the woods into which the bitch had gone as it ran. The man had on white riding trousers, a black coat and a straw hat. He was tall and held a gun in his hand.

"Ah, boy, what are you doing here?" he asked.

"I am cutting pine, so that I can carry back the needles to the convent."

"That is good, the pine is good here. Have you seen my bitch, a black and white one?"

"Yes, she left just as you arrived."

"Good, she has several puppies who are like her, fat and beautiful. They are not far from here. Would you like one of the puppies?"

The boy said he would if the man would give it to him as a present.

"Of course," said the man. "Come, we will talk over there."

The boy forgot his work and thought only of the generosity of the man who was going to give him the puppy.

They walked a short distance until they came to a large and heavy door. The man opened it, saying, "Enter, boy, look, here are the puppies."

In a corner the boy saw five puppies. They were black and white and old enough to be taken from their mother.

"Which of them do you like best?" asked the man.

All five were beautiful. The boy looked at them and said, "This one, Señor. He is the most beautiful."

Pl. 10. *Rezadores* in the church doorway: at the right, Tata Julián, Alcalde Rezador; left, Roque Matías, First Rezador. At the right is one of their staffs of office, and on the steps is a *pichacha* or censer.

Pl. 11. "El Rey," Macario Bautista, the calendar priest of Todos Santos.

Pl. 12. Tata Julián, Alcalde Rezador, and an *escuelix,* in the doorway of the church.

Pl. 13. The two crosses, seen through the doorway of the church.

Pl. 14. The Year Bearer Ceremony as it was depicted by the ancient Maya in the Dresden Codex.

These pages (25–28) of the Codex may be explained as follows (according to Förstemann, pp. 120–31, but in much simplified terms): The hieroglyphs on the left of each page are day signs for the last day of one year and the first of the following, each repeated thirteen times. The four pages are said to cover thirteen 52-year cycles. Other glyphs imparting calendar lore are at the top (sixteen to each page, rather obliterated) and between the pictures. The four top pictures show a priest wearing the mask of a beast of prey and a tail. In his right hand are the staff of office and, in two pictures, a copal pouch; in his left, either a rattle or a fan. He carries on his back in each picture the figure of a different god—presumably each of the four Year Bearers or, to the Mames, the Alcaldes del Mundo. The skull-faced one, in the fourth picture, is a god of death. (Thomas, I, p. 67, suggests that the priest is marching in procession to the chief's house or to the sacred heap of stones outside the village.) The middle pictures each show, right, a house, one wall marked with a cross; sitting before it, a priest or god, wearing a gala mantle; and left, an altar on which incense burns. Before the figure are vessels of food for the sacrificial feast—it is suggested, corn, an iguana, birds, squash or fruit, a fish, and bones perhaps symbolizing an animal. The lower pictures each show, left, the hieroglyph for a heap of stones (and also for the 360-day year) surmounted by a tree. In the first picture, the top is carved in the shape of the head of the long-nosed god carried by the animal-priest above; in the other three, the tree is leaved and draped with a mantle and breech-clout, a serpent coils about, rain symbols are on the trunk, and on the drapery are footprints, perhaps representing that the stones and tree are the goal of the procession. The god or priest at right holds a decapitated fowl and, in three pictures, is casting grains of corn in divination. Before him are, again, vessels of offerings (in the fourth picture, a haunch of venison). (The plate is from Gates's redrawing of the Dresden Codex. The Codex was found at Vienna in 1739 and presented to the Librarian of the Royal Library of Dresden. Its earlier history is unknown; not until the latter nineteenth century did it become known for what it is. It is in the State Library of Dresden, having survived the last war with only slight water damage. See also p. 99, footnote 1, and pp. 102–3, fig. 1.)

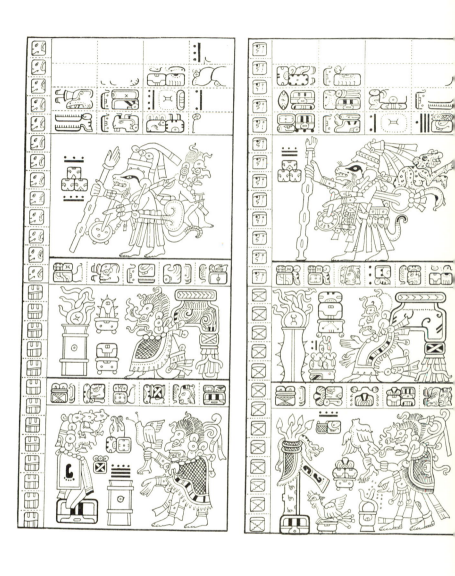

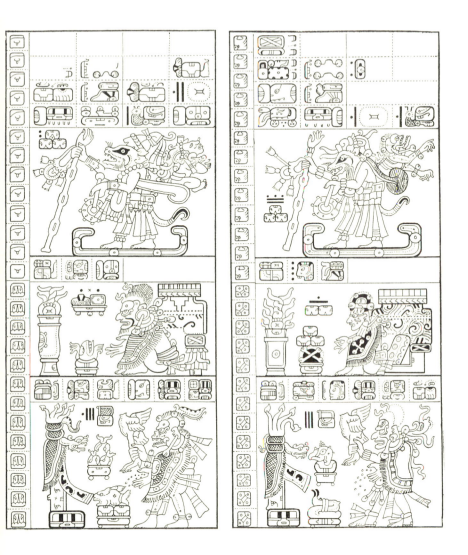

Pl. 15. The two crosses at the foot of the pyramid of Cumanchúm.

Pl. 16. The *mixes*, used for divination. Note the medicine bag of the *chimán* and the quartz, marbles, and dice.

Pl. 17. Fiesta: Indians standing in line to pull the bell-rope for
good luck on Todos Santos Day.

Pl. 18. Fiesta: A rider tying a live rooster to the rope above for the *corrida de gallos.*

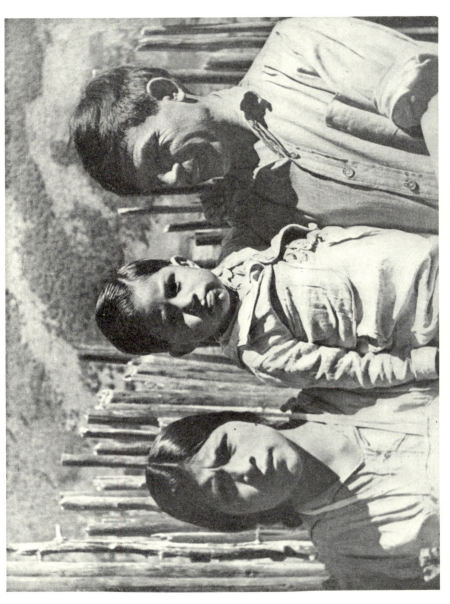

Pl. 19. A *ladino* with his Indian wife and their son.

Pl. 20. Two municipal *mayores*.

Pl. 21. A *mayor* of the religious body, with his staff of office.

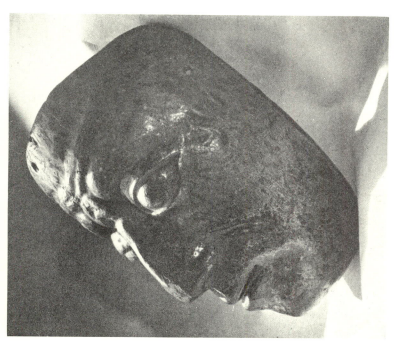

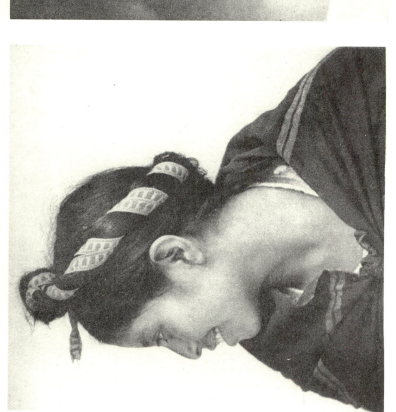

Pl. 22. (a) A Mam woman.

(b) An unpainted carved oak mask which belonged to Patrona's grandfather.

"Pick him up. I give him to you as a present."

The boy had nothing to tie him with, so the man opened a chest and took out a metal chain. This frightened the boy. He then noticed that the room was filled with metal farm implements, *panela* [brown sugar], clothing of all kinds, and everything that the people of the pueblo liked.

The man chained the dog and gave it to the boy, saying, "Wouldn't you like to take with you a machete, some sugar, or anything else that you desire?"

All this generosity was too much for the boy and he began to suspect the man. He thought of this house, quite apart in the woods, that he had never seen before, and he thought with suspicion of the dog and the man's generosity. It occurred to him that possibly this man had some evil purpose. He wished he was outside the house, and said to the man that he wanted to go and fetch some more pine needles. So the man opened the door and said, "Good-bye."

The boy went to where he had cut the pine, fastened the puppy to a tree, and gathered his load together. Soon he was marching on his way back, the chain in his right hand, the puppy trotting along at his side, and the pine needles in a sack on his back.

As they walked along he noticed that dawn was about to break. He was happy in his heart for now he was the owner of a black and white dog.

After they had gone a short distance and the sun was about to show itself, the puppy commenced to tremble and pull at the chain. The boy was deep in thought. He looked up and saw the sun just rising and then looked down and saw that the puppy had vanished. Maybe this was all an illusion, he thought, for he did not have even the chain.

Without doubt, however, this had not been an illusion, for we all know that in the mountains live *gente* and they are the *dueños de cerro*. The boy did not live long. Within a year he was dead.

# 8

## The Chimanes as Soothsayers and Curanderos

### 1

EVERY *chimán* is a soothsayer. Divination is at the base of everything he does. No matter what he is called upon to do—to cure sickness, foretell events, lift a spell from someone, cast one upon someone else—he first consults his *mixes*. Consulting the *mixes* is the same as calling on K'mané, the god of the *mixes*. The charge is from ten to twenty-five cents.

The *mixes* appear to be bright red dried beans. (*See plate 16*.) Don Pancho told me they come from a plant called *palo de pito*.[1] They are carried in a specially woven cotton cloth the size of a small napkin, or in a small bag made of this cloth. The cloth is white with four red lines woven in it which, I imagine, symbolize the four Alcaldes del Mundo. Mingled with the beans are crystals of quartz and often glass marbles, grains of corn, dried black beans, and coins. Chimán Domingo Calmo had, in the bag with his *mixes*, four large crystal lumps, which he put on the four corners of the table, and I imagine that they too symbolized the four Alcaldes. Chimán Manuel Andrés of Santiago Chimaltenango had four black beans combined with his *mixes*.

I found three systems for consulting or casting the *mixes*. Domingo Calmo, Rafael Calmo, and the Chimán Nam, as well as Pedro Pérez of San Juan, used one system; Pascual Pablo used another. In Santiago

---

[1] Goubaud (p. 11) says they are seeds of this plant, which he identifies as *Erythrina corallodendrum*. La Farge says of divination in the pueblo of Santa Eulalia (in *S. E.*, p. 182): "The correct outfit consists of a quantity of *tzité* seeds mixed with a few crystals. As far as I could make out from divinations here and at Jacaltenango, the crystals have no particular significance in the count but add a touch of style to the equipment. Lacking both, grains of corn will do."

Chimaltenango, Manuel Andrés used still a third system. The various other *chimanes* of Todos Santos, apart from these mentioned, used one or the other of the first two.[2]

2

### Chimán Rafael Calmo's System

Given by Don Pancho

Hold the *mixes* in your right hand, raise them to your forehead and say, "Dios Padre," then to your chest and say, "Dios Hijo," then to your mouth and say, "Dios, el Espíritu, Santo de los Mixes." Then hold them in your hand saying, "Santo Jesucristo, Dios de los Mixes, Dios del [whatever day it is], this man [or woman], desires to know . . ." etc., etc.

Put a clean cloth on the *costumbre* table and on this pour out your *mixes*. Move them around with your hand, saying, "Are you there, Dios del Cielo? May my mouth tell the truth." Then take a handful of *mixes*, saying, "To you, K'mané." Then put a handful on the table apart from the others; from these take four at a time and put them in a pile, and repeat this until you have four piles of four *mixes* each, arranged in a square. Then put what is left over in the centre. Touch each pile with your hand, saying "K'mané, Noj, Ik, and Cuman T'ce." Then count what has been left in the fifth pile in the middle. If the number is even, put them to the right; if odd, to the left. Leave the fifth pile and gather up the other four piles now and put with the original *mixes* and repeat as before, doing it twenty times. The only difference in the counting will be that each new handful must be given the name of each of the twenty days in order, commencing as I have told you with the day *k'mané*. When this is finished, there will be the two piles remaining, to the right and to the left. Count the pile that has the even numbers; they are good. Then count the odd numbers; they are bad. Remember that each pile is counted one by one, according to the calendar of twenty days, commencing with *k'mané*. If there are more than twenty, begin

[2] For a chart of the days for casting the *mixes* given by three different *chimanes*, see the Appendix, pp. 248 ff.

Fig. 4. Divination, from the Codex Borbonicus.

Though the Codex Borbonicus is Aztec rather than Mayan, this picture contains interesting parallels to Todos Santos divinatory practice as observed by the author. According to Seler (II, pp. 81–82), the two figures represent the gods Cipactonal and his wife Oxomoco, soothsayers, doctors, and inventors of the calendar. They carry gourds for tobacco on their backs, and Cipactonal, right, also has such priestly implements as a pointed bone, a copal pouch, and a "spoon for dispensing incense" (cf. the *pichacha*). Oxomoco holds a bowl from which she casts "grains of corn" (cf. *mixes*). The two deer-headed objects jutting out at the top, says Seler, probably denote lancettes. Hamy says, in his commentary on the Codex Borbonicus (p. 14), that the deities are consummating a sacrifice in a cave, before which they have planted their golden staffs (the deer-headed objects?). The pointed tool held by the god is described by Hamy as a maguey spine used for administering the sacrificial thrust. (The drawing is from Seler, II, p. 83, where it is reproduced after the Codex Borbonicus. As with other Middle American codices in Europe, the precise origin of this one is unknown; the Bibliothèque du Palais Bourbon, Paris, acquired it in 1826.)

again with *k'mané*. If there are more in the good pile, then the day with which the count ends is the important day for prognostication, though the day of the bad pile also figures. If there are more in the bad pile, the day with which the count ends is most important and probably indicates bad luck. The day on which the *chimán* consults the *mixes* is also important.

### 3

### Chimán Pascual Pablo's System

Given by Don Pancho

When the *chimán* is ready to cast the *mixes*, he sits at his table in his room, and the questioner sits without. He holds the *mixes* in his right hand and begins with this invocation:

"Nombre de Dios, Santa Vara, Santa Letra, Santa Justicia, Dios Jesucristo, Santa Vara, Santa Justicia, Dios T'ui Cumanchúm, Dios Akbal [or whatever day it may be], appear to me so that I may tell the truth. Four Alcaldes del Mundo, appear to me so that I shall not tell a lie. This man [or woman] wishes to know."

When he finishes the invocation he raises the *mixes* in his right hand to his forehead, saying, "*Malaya, Dios*," then to his solar plexus, saying, "Santa Vara," next to his left breast, saying, "Santa Letra," then to his right breast, saying, "Santa Justicia." He repeats this prayer five times, touching the *mixes* to each of the four parts of the body mentioned.

On the *costumbre* table he puts a clean cloth, and on this he puts his *mixes* and moves them around with his right hand, saying, "Ah, *malaya*, Dios K'mané, tell the truth." He then looks at the *mixes* intently and grasps a handful, putting it to one side. From then on he counts in pairs, giving each pair the name of a day commencing with the day *k'mané*. If the counting ends with one instead of a pair, it is counted as a pair. Then he makes a mental note of the day that ends the count.

The second invocation begins, "Nombre de Dios, Noj, tell me the truth." Then he repeats what he did before, commencing with the day *k'mané*. The third invocation begins, "Nombre de Dios, Ik, etc." and the fourth, "Nombre de Dios, T'ce," etc.

181

When he has done this four times, each time naming one of the *alcaldes del mundo* and then counting the pairs, always commencing with *k'mané*, he has a good picture of what the answer to the question will be. If it so happens that each count ends on a good day, the answer will be very good. If it is even, two good days and two bad, then the day on which he casts the *mixes* will have to be taken into consideration. If there seems to be no inclination either way, then it is not a good day for the person concerned. If the *mixes* give good answers but the day of the count is bad, then it is necessary to have prayers, candles, and a little copal.

4

*Chimán Manuel Andres' and Other Systems*

The third school was represented by Chimán Manuel Andrés, from Santiago Chimaltenango. He cast the beans for me twice, and once each for my *mozo* and for a *gringa* friend.

From the handful of *mixes* he would count two by two, but at the end of the count he always left four. For example, if there were six beans left he would take two and put them in the even pile, and if there were five left, he would put one in the odd pile.

Chimán Domingo Calmo did the *mixes* many times for me. The first time he counted twenty times. The only exceptions to this were when I told him my dreams and asked if they were good or bad. He told me they were bad and then counted the *mixes* only thirteen times. When he moved the *mixes* around with his hand he addressed them fondly as "Nana T'ui." If one bean lay on top of another, it meant very bad luck. If the two piles of odd and even beans came out even, it meant bad luck.

· · ·

There are other methods of divination. There is, for instance, one in which the *chimán* sees things "as in a flash of lightning." This power, which few of the *chimanes* now have, is sometimes used in conjunction with the *mixes*.

182

Another method is illustrated by the following example: One day my neighbour Patrona lost a chicken, the third in two months. She was frantic and asked me what to do.

I said, "Chimán Tata Domingo Calmo is coming to see me, and I will send for you when he arrives."

When he came I asked him if he would help her as a favour to me, and he acquiesced. He sat on a low chair and questioned her as to when she had last seen the chicken and who she thought might have stolen it. He then rolled up the trouser of his right leg and put his left hand on the calf of his leg below the knee. He shut his eyes and mumbled so low into his beard that I could not hear what he was saying. After about three minutes he told her the hen was still alive and probably shut up in some-one's house, and that later the thief and his family would eat it. He hinted at who had stolen it. Later I questioned him about his method and he said the muscles in his leg could speak.

In San Juan Atitán, one of the chief *chimanes*, a very old man, divines by the aid of a cross suspended on a string held over a cup of water. He enumerates the twenty days by counting how many times the cross touches the side of the cup. His invocation, as far as I could understand, was to the four Alcaldes and to San Juan.

5

Although the *mixes* are always consulted in the treatment of disease, the *chimanes* frequently combine this with other methods.

They all seem to have an excellent knowledge of herbs and they all practise as *curanderos* (healers).[3] Bloodletting, too, is a common practice among the *chimanes* of Todos Santos.[4] Some *chimanes* also have great skill in setting bones and dislocations. Massage too is often used, generally when the patient is in the sweat-bath. For treating infections,

[3] There were *chimán* specialists: from our point of view, those who were better for sprains or broken bones, diagnosticians, bleeders, veterinarians, etc. They all did a little bit of everything, though.

[4] Cf. Landa, p. 47: "The sorcerers and physicians cured by means of bleeding at the part afflicted, casting lots for divination in their work, and other matters."

however, the *chimanes* are worthless; they have no idea of sanitation or antisepsis. I treated personally many cases of infection, of really bad infection. Most of these patients had been to *chimanes* before they came to me. I was the last resort.

As an example let me give the case of Tomás Mendoza, a *principal*, who had an infected foot. I saw him limping along one day and told him to come to me, that I could fix it. But he did not come. Two weeks went by and his foot became so swollen that he could not walk. Meeting him riding a horse on the trail, I told him he had better come before it was too late. Another week went by, and then his wife came to me and said that Tomás was suffering intensely. She asked if I would go to see him, as he was too sick to come to me. I told her that he had waited a long time before coming to me and he could wait a little longer; I would come late in the afternoon. When I arrived, I found Chimán Pascual Pablo there. The *chimán* watched everything I did. The infection had gone up Tomás' leg; the foot and leg both were very much swollen. In three days the swelling had gone down and in five he was cured. After that the *chimán* himself sent me many patients.

## 6

Besides the *chimanes*, there are people called *pulseras*, who feel the pulse, tell what is wrong with the patient and whether he will live or die. Most *pulseras* are women. Rosa Bautista (*see plate 9*) was a *pulsera* as well as a midwife and had an amazing knowledge of herbs, of the calendar, and of all *costumbres*.

Most illnesses are attributed to *susto* (fright) or to someone's evil thoughts or the casting of a spell.

All *chimanes* are supposed to indicate immediately if the patient will live or die. If they predict death, both family and patient accept the verdict. The patient then ceases to eat and prepares for death, and the family for its part ceases to feed the sick one. One way or another, the patient usually dies soon.

In October, 1946, I was called in on a case of serious burn and shock. Three *bombas* (home-made "bombs" that the Indians use for celebrations) had exploded near the leg of a young man named Manuel Pablo. The flesh was blown open from ankle to knee and the foot and leg were burned so badly on one side that I feared for his recovery. They had called in Chimán Rafael Calmo, who had cast the *mixes* and said that Manuel would not live. The wife called me in the next morning. Over the leg was a filthy cloth and the wound was covered with flies. Because of what the *chimán* had told him, the patient had already given up hope and was prepared for death. He was suffering from shock, pain, and fright. I told him he would not die if he did what I told him to do, but that his wound would take a long time to heal and that he would have to have patience. He accepted my verdict, and the expression on his face was most rewarding. It took a long time for the wound to heal, but it finally did, and Manuel and I became fast friends. He sent me many patients and stuck by me faithfully when I was accused of being a *bruja*.

A tropical country like Guatemala has its share of poisonous snakes, and it is only natural that the *chimanes* should be called upon frequently to cure snake-bite. Their method of treatment is indicated by the following example.

In March, 1947, a child of my neighbour Patrona was bitten by a snake while he was with his father near Concepción. He was taken to a *chimán* near there and cured. I told this to Tata Julián, the Alcalde Rezador, when he came to call that evening. He told me that there were just two *chimanes* who could cure snake-bite, one at San Juan Atitán and the other near San Martín. If anyone is bitten he goes to the nearest *chimán*, who ties a number of loops of cord on the patient's leg. If the man is bitten in the foot, the *chimán* ties one loop at the ankle, another below the knee, and another above the knee. Then he makes an incision at the snake-bite and permits bleeding. He now unties one of the loops and lets the blood flow there, then unties another and lets the blood flow at that place, and so on. Sometimes snake-bite is also cauterized.

"Every year, Señorita," Tata Julián told me, "the *chimanes* of San Juan make *costumbre* and summon the snakes, who come from all directions at their bidding."

"What do they summon them with?" I asked.

"With *chirimías* made of reed. The harmless snakes they let go, the others they kill."

Another method of curing snake-bite was described by Chimán Pascual Pablo. Don Pancho had asked him: "Tata Pascual, are there *chimanes* today who can cure snake-bite?"

"Today, no, there are none, but formerly, yes," the *chimán* said. "In San Juan Atitán there used to be *chimanes* who could cure snake-bite. Formerly I too used to know how, but now I don't remember. Formerly, when I was a young man, I knew all about it, but now I am forgetting things. There was a time when a *chimán* would play a *chirimía* and pray and then the snakes, large and small, would come to him. Some were dangerous snakes, others less so, yet all came. I would have misgivings that one would come that I feared. Ah, wicked, indeed, is the bite! Now this is what one must do. Catch a snake and press a forked stick down on the snake's throat. Then with a knife cut the skin around the throat and pull it off as one pulls bark off of a branch. Be sure not to kill the snake. Keep the skin and put it in a pot with water. If the patient is very sick, very little water. Then pray. Put poultices of this water on the wound."

.  .  .

I found no instances of treatment of "psychological" complaints by *chimanes*. But I noted two instances of lay treatment.

The *ladinos* and some of the Indians have a pleasant treatment for listlessness. If a man has no energy and finds he does not want to work, he goes to the Todos Santos River with an armful of flowers. He then sits on its bank and throws a flower upstream and follows the blossom with his eyes until it is out of sight downstream. He does this for about twenty minutes and repeats it every day until he is better.

"Sadness of the heart" is a common complaint among the Indians. This is usually "cured" by a special medicine sold in Huehuetenango, called *Remedio para Tristeza de Corazón,* "Remedy for Sadness of Heart." I bought a bottle, and found it deep red in colour, with a very sweet taste suspiciously like port wine.

# 9

## The Calendar and Its Ceremonies

### 1

THE MAYAN CEREMONIAL CALENDAR is commonly known among the older men and women of Todos Santos and is referred to as the "calendar of the *chimanes*" (*guaxakláj xau*). Usually, however, the Indians reckon the passage of time by neither the Mayan nor the Gregorian year but (and for them it is more exact) by the simple agricultural year. The Gregorian year is not entirely disregarded; the induction into office of the civil and religious officials is on January 1, and some, but not all, of the Christian fiestas fall on their "right" dates. But if you question an Indian as to the date of a certain fiesta, he never refers to the month of our calendar in which it is held but says, "It is when the corn is green," or "It is held in the rainy season, during the twenty days when there is no rain," and so on, in terms of the agricultural calendar.

The native calendar, as it has survived from Mayan times, consists of a year (*ab[1] ij*) of 360 days, plus a five-day period[2] added to the end of the year and considered evil. The 360 days are divided into eighteen months; a month is *tequin[3] ij*, or *wen en[4] ij*, or *xau*, which also means "moon." Each month is composed of twenty days; a day is called *ij*, which also means "sun." Every fifth day is called an *alcalde*, so that there are a total of four *alcaldes* in a twenty-day month. These are the four *alcaldes del mundo* (*t'uit tor*). The other sixteen days are called *mayores*, and *batz*, the twentieth day, is also called *casalera del mundo*.[4a]

---

[1] Cf. the Mayan *haab*, "calendar year."
[2] Identical with the Mayan five-day added unit, *uayeb*.
[3] Cf. the Mayan *tzolkin*, "a period of 260 days."
[4] Cf. the Mayan *uinal*, "a period of twenty days," i.e., a month.
[4a] See Chimán Pascual Pablo's explanation, p. 137.

The Mam *chimanes* have no knowledge of the month names or the number count still used with the Mayan calendar in other parts of Guatemala.[5] I have questioned many old *chimanes*, not only in Todos Santos but also in San Martín, Santiago Chimaltenango,[6] and San Juan Atitán. They all say that the number count was never used by their people. Yet they insist that other tribes use the number count. It is a very curious fact that even among *chimanes* ninety years old or more, there is no knowledge of this count in connection with their calendar.

The four *alcaldes del mundo, k'mané, noj, ik,* and *t'ce,*[7] alternate in the role of introducing the new year and are called Year Bearers.[8] The *alcalde* that introduces the year is considered the most important day of the whole year. In the esoteric interpretation, however, *k'mané* is always the most important day, whether it is the chief Year Bearer or not. On this day, which comes every twenty days, people burn candles, pray, and make offerings of flowers and other objects at the church and at Cumanchúm (*see plate 15*). The Alcalde Rezador and the Chimán Nam always perform *costumbre* on each of the *alcalde* days, but on *k'mané* and the chief *alcalde* day for the year they perform a more elaborate *costumbre* and more *rezadores* participate.

The *chimanes* recognize a starting day in the use of their calendar; this is always *k'mané*.[9] During 1946 and 1947, the first day of the new

---

[5] See Goubaud, pp. 8–18; La Farge and Byers, ch. 18; Rodas, Rodas, and Hawkins, pp. 11–18.

[6] Wagley found the same condition existing in Santiago Chimaltenango, according to La Farge, *S. E.*, p. 170, footnote 6.

[7] These correspond to *ik, manik, eb* and *caban,* the *bacabs* or Year Bearers used by the Mayans during the Old Empire, and also used by the Old Quiché. See Morley, p. 301; La Farge and Byers, p. 176. (See p. 77, footnote 6, of the present work.)

[8] Cf. Landa, p. 60: "Among the multitude of gods worshiped by these people were four whom they called by the name of *Bacab*. These were, they say, four brothers placed by God when He created the world, at its four corners to sustain the heavens lest they fall. They also say these *Bacabs* escaped when the world was destroyed by the deluge. To each of these they give other names, and they mark the four points of the world where God placed them holding up the sky. . . ." (Also see plate 14 of present work.)

[9] The Ixil calendar commences with *ee*. I find great similarity between the calendar of the Ixiles and the Mames. (See Lincoln, p. 107.) I thought at one time that *k'mané* and *cuman ee* were one and the same. Though they both are the day *ee*, there is a distinct difference in the pronunciation of their names.

year was March 10. The Year Bearer for 1946 was *t'ce* and for 1947 *k'mané*.

The twenty days are regarded as gods, the most important god being K'mané and the next most important, co-equal among themselves, Noj, Ik, and T'ce.[10] These four gods are also the names of the four most important mountains which surround Todos Santos.[11]

2

## The Day-Count

By questioning, I obtained the following information concerning the day-count:

Chimán Nam Macario Bautista stated: "I know of the count of 1–13 of the *chimanes* of Concepción, but that is not known to me or to my father."

Chimán Rafael Calmo answered: "I know of the count of 1–13, but it is not done among my people. We have only the count of 1–16 and 1–20."

"Why should there be a count of 1–16?" I asked.

"Because of the twenty days, every fifth day is an *alcalde del mundo*, and the four days between are *mayores*. The 1–16 count is useful when one asks the gods to punish someone. Each *alcalde* has four *mayores*. Two *alcaldes* plus eight *mayores* are ten. All the *mayores* together make sixteen. These sixteen are very useful, as I said, when one asks the *dueño de cerro* to punish someone."

Chimán Pascual also denied any knowledge of the thirteen count: "No, I do not know the count of 1–13. Only on the coast do they know such numbers, but there it is not 1–13, but 1–19. No *chimán* of this pueblo knows the count of 260 days of the calendar. Possibly other people who speak another language do. No one in the pueblo knows it. We

---

[10] *Batz* also is an important day; see p. 137.
[11] For lists of the calendar and the meaning of the day names, see Appendix, pp. 251 ff.

know just the count of twenty days, the months of twenty days. The year of the *chimanes* has twelve months, maybe eighteen months."

Chimán Domingo Calmo agreed with the others: "The *chimanes* of this pueblo do not know the count of 1–13, nor did my father know it. The *chimanes* of Jacaltenango and Concepción know this count; but our ways are different."

3

*The Five Evil Days*

Every *chimán* I questioned said one of two things: either that there are five days that end the year, namely the retiring *alcalde* and the four days *k'nel, t'coj, t'ciik,* and *batz;* or that there are four days that end it, namely the last four.

In 1945, the Year Bearer was *ik. Ik* not only introduced the year but ended it as well, on March 5. Instead of the next four being *akbal, kets, kan,* and *kimex,* which would be the proper order, they were *k'nel, t'coj, t'ciik,* and *batz.* Then came the new Year Bearer, *t'ce.*

I asked several *chimanes* why they did not continue with the days *akbal,* etc. They said, "We have been taught that the last four days are always *k'nel, t'coj, t'ciik,* and *batz.* Who ever heard of an *alcalde* entering except on the day *batz?* He is a very important Señor, *batz.*"

The Indians feel the last four or five days are evil. During these days they stay at home, do not work, eat little, and abstain from sexual intercourse.[12] On the day *t'coj,* they go to their *chimanes* and confess their sins. All sins must be confessed before the new year begins.

*Chimanes* perform *costumbres* at the *cerros* and in their houses during the five evil days. *Chimanes* abstain from sexual intercourse for ten days before the New Year.

Chimán Domingo Calmo told me: "During the last four days of the

---

[12] Cf. Landa, p. 70: "For the festival of the chiefs, the priests and the leading men, and those who wished to show their devoutness, began to fast and stay away from their wives for as long time before as seemed well to them."

year there is no justice in the world. Nothing is received; there are no *alcaldes*. A *chimán* cannot work with his *mixes* for he will be punished and die. The world is suspended until the new *alcalde* of the year enters. Then the month changes, the *chimán* sacrifices a rooster[13] and burns its blood with copal, and the people eat meat, so that in this way no harm will come to us during the whole of the coming new year."

On the day *batz* in the evening, the *chimán* receives people in his house, for this is the *chimán's* own night, the night when the Spirit or *dueño de cerro* will come and answer questions and make prognostications for the year to come. This is the night of the big fiesta (*Xoj K'au*) of the *chimanes*,[14] which welcomes the new Year Bearer for the year to come.

### 4

This is what the *chimanes* Pascual Pablo and Rafael Calmo told me they did on the final five-day period of the year in 1947:

| | PASCUAL PABLO | RAFAEL CALMO |
|---|---|---|
| March 5: *CUMAN T'CE* | We take leave of the Alcalde del Mundo, Cuman T'ce. He is not sent away, yet we are sad and drink a little. We burn copal, send off skyrockets, and perform a mass at the table during the night. | We take leave of the Alcalde Cuman T'ce with skyrockets. |
| March 6: *k'nel* | We salute the Alcalde K'mané who will enter. This will be a good year which will give health and money. | We pray for the Alcalde K'mané who will enter the new year. Everything will be good. |

[13] Cf. ibid., p. 62: "Thus incensing the image, they cut off the head of a fowl, and presented it as an offering."

[14] Each *chimán* receives in his house. Tata Julián said to me, "When I was a young man I went with my family on the night of the *chimanes* to pay our respect to the Chimán Nam. Nowadays some people forget the Chimán Nam Macario Bautista. This may bring misfortune on our pueblo." Ceremonies on the night of the *chimanes* are described below (pp. 204 ff.).

| March 7:<br>*t'coj* | The people who have debts will come and they will have to pay a fine. They will have to tell the *chimán* their sins. | They will pay a fine, those who have sinned, and they must tell their sins before all those present. |
| --- | --- | --- |
| March 8:<br>*t'ciik* | We say prayers for the new Alcalde del Mundo and ask that there will be no cases of people talking like dogs. | We say prayers for the new Alcalde del Mundo, that he will close the mouths of the people who speak like dogs. |
| March 9:<br>*batz* | This day we pray to the Alcalde who is to enter, that he will give health and everything good to the people. In the night when the first rooster sings, we send off skyrockets, have drinks, and play music. The *chimán* summons all the *dueños de cerro*, so that Santo Mundo will come and tell us what will take place during the coming year. | We light a candle for the Alcalde who leaves, and for the Alcalde who will stay at the table with the *chimán*. |

## 5

### Ceremonies at Chimán Rafael Calmo's House
Given by Don Pancho (March 7, 1947: *t'coj*)

At six in the afternoon, I received a message from Chimán Rafael Calmo to come to his house as the Spirit would come that night. I was instructed to bring *cera* and *sebo* candles and a bottle of *aguardiente*.

I arrived at his house around seven-thirty. There were present only the *chimán*, his wife, and a young guitar player. Rafael received me with warmth and I gave him the candles and *aguardiente*. He thanked me for them and put them on the *costumbre* table.

He told me to sit in the only chair in the room and said, "I sent for you to come, for the Spirit will come this night and you can hear what he has to say."

"Are more people coming?"

"Yes, a rooster and a turkey will come." He was busy making the decorations for the doorway of the *corral* and the altar. He was sewing oranges to the pine boughs, two by two.

At about ten o'clock, a family consisting of husband, wife, and four children entered. The man carried a large turkey in a sack on his back, and the oldest daughter carried two roosters with their feet tied together. They gave these to the *chimán*.

At eleven o'clock, the *chimán* was ready to make the sacrifice. He asked for a piece of a clay pot and a knife. He then lighted several candles and placed them on the *costumbre* table which served as altar. The newcomer handed the candles, the copal, and a litre of *aguardiente* to the *chimán*, who laid them on the table with a great deal of respect. Soon he took the candles and called on his wife to help him. They cut each candle into four pieces and threw them into a clay pot. He then threw in the copal, after breaking it up into small pieces. Then he asked for the first rooster. He took it in his right hand, holding the feet in his left hand.

He now addressed the table: "Ah, *malaya*, Dios, our Jesucristo, Santa Mesa T'Chimolal, let there be a little health for Sebastián Jiménez and his family [mentioning all their names]."

He thereupon uttered some words in Mam that I did not understand. All this time Sebastián and his family remained in a crouching position with their heads bowed.

The *chimán* then passed the head of the rooster over the head of each member of the family and uttered the following invocation: "Ah, *malaya*, Caballero T'ui K'oy, Caballero T'ui Bach, Caballero T'ui Xolik, Caballero Cilbilchax, give health to this family. Ah, Dios, Santo Jesucristo. . . ." In Mam he added *"t'chimolal"* and other words.

Then again he spoke: "Ah, *malaya*, Santo Mundo, give to Sebastián a hen, a turkey, a mule, anything he wants. Look after his animals that they may have burdens to carry, guard him on the road. Santa Mesa, receive Sebastián Jiménez who is here with his family, grant them health, food, money, advice."

The *chimán* then sat down on a small stool, his wife took the rooster

194

by the feet, and the *chimán* grasped the head with his left hand. Holding the knife in his right hand, he slit the neck of the rooster. The blood flowed onto the candles and onto the copal in the clay pot. When the rooster was dead they collected the pot and the rooster, and laid them in front of the altar-table. With his hands the *chimán* then stirred up the candles and copal so that they would be covered with blood just as his hands were. He then asked for a *doblador* [corn leaf], took some of the copal and pieces of candles soaked in the blood, and wrapped them in a leaf like a tamale. Then he tied it with a piece of maguey fibre. Now he took four candles and some copal and wrapped these together in a piece of material supplied by Sebastián, with the tips of the candles sticking out. The *chimán* uttered something in Mam after that, and when I asked what he had said, he answered, "What is in the bundle Sebastián must burn, partly in front of the cross outside the church and partly at Cumanchúm, and in this way my work for him will end."

After Chimán Rafael had given the bundle to Sebastián he took some more candles, cut them into four pieces, and with the copal threw them into the pot as before. He took another rooster and sacrificed it as before, first holding it over the heads of the members of the family and repeating the prayer previously uttered, except that he added: "Remove their sickness; remove their suffering; remove their affliction; remove the harm done by the caprice of the *gente* and close the mouths of the *gente* who talk against this poor man. Ah, *malaya,* Santa Mesa, give him a turkey, a pig, a dog, a hen, a cat; ah, *malaya,* Santo Mundo, Santa Mesa, give him corn; give him beans; give him chili; give him salt; give him *bebida;* give him potatoes; ah, *malaya,* Santo Mundo, Santa Mesa, give Sebastián his strength so that he can work; seed his corn, his potatoes, his beans, his squash, his herbs."

Then he sacrificed this rooster and let the blood fall on to the candles and the copal. After several strong flaps of its wings, the rooster died, and the *chimán* folded its wings around its body. He then made another tamale, putting into the cloth the same things in addition to a flower that was on the altar. This flower was a red one, an *amapola* [poppy].

He sacrificed a turkey in the same way except that he gave each member of the family a poppy to hold during the ceremonial sacrifice. When the ceremony was over he took back the poppies. He then made the same kind of tamale as before out of the candles mixed with copal, and added a flower. This tamale, however, he kept on the table. The other two he gave to Sebastián.

The *chimán* then gave us all coffee and *aguardiente,* and turning to me, said, "With your permission, Don Pancho."

Thereupon Rafael Calmo entered his *corral,* where his table was. The decorations had been placed around the door. Over the door hung an old dirty black rug, full of holes. In this room he thus addressed the gods:

"With your permission, Santa Mesa, ah, Dios, Santo Jesucristo, Señor of the World, Alcalde Cuman T'ce, you are going to leave, and you, Alcalde K'mané, you will enter. Make a slight appearance. With your permission, Alcalde Ik, Alcalde Noj. With your permission be it. Ah, Dios, Caballero T'ui K'oy, Caballero T'ui Bach, Caballero T'ui Yembel, Caballero Cilbilchax, Caballero T'ui Cumanchúm, Caballero T'ui T'suts, Caballero Punliak, Caballero Chan Chuyé, Caballero T'ui Xolik, Caballero T'ui Talchej, Caballero T'ui Soch, Caballero Xétajo, Caballero T'sipego, Caballero Tincoig, Caballero Tiqnak, Caballero Xemolak, Caballero Xepaxá, Caballero Xemina Cruz, Caballero Chalajuitz, Caballero Xinakabiok. Ah, Dios, speak a few words for it is impossible to understand if there is just a mumbling. With your permission, Don Pancho. . . ." The rest was in the Mam language.

Now the light was put out and there was a moment of silence. Then a sound like the flapping of the wings of a bird was heard, and shortly after the voice of Rafael, though he tried to change it by making it more feminine.

"Good evening, Don Pancho," said the supposed Spirit.

"Good evening, Señor," I said.

"How are you and your family?"

"They are about as usual, thank you."

"You have come to visit me?"

"Yes, speak to me a little."

"Don Pancho, I have come from far, far away, far away, and I am tired, for we Spirits are wind."

I had no respect for him, for there was no Spirit there except Rafael Calmo. He expected to gain something from me and from all the Indians sitting there on the floor, full of faith.

So he talked to me in Spanish, and then to the Indians in Mam. I was seated near the curtain and could observe everything very well. There were eight Indians in all, full of respect and deep faith. The Spirit would reprimand one, give advice to another, and prognosticate for another. Each would say, *"Bueno,* Ta." The voice changed twice while he was talking to the Indians. He spoke for about half an hour and ended by saying, "It is true, Don Pancho, and now we will send off a sky-rocket."

Then I said, "Yes, Señor, it will be delightful."

"With your permission, Don Pancho, will you take a small drink?"

"Yes, Señor, and do you take one too," I said.

His fraud was so obvious that it was difficult for me to speak respect-fully to him. He spoke to the Indians a short time and then said to me:

"Burn a little copal so that your wishes will turn out well. Do you know of what I speak? Let me foretell this for you. Your Señora will not leave her position in the school. Señor L—— is gossiping against you, but he has no reason for doing this. Every *alcalde*-day, *k'mané, noj, ik, cuman t'ce,* burn your candle in the church. Señor L—— will unques-tionably leave his job this year. This year a young *ladina* woman with shoes will kill herself over a man, at El Calvario. Another *ladina* woman also will die. The day after tomorrow it will rain.[15] That is all, Don Pancho."

To his wife he said, "Chucia Bank, *sopla el fuego* [stir up the fire]."

Near me I heard a sound of something he had rolled away,[16] and I wondered if it had been an orange.

---

15 It did.
16 Perhaps to suggest the departing Spirit?

Immediately afterwards, the room was lighted up again and everyone started to say good night to one another. The *chimán* sat outside his little *corral*, with the expression of one who knows everything and is quite pleased with himself. He gave us a little more coffee and *aguardiente*, and as I was leaving he said, "The Spirit did not come the way it will Sunday night, so come Sunday." I accepted and thanked him.

6

*Ceremonies at Chimán Pascual Pablo's House*
Given by Don Pancho (March 8, 1947: *t'ciik*)

I went to the house of Chimán Pascual Pablo at seven in the evening, carrying the necessary things: copal, candles, and *aguardiente*. His house is beyond El Calvario and is small, with a thatched roof. His nephew came out to meet me and very respectfully asked me to enter. I found the house full of people. They looked at me with suspicion, without pleasure. I offered each a cigarette, and this seemed to ease the tension. The *chimán's* nephew told me that the *chimán* had gone out for a short time with one of his pupils to officiate at a rite and that we were to await his return.

At ten o'clock the *chimán* arrived with his wife. Both were a little drunk. As he entered he saluted and embraced me. The effect was extraordinary, for they all saw then that he treated me as a personal friend.

"You have come," he said.

"Yes, I have come to see if I can learn properly."

"Good, sit down. I had just gone out to serve as a *fiador* for the pupil to whom I had sold a table. Yes, I have taught this pupil well, yet he is still lacking although he knows his office well. Because of this I wish to teach him everything. Come here, sit near me and learn well, for in another month you are to receive your table."

I could see that the *chimán's* own table, serving as an altar, had an arch of pine above and in front of it; on two poles framing the doorway was hung some white material, and next to the table stood a small chair.

The *chimán* said, "I shall speak Spanish to you, but to my people our own tongue."

The *chimán* then took the copal and *aguardiente* I gave him and put them in front of the table, over which was another arch, of pine boughs hung with oranges and bananas. Then he began:

"Ah, *malaya,* Santo Mundo, Santa Mesa, Santa Justicia, Dios, accept the offering of Don Pancho here. Grant wealth to him and to his family. Take care of him, Padre Mundo. Give him food, clothing, and work. Defend him, Father T'ui K'oy, T'ui Xolik, Father Cilbilchax, Father T'ui Bach, defend Señor Don Pancho from harm. Close the mouths of the *gente* and those of his family."[17]

He then went to his place in front of the table and took out two candles, saying to me, "Light these and put out the light of the *ocote.*"

Another man then gave him a large bundle of candles, some copal, and a litre of *aguardiente*. These the *chimán* put on the floor in front of the table. He now took the *aguardiente* and copal in his hands, and the man sat down in a crouching position in front of the altar, which was lighted by the two candles. Before this the room had been lighted only by *ocote*. The *chimán* received each one with the same prayer he received me with. When he had finished with one he would turn to another.

Of four people who now entered, one was a young woman of about twenty years who carried candles and copal. When the *chimán* saw her he said, "Why has your husband talked against me? He says that I am not a *chimán,* only a drunkard, that what I receive I just drink. No, when I drink, it comes from my own money. Your husband is a bad person. These candles you have brought are not for my table. Possibly they are for the devil's, so go burn them in the patio."

The young woman went out, and all the Indians in the room whispered among themselves. I then asked the *chimán* what it was all about.

He answered, "The husband of this woman has been speaking ill of me. Why does she come? Her presence is not good for my table, and for

---

[17] The *chimán* had suggested that Don Pancho's wife would be opposed to his learning to be a *chimán*.

that reason I have sent her into the patio. What do the people say? Well, that he is badly brought up, a worthless young man. Why doesn't he come himself with candles and not send his wife? His wife has been possessed by evil spirits; she is always complaining and timorous and asking my pardon."

Then I spoke to the *chimán* and said, "Poor thing, won't you forgive her?"

Thereupon he spoke in Mam and said, "Well, she may enter, but she must leave her candles in the patio."

Many more people now came with similar presents. The bottles of *aguardiente* ranged in size from small to large. The *chimán* received and greeted each one in the order in which he came. He was about to commence with the sacrifice of the roosters when the young woman, the one who had gone out to light her candles, returned and with her came her husband. They both knelt in front of the *chimán* and the husband talked to him in Mam.

The *chimán* reprimanded him, saying, "You are bad and wicked. Never will I intercede for you; it is unnecessary. Why are you saying these evil things about me? You speak like a dog; you have no respect; you are badly brought up. Repent for what you have said, or my table will punish you, and if this happens it will be your fault. Never ask the Spirit for food, for he has no food for you. This kind of thing annoys me, so repent! I see you are crying like a baby."

The two begged for forgiveness and the *chimán* said, "Tomorrow we will talk things over. Now I have work."

The candles were then taken off the table and put on the pine needles on the ground. A tablecloth of white with red and black lines was now put on it. It was a *tortilla* napkin. Upon this were laid in succession a wooden cross, the cross of the ceremonial table, a small gourd cup, and a large candle. Below the table were several clay pots. The *chimán* then ordered his nephew to send off a skyrocket.

Everyone had brought candles, and each one was ordered by the *chimán* to light two. When this was done the room was filled with the light of burning candles. He now asked for some leaves, and the large leaves of the *ortiga* [nettle] were brought. He laid two of these in front of the altar, on the pine needles, and upon them put six balls of copal, in this design:

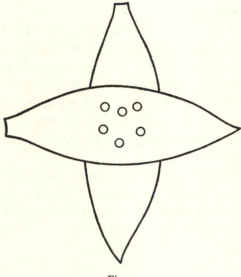

Fig. 5.

"Move your chair closer," he said to me, and to his nephew he said, "Come here and help me, I have received and greeted every one here. Give them all a drink now."

He then took the first rooster and put it in front of the altar, saying: "Ah, *malaya*, Santa Mesa, Santo Mundo, Santa Justicia, Dios, receive this from José Pablo. Grant him health and grant health to his family. Ah, *malaya*, Caballero T'ui Bach, Caballero T'ui K'oy, Caballero T'ui Xolik, Caballero Cilbilchax, accept them. Santa Mesa, give them health, food, money, and work. Give everything necessary and defend them against evil-wishers in the pueblo. Ah, Dios del Cielo."

All this was uttered in front of José and his family while they all knelt in worship and respect. The *chimán* now handed the rooster to his nephew, took some copal, broke it up into small pieces, and put six of the pieces on the crossed leaves that lay in front of the altar. Out of his bag he drew his clasp-knife and opened it. Holding the head of the rooster with his left hand, he parted the feathers with his right hand and slit the bird's neck, letting the blood pour over the copal in the *pichacha* and over the leaves.[18]

When the blood ceased flowing, the *chimán* laid the body of the fowl on the pine needles in front of the altar. In all, he sacrificed thirteen roosters on that day. The invocation following each sacrifice was always the same except for the names of the donors.

After the roosters had all been laid in front of the altar, the nephew pulled the white curtain so that it covered the door of the *corral*. Pascual Pablo now lighted a large candle, the only one of its size, and then uttered his invocation:

"Ah, *malaya,* Santa Mesa, Santo Mundo, Santa Justicia, Dios, ah, Santo Mundo, grant health to the people who are here. Ah, *malaya,* Santa Justicia, Dios del Cielo, come, Spirit. Come this night to tell us the truth. Alcalde K'mané, Alcalde Cuman T'ce, Alcalde Noj, Alcalde Ik, appear. The people are waiting for you."

He then gave me the large candle and said, "Do you invoke the *dueños de cerro*. If you forget anything, I will help you."

Throughout all this time the spectators had been standing, but when I took the candle and stood it in front of them they all knelt as if the candle commanded great respect. I began, "*Malaya,* Santo Mundo, Santa Mesa, Santa Justicia, Dios, good Spirit of God, these people wish to have knowledge."

Then I raised the candle above all the people who knelt before me, and continued, "They desire to know your prognostications for the coming year. Ah, *malaya, dueños de cerro,* come, and tell us a little of what is true tonight."

Then I named the four most important mountains, and the others too.

[18] If the rooster does not die immediately and flaps his wings, this signifies good luck for the one who brought it. But if it dies without a struggle and not much blood pours out, this signifies that the man who brought it or one of his family will die.

In the main I repeated what the *chimán* had said. When I reached the last part, the *chimán* began where I had stopped, but spoke in Mam. The light and fire were extinguished. The *chimán* asked for the candle and told me to sit next to him in the room behind the curtain, and not to be afraid. He himself put out the candle. We were in complete darkness, except in so far as the light of the moon penetrated through the cracks of the wood-slat walls. There was complete silence. All waited hopefully for what would come. I was seated very close to the *chimán*. I could feel his body begin to tremble as if from chills, and I could hear his teeth chattering. I heard a knocking in the table, and immediately the *chimán's* body stopped shaking and he was still. Soon I heard the voice of the *chimán* say a word in Mam. His wife outside then said, "Enter, Ta," and he answered, "Are you there, Chucia Chuán?" Then she again spoke, saying, "Enter, Ta."

The Spirit[19] talked to each one present in Mam, and then said to me, in Spanish, "Don Pancho, you will receive your table, but this is not to be played with. Think well about the matter, for when you have once received a table you have received it for ever. There are many vows that a *chimán* must take. Remember, *chimanes* are never rich. If you want to be rich, it is better not to become a *chimán*. You must take four poles and make a special *corral* for the table, and the table must always be in this *corral*, never in the house of a *ladino*. Good-bye now [to all], I shall come tomorrow to tell of the year to come."

After that, silence. Then the *chimán* ordered light to be made, the fire lit, and coffee to be given to the people, but to me he gave a drink of *aguardiente*, saying, "The Spirit has not appeared in the way he will tomorrow. Tomorrow he will be more contented and give us much more information."

He then ordered a skyrocket to be set off. We all took coffee and drank more *aguardiente*. Two older men played music on a guitar and a violin. Then the *chimán* said to me, "You must dance a little with me for we are all here together as one."

19 Don Pancho was convinced this actually was the Spirit.

203

I accepted and he ordered the musicians to play. He rose and I did too. The people moved back, leaving a small space in the centre of the room, but very small because of the size of the house. We danced together and yet apart, each with his arms folded in back, and the people watched us with great respect.

When we stopped the *chimán* exclaimed, "Don Pancho, *ladino,* knows how to sing. Won't you sing us a song?"

I asked for the guitar and inquired whether they would like a *ladino* or an Indian song. Indian, they all said. So first I sang what they wanted, and then I sang a *ladino* one. When I finished they all expressed their appreciation, and the *chimán* said, "Many thanks, Don Pancho, for your visit. We will talk later about certain matters and arrange things." He was referring to the table.

"Good," I said, "I do not want to withdraw. I know well that it is a delicate matter to receive the table, but I am a serious person and I should like very much to serve the *todosanteros,* to whom I am very much attached."

"Come with your family tomorrow then," he said, "and help us eat the chickens. It is very important to do so. If all your family cannot come, at least bring your wife."

I accepted with pleasure and the *chimán* ordered his nephew to give me *ocote* to light the way home.

At midday the next day Dorotea, the niece of the *chimán,* came to tell me that the *chimán* was expecting us. We ate bowls of *masa* made of chicken, and *tortillas, batido,* and coffee. We talked a great deal and we had a good time.


7

*Ceremonies at Chimán Domingo Calmo's House*
(March 9, 1947: *batz:* "Night of the Chimanes")

About a week before the occasion, Chimán Domingo Calmo stopped by my house and invited both Basilia and myself to come to his house on the Night of the Chimanes, March 9. I was quite surprised, for I had seen very little of him and certainly did not expect an invitation to his house. We both accepted and I told him I would bring the necessary presents.

On the day *batz*, March 9, I bought a litre of *aguardiente*, some copal, and candles for both Basilia and myself, and I decided to take the *chimán* also a white rooster which I happened to have.

That evening, I asked Patrona if she wanted to come with us, and she said, "No, Señorita, if it was any other *chimán* I would go with you, but not Tata Domingo, for he is a *brujo*. He was my *chimán* once, but he did something against me. Maybe my Domingo told you how he took a piece of my hair and *huipil,* and about my son who died. For that reason, Señorita, I do not want to go."

About seven-thirty, Basilia and I went with our gifts. It was pitch-dark, and we picked our way by the light of the flashlight along the narrow path. Most of the stars were blotted out by clouds. We could see light coming through the wide cracks of Domingo's house and we could hear the guitar playing. As we pushed open the door and entered, most of the faces that greeted us were hostile. I saw no sign of Tata Domingo.

His stepson[20] greeted me: "Good evening, Señorita, are you just passing by?"

"I am here because Tata Domingo invited me to come. Where is he?"

"He is just taking a rest."

I looked down on the floor and saw the *chimán* and his wife, rolled up in blankets, fast asleep. I was given a chair near the fire, and I put my gifts near the *corral* of the *chimán*, which was in the usual part of the house, in the corner opposite the door. It was covered with pine boughs, and around its door were strung oranges and bananas. Inside, the table-altar was framed in pine covered with the same fruit. On the altar, one candle and some copal were burning, and there was a cup for *aguardiente*. Two men played guitars next to the room of the *chimán*. By the fire in the centre of the small room, on my right, was a friendly Indian from Momostenango, and on my left were the sleeping *chimán* and his

[20] The one whose cut wrist I treated on Todos Santos Day—see p. 211.

wife. Everyone around the fire stared at me as if I were a ghost. None was actively hostile, but they were all distinctly unfriendly. I passed around cigarettes and then they became a little more amiable. María, the wife of the *chimán,* came out of her drunken doze and greeted me with affection. The *chimán* awoke—he was a little drunk himself, and decidedly in need of a sweat-bath, or any kind. Although he greeted me with warmth, I felt instinctively that he wanted to get rid of me as soon as possible. He asked me when I had arrived and when I was going to leave.

I said, "I shall leave when I feel it is the time to leave."

He thanked me for the *aguardiente,* thanked Dios, kissed the bottle, and put it on the floor beside the altar. He then fixed a sort of stool-chair in front of the door of his *corral,* which was just large enough to hold a chair and his table-altar. His wife, who was next to me, would occasionally pat me and then relapse into a drunken doze. The *chimán* himself sat in his chair quite drunk, and I felt I could read what was in his mind. He had invited me, never thinking that I would come; I had brought generous gifts but still he wondered how he could get rid of me. His stepson spoke to him in Mam, and Basilia afterwards translated for me: "Oh, say a few prayers and then she will go."

But María, his wife, said, "No, you must summon the *dueño,* for she has been kind to us."

All the Indians were watching and listening. The *chimán* went outside to relieve himself, and when he returned he had me move even closer to him, so that I sat in the doorway of his *corral.* He put my copal in a dish and Basilia's and my candles on the altar, as he spoke our names. Then he took the white rooster in his arms and prayed over it, holding it up towards the altar and now and then kissing it. He made a long prayer, mentioning first the four holy mountains, then all the others and all the volcanoes of Guatemala. He mentioned localities of Guatemala: Momostenango, Chichicastenango, Quiché, San Juan Atitán, Chiantla, Santiago Chimaltenango, Concepción, Santa Ana Huista; then he mentioned Nueva York, my name, and Basilia's. Out of his medicine-bag he finally took a knife in a leather sheath. He asked his wife to hold the rooster, first kissing it again on the head. He placed the head on a flat stone while María held the body. Putting his left hand around the rooster's head and neck, he plucked off one white feather and put it in the bowl with the copal. Then he stretched the neck and at the same time cut it part way through with his knife. He held the neck over the bowl of copal and I could hear and see the blood pouring over the copal. I knew I must keep a poker face; they were all watching me. When the blood stopped dripping, he held the rooster by its feet over the bowl. It flapped its wings wildly, spattering blood in all directions, some on my face and on my legs. Its wings then dropped and spread out, making the form of a cross.

The *chimán* now laid the rooster to one side and sat silent a moment, looking at me. I saw his small eyes, greedy and cunning, and absolutely nothing spiritual in his face. I thought to myself, "How the liquor has brought out the worst in you!" His thoughts of me were not complimentary either, I was sure.

He filled his *pichacha* with red coals, and put a black rug over the entrance to his *corral*. All the lights were put out. He began to pray in Mam and to summon the *dueño de cerro*. I could smell the burning blood, and then I heard his voice change. I could tell he was talking into a clay pot so that it would sound strange. There was none of the sincerity in his voice that had been apparent in the sound of the Spirit I had heard the year before in the house of the *chimán* at Santiago Chimaltenango. He made a swishing sound, rather like the wind, and this he continued to do all the time. All the people exclaimed, "Enter, Ta." His wife kept up continuous talk, although I could not understand what she said.

The *chimán* said in Spanish, for my benefit, "I am *el espíritu*, I am *el dueño de* T'ui K'oy, I am *el dueño del cerro*. My house is in the *cerro*. I am also *el dueño de todos los cerros*."

These he then named, and all the volcanoes, all the cities, including Nueva York.

"Do not be afraid of me, Matilde, *cristiana*," so the "Spirit" spoke, "I have come to talk to you, to give you what you want. Your family are well and your mother is in good health. They are all awaiting the day when you will return to them. Have no fear, Matilde, *cristiana*, let us talk."

I said nothing for I realized what a fake he was. Then, very rapidly, he said, "*Cristiana*, why won't you talk to me? I have come from my *cerros* to talk to you."

I still said nothing, which I am sure upset the old *chimán*, and for that I was delighted.

"I am going now, *cristiana*."

Then I said, "*Adiós,* Ta."

The fire was started up again and the candles were lighted. The *chimán* then came out, beaming all over, and repeated again what the "Spirit" had said. Basilia and I got up to go. I was very much amused and, at the same time, irritated that he did not have the decency to offer us coffee or a *trago* from the bottle I had brought.

When we got back to the house I sent Basilia for Patrona and told her all that had happened. She said: "Señorita, they never gave you coffee or a *trago* from your own *aguardiente*? Señorita, he is just what I told you, *chucho* [dog] and a *brujo* and all he thinks of is to get as much *aguardiente* as he can for himself. His Señora, María, is a good woman, but the wife he had before was a pig. Her name was Odette and all she thought of was *tragos* and meat. She ate nothing but meat. She used to get so drunk that when the time came for them all to eat the roosters she would give a bowl with a tiny piece of meat to each guest and then she would sit in front of the cooking pot that held the roosters, put both hands in, and cram the meat down her throat. Half of it fell down her front, she was so drunk. The *chimán* would say, 'Odette, you must not do that,' but she paid no attention and simply ate more. She was a bitch and a pig, and became swollen with *tragos* before she died." I told Patrona I couldn't understand why they didn't give even Basilia a *trago* or a cup of coffee.

# 10

## The Fiestas and Dances

1

THE MOST IMPORTANT fiesta of the whole year is the Fiesta of Todos Santos, which lasts three days, from October 31 to November 2.

Of the three days the most important is November 1, Todos Santos Day—All Saints Day, as everywhere in Christendom. On this day teams of horsemen compete in the so-called *corrida de gallos*, "rooster race," and groups of dancers dance in front of the church.

Not only do the *todosanteros* fill the pueblo to overflowing on these days, but Indians from villages near and far come, dressed in their best, bringing something to trade or sell so that they will have money for *aguardiente*. The market place, with its picturesque thatched roof, is then crowded with Indians and *ladinos*. (*See plate 3.*) The latter come to sell fruit, *pan dulce,* sweet drinks, candy, nuts, sugar cane, eggs, chickens, potatoes, meat, cigarettes, material for clothing, and all manner of ribbons and trinkets to tempt the Indians. *Finca* agents roam about looking for drunken victims to sign up for work.

Early on the morning of the first day, the Maryknoll Father, from Chiantla, holds a mass in the church. But before dawn the *rezadores* have already sacrificed turkeys at the *cerros* and the other places where *costumbre* is performed, and the dancers have already been blessed by the Chimán Nam in the house of the Alcalde Rezador.

After the mass the teams of riders assemble in preparation for the *corrida de gallos*. The race is held on the main road that passes through the village—altogether, two or three city blocks long. Across this road are stretched two ropes, and on these live roosters are tied by their feet, high enough so that their heads are within reach of a galloping horseman; for the object of the contest is to see how many chicken heads each team can jerk off. (*See plate 18.*)

The race lasts from nine to noon and again from two to five. Usually about six teams participate, and there are about twenty men in a team. Most of the horses are rented from other pueblos, as few *todosanteros* own horses.

The horsemen are dressed in their best, with red bandannas tied around their heads and over their mouths. From their hats hang red ribbon streamers; wrapping their arms and crossed on their chests and backs are red ribbons. From their waists hang the ends of their broad red sashes.

Crowds line the course and perch in every window, tree, and other spot from which a view of the race can be obtained. It is the hope of everyone that many riders will fall from their horses and add to the excitement of the fiesta. The riders are all so drunk that they can hardly keep their seats, and the hopes of the crowd are invariably gratified.

Each rider is uplifted with pride and with *aguardiente* and, though his seat is insecure, with courage, for he has been blessed by his *chimán,* as has been the course he will soon gallop.[1] The *dueño de cerro* will protect him, for the *dueño* is the god of this race.

The dancers, in their beautiful rented costumes, dance all day and evening in front of the church, each group surrounded by crowds of admiring Indians. Numbers of Todos Santos Indians line up for the privilege of pulling the church-bell rope, for they feel that if they ring the bell luck will be theirs for the year. Sometimes the bell rings for an entire afternoon. (*See plate 17.*)

By late afternoon, many Indians have fallen off their horses. In 1947, nine riders fell off, six of whom thus became my patients. Just before the noon meal on Todos Santos Day, a drunken young man came begging me to minister to his father, who had fallen off his horse. His father turned out to be Telespio Mendoza, son of Chimán Domingo Calmo's

[1] See p. 214 f.

wife by her first marriage. I went to his house and found a crowd of drunken wailing Indians about the victim, who was lying outside on the ground. They told me he had fallen on his head and a horse had stepped on his wrist, which hung there ripped open. Telespio Mendoza was unconscious and covered with blood. I could see the artery was not cut, though the wrist was bleeding badly. I did wonder, however, about the nerves and the tendons.

Beside him on the ground was sitting a dignified old man with a beard. I did not know him but recognized him as some *chimán*.

"I also cure, Señorita," he said.

"Yes, *chimán*, I know you cure, and cure well."

The drunken son and the wife of the injured man were wailing, fearful that he would die. I told them to stop crying, that Tata Mendoza would not die and that I needed their help. First, I used boiling water and soap. The crowd kept at a distance to give me light. The *chimán* motioned the crowd further back and I spread on the earth a newspaper in which my instruments and medicines were wrapped. On this I put my equipment and started to work. I washed around the wound but did not clean it, for it was bleeding too profusely. Then I poured sulfa powder into it. The *chimán* wanted to know what the powder was and I explained to him that it was a powerful medicine that could cure people. He asked me to put on more, and to please him I did. Then I bound the wound tightly and told the family to hold the injured man's hand high for at least an hour; if it continued to bleed, I told them, they should come and get me. Mendoza's head was so covered with dried blood that I had to cut off a lot of hair before I could find the wound. It was not deep. I put the hair on a piece of paper and instructed the *chimán* to see that it was burned.[2] When I poured the iodine on the wound the patient came to and asked his son what was happening. The son spoke in Mam but used my Spanish name. Mendoza closed his eyes and lost consciousness again. I told the *chimán* to move him inside and cover him with a blanket, I would come the next day to see him.

[2] Hair may be used to cast a spell; see p. 161.

By nightfall most of the Indians of the pueblo were drunk, quite drunk. The *policias* were kept busy locking up those who had become violent. The others were helped along or left to lie where they fell. Marimbas played all night long and the dancers danced most of the night.

. . .

I can best explain how a *cuadrilla* (group or team) of riders is formed by quoting the description given me by one of the captains of the riders, Estanislaos Pablo:

"During the fiesta of Todos Santos, if a man watching or participating in the contest of riders gets the idea he would like to form a *cuadrilla* of his own for the coming year, that thought has been put in his head by the *dueño de cerro*. He realizes at once the importance of this, goes to his house, and that night talks it over with his family. They do not reject the idea; on the contrary they welcome it and plan how they can raise the necessary money for the expenses. They also go to seek advice from their *chimán* on how to form the group.

"The man must find a marimba,[3] buy *aguardiente*, and, on the night of the eighth day after the fiesta, invite twenty or thirty friends to his house. After a few tunes have been played on the marimba, he addresses those present: 'Señores, I am thinking of forming a *cuadrilla de corredores* for the coming year. As you know the idea has been given to me and I must consequently accept my obligation. This is the reason I have called you together here. I hope you will join me and we shall then all be together.' Then long discussions begin. One man will say he cannot do it as it necessitates the outlay of much money and he is poor. Another that he is unable to join for fear harm will come to his horse, etc., etc. After the marimba has been played some more and all have danced, one will say it is getting late and he must go. Then, at this moment of si-

---

[3] The name is applied to the ensemble consisting of the instrument—the xylophone-like affair known to us by the same name, but much longer than ours—and the three or four musicians needed to man it.

lence, the *capitán*, the man who wishes to form the *cuadrilla*, will speak, saying, 'All has been arranged. Here are bottles of *aguardiente*, one for each of you. If you accept a bottle, it is the same as if you have given your word that you will participate in the *corrida de gallos*.' All who accept bottles promise not to break their word, for if they do it will cost them their lives. They will be killed in one way or another. If you break your promise or leave the group, you will die that same year. The people, after they are given *aguardiente* in the house of the *capitán*, are bound to respect their promises.

"The group is usually formed of twenty people or less who wish to take part and have made their promises. The *capitán* then takes a rooster and holds in his hand a *pichacha* full of coals and copal. The men all form a circle around him so that he stands in the centre. He cuts the throat of the rooster so that the blood flows on the copal and he burns this in the *pichacha* as he utters the following invocation: 'Caballero Santiago, Caballero San Pedro, Caballero San Miguel, Caballero San Marcos, Caballero San Juan, Caballero San Antonio, Caballero T'ui K'oy, Caballero T'ui Xolik, Caballero T'ui Bach, Caballero Tres Cruces!'

"Then he swings the *pichacha* in the face of each man. When this is finished he lights as many candles as there are riders and places them on the floor.

"Throughout all this time the wife of the *capitán* has plucked the rooster and prepared it for cooking. The men talk and smoke until the rooster is cooked, for it is necessary that each man should eat a piece of it. Throughout this ceremony all smoke, drink *aguardiente* and coffee. By this time it is late, and when they leave, it is with faith and assurance that they will not falter in keeping their promises.

"About June, the *capitán* calls all these people back and waits for them in his house with a marimba, cigarettes, and a supper of *tortillas* and beans (unless he has enough money to buy mutton). These reunions are called *ensayos* [rehearsals]. They dance all night and then, when there is a moment of silence, the *capitán* tells those present what has to be arranged. They must name a *capitán segundo* and two others called *mono primo* and *mono segundo*—First and Second Monkeys. These last two must keep the contestants informed as to what is happening. They also have to burn with copal in front of the big cross the heads of the roosters pulled off in the contest. The *capitán segundo* is to take the place of the *capitán* if he is killed, for only death could stop the *capitán*. This rehearsal, then, is only for the purpose of naming the Second Captain and the two Monkeys, and to give all those present the opportunity to say whether or not they still have the desire and intention to go ahead, and to insist that only death would stop them.

"One month before the fiesta, all return again to the house of the *capitán*, where he awaits them with the accustomed dinner, cigarettes, large quantities of *aguardiente*, and the marimba. The object of this reunion is to kill another rooster. They form the same circle as described before. When this is finished all go inside the house, for what has hitherto been described takes place in the patio of the house. Each man lights five candles and puts them in the corner of the house where a special place has been cleared for them, with flower decorations and a cross. They discuss such matters as where they can rent horses, who has saddles, and so on, until everything has been arranged. Before leaving, every man promises to bring two roosters for the contest.

"Five days before the contest each rider looks for his *chimán*, that the latter may pray on each of the next five nights, especially on the last night just before the race. During these five days and nights, and until the end of the contest, the rider must refrain from sexual intercourse. On the last night prayers are said over the route by the *chimán*, who has also sacrificed a rooster, soaking the copal in the blood, and this he burns at three places on the route of the contest: where the riders will start, where they will finish, and in the centre, where the roosters are to be hung up by their feet. The *chimán* also lights candles, so that the *dueños de cerro* will give understanding. There will be many candles when all are burning, for each *chimán* may officiate for several riders. The *chimán* puts into the *pichacha* copal that has been saturated with blood, and makes his invocation:

" 'Here, ah, *malaya*, Dios, is so-and-so [the rider]. Guard and protect him from all harm. Ah, *malaya*, Dios, may no harm come to the horse, ah, *malaya*, Dios, may so-and-so not hurt his head, or break his arm or leg. Ah, *malaya*, Dios, may he not be killed. Ah, *malaya*, Dios, may no blood flow. Ah, *malaya*, Dios, may the horse not break its leg or its head. Ah, *malaya*, Dios, may all turn out well. Ah, Dios, protect the people. Caballero Santiago, Caballero San Pedro, Caballero San Miguel, Caballero San Marcos, Caballero San Juan, Caballero San Antonio, Caballero T'ui K'oy, Caballero T'ui Xolik, Caballero T'ui Bach, Caballero Tres Cruces. Protect so-and-so. See that he receives no blows, that he and his horse will not be killed.'

"Throughout all this time the *chimán* takes many drinks, for the riders give them to him as they go from one place to another. When they reach the last place, the riders as well as the *chimanes* are very unsteady on their feet, for by this time they have consumed great quantities of *aguardiente*. When the invocation is over, they lead the *chimán* to his house and they go to theirs to prepare for the contest and to eat. Over their clothes they put as many red ribbons as they can find and tie red handkerchiefs over their mouths as well as around their heads."

2

There are three main dances given at Todos Santos: the *baile de moros*, the *baile de venado*, and the *baile de toro*. The Indians all adore these dances and know every detail connected with them. They form an important part of their ceremonial life. Every child aspires to take part in these dances when he grows up, for participation in them will entitle him to wear cock feathers in his hat from that time on.

Since these dances have been frequently and adequately described,[4] I shall not describe them here, but instead I shall give two versions of how a *cuadrilla* is formed for these dances. The procedures differ but slightly

[4] See La Farge and Byers, ch. 12; also Rodas, pp. 80–85.

from that connected with the formation of the *cuadrilla* for the *corrida de gallos*. The first account was given me by my neighbour Margarita Elón, an Indian, whose husband and father were both well-known dancers; the second, in the form of a story, by a carpenter named Rafael Gómez, an Indian with a little *ladino* blood.

3

Given by Margarita Elón

If one of the spectators at a dance suddenly has the idea that he would like to form a *cuadrilla* of dancers, it is as good as done, for this thought is put into his head by the *dueño de cerro* who is the god of dancers. It is a command. If the man has no money and no land to sell, that is not important, for he can get money from one of the many agents of the *fincas* who are always present in the pueblo. He can pledge himself to work so many months on a coffee *finca*, or he can sell his mule or house. Once this idea of forming a *cuadrilla* has entered his head, he must do it or else die. Once it has entered his head, he may die anyway, but the *cuadrilla* will continue until the twenty days of dancing are completed.

First, of course, the money must be found, then a marimba that is willing to enter into a contract for a year. Eight days after the fiesta of Todos Santos, the man must invite his *chimán* and the friends whom he wishes to have take part in the *cuadrilla*. It is best to choose the type of dance that will last two days and three nights without stopping.

When all have gathered in the house of the *capitán del baile* or Dance Captain, that is, of the one who has formed the *cuadrilla*, they are fed, given *aguardiente, batido,* and cigarettes. The *capitán* speaks to one person after another of the obligation he is under to form the *cuadrilla*, and entreats them all to take part in it. Those who promise that they will take part in the dance receive a bottle of *aguardiente* from him, and this constitutes their contract, not only with the *capitán* but with the *dueño de cerro*.

If the *capitán* has luck he will be able to form his *cuadrilla* at the first gathering. If not, he must try again within a month [twenty days] and if that is not successful he must try the following month until he succeeds, for it must be done.

As soon as enough men have accepted their bottles of *aguardiente,* the *chimán* calls them all into the patio of the house. There they all form a circle around the *chimán* and he sacrifices a rooster, saturating the copal in the *pichacha* with its blood. While this is burning in the *pichacha,* he utters the following invocation:

"May the *dueños de cerro* receive with love the *cuadrilla de moros* that has been formed this day. Caballero T'ui K'oy, Caballero T'ui Xolik, Caballero T'ui Bach, Caballero Cilbilchax, Caballero T'ui T'suts, Caballero Punliak, Caballero Chan Chuyé, Caballero T'ui Talchej, Caballero T'sipego, Caballero Tiqnak, Caballero Xemolak, Caballero Xepaxá, Caballero Xemina Cruz, Caballero T'ui Cumanchúm, Caballero Chalajuitz, Caballero Xinakabiok, Caballero T'ui Yembel, Caballero T'ui Lom, Caballero Tincoig, Caballero T'imulé. May the *dueños* receive with love the *cuadrilla* which has been formed today. The dancers by their dancing are showing their respect and love for the *dueños de cerro.* We beg health, food, and money for all of us present and for the pueblo. These men will dance with devotion for you, and do you, gods, guard them as you would your own family."

The *chimán,* standing in the centre of the circle, then swings his *pichacha* in front of each man so that he is bathed in the smoke of the burning blood and copal. Then all go inside of the house to drink, smoke, and talk.

Each month they must meet at the house of the *capitán* and practise. Each time they dance two days and three nights, and are instructed by an old man who has the proper knowledge. During this time they must not have sexual intercourse. If they do they will die. When the last month arrives they decide which day they will go to Totonicapán to get their rented costumes. The night before they go they are obliged to take sweatbaths, and after this they all meet at the cross in front of the church. The *chimán* sacrifices a rooster and, as he swings his *pichacha,* he begs the *dueño de cerro* to bring good luck to the men on their journey; to see to it that no snake will bite them; that they will not have cramps; that they will not lack for food; that the weather will be good; and that they will not suffer from the cold. The dancers swear to keep their promises to be on good behaviour, and to practise sexual abstinence until the end of the dance, which lasts twenty days.

They now all go together to Totonicapán and usually return in five days. They come back carrying skyrockets, copal, candles, *aguardiente*, and their costumes. When they arrive at the cross of El Calvario, each one burns a little copal and prays to the *dueños* to help him so that his thoughts will be good during the dance and to receive him with love during the dance. Then each sends off a skyrocket to announce his arrival, and all march to the house of the *capitán*. Later each one goes to his own home.

The next day they again meet at the house of the *capitán*, where they have what is called the *ensayo general* [dress rehearsal]. They go there with red bands, crossed, on their chests and backs, red bands around their arms, red stockings, and new hats. The marimba players are there to play music, and the *capitán* feeds them all. After they have danced and eaten, they talk and choose the one who is to be the first of their group to be visited. This means that within the next three days they will visit the house of every member of their *cuadrilla*. Each member of the *cuadrilla* must feed the others and give them coffee, *aguardiente*, and cigarettes. After this he puts on the costume he obtained in Totonicapán, does a few dance measures to the accompaniment of the music of the marimba, and presents a litre bottle of *aguardiente* to his *cuadrilla* (to be used during the twenty days of dancing). Then he sends off a skyrocket. This custom of visiting, and all the rest, is called *xuk*.

When all are in their costumes, a procedure which takes two or three days, they go to the house of the *capitán* while he dances and sends off his skyrocket. Certain ones dressed as monkeys go on horseback to announce to the people that they will start dancing that day, and invite them to come. As they leave the house together, they send off another skyrocket, and they go directly to the church. Between the church and the big cross they dance, and they do this likewise in front of the *juzgado*. This is called *presentar la ropa* [displaying the costumes].

The night before Todos Santos Day, the dancers dance all night long in the house of the Alcalde Rezador. Here they partake of food and drink with the body of religious officials, the *principales,* and the Alcalde Municipal. Before dawn they and their *chimán* climb to a *cerro* and pray to the *dueño de cerro.*

When the fiesta of Todos Santos is finished everyone dances at the different houses of the dancers and sometimes at San Martín. When the twenty days are completed they all gather again with the *chimán* in front of the big cross at the church. He sacrifices another rooster and prays to the *dueños,* telling them that the dancers have kept their promises. After that they go to the house of the *capitán,* dance, and drink *aguardiente.* They then remove their costumes, shake the dust from them, and pack them to be returned to Totonicapán. They drink more coffee, eat a little, and are then freed from their vows of sexual abstinence.

Most groups dance twenty days but there are a few that dance longer, depending upon their vows.

### 4

Given by Rafael Gómez

Much time has passed since what I shall tell of took place. They organized in this pueblo a group of dancers. To do this the *capitán* began by inviting his friends to his house, where they were expecting a marimba player and *aguardiente.* After they had listened and danced to the marimba the *capitán* spoke to each one present and handed him a bottle of *aguardiente.* If this bottle was accepted and taken home, that constituted a promise that the person accepting it would be one of the group of dancers. If anyone accepted the bottle and did not keep his promise, he would without doubt get sick and die.

Among those that the *capitán* had invited was a poor young man twenty-two years old. He accepted the bottle of *aguardiente* with the rest of his friends. This young man was very poor and he realized that it would not be easy to obtain money to buy things necessary for the dance. To rent a costume would be expensive, as would the skyrockets, candles, copal, rooster, and *aguardiente,* and the obligation each man was under to receive his group at his house and feed them. The food on such an occasion must consist of mutton, potatoes, coffee, *tortillas,* and *aguardiente.*

Each time a rehearsal took place the young man was worried as to how he was going to get the money for the necessary expenses. The time passed and he could find no way to raise the money. Soon the time came for all to go to Totonicapán to bring back the rented costumes. This poor man could not leave with his companions and he realized only too well that he could not keep his vow and that this meant death. He had exhausted all his resources for raising the money, so when he saw his companions leave he went with a heavy heart to the *cerro* of T'ui Bach to cut some wood. When he got to the top, he sat on a stone and gave way to his grief. He cried a great deal, for his heart was sad that he could not go with his companions to fetch his costume, that his lack of money kept him from going.

As he sat there lost in sorrow, with his head between his knees, he heard a voice say, "What is the matter, young man?"

He raised his head and saw a tall man with a white face, dressed in an elegant red suit and hat. The man said, "What has caused your tears?"

The young man, speaking in Mam, told him all his troubles, that all of them came from his lack of money. The man said, "Listen, if you wish, I shall give you your costume and all that is necessary, even money, on condition that, when the dance ends, you will come to my house and work for me."

The young man pondered the offer a little and then asked what the work would be like. The man answered that the work would be easy, the kind of work a man does around a house. The young man then agreed and the man in red withdrew, saying, "Wait here for me; I shall bring you your costume."

In a short time he returned with an elegant *moro* costume, exactly what the boy needed, only more beautiful. He said to the young man, "When your friends returning reach the cross of El Calvario, they will shoot off skyrockets to announce their arrival. Go there, and when you get there behave as if you had come by the same road. Send off your skyrockets and burn copal with your friends at the cross, engaging them in conversation as if nothing had happened."

The young man received the costume, skyrockets, *aguardiente,* and money, and went to his house contented and happy, even though he knew that after the dance he would have to fulfil his obligation.

When the day arrived for the return of his friends, the young man, with his costume on his back, joined the group at the cross of El Calvario at the entrance of the pueblo and sent off his skyrockets with the others. His companions asked why they had not seen him on the way and remarked on how true and strong his skyrockets were, but they did not bother him any further.

When the main day of the dance came, he was looked up to by all his companions, as he had the best of everything and his costume was by far the most beautiful. It was greatly admired by all because it was so elegant. They wondered how he could rent a costume of such elegance, for they knew he was poor.

When the final day of the fiesta, the twentieth day of dancing, had arrived, they gathered together in their costumes, as always, in front of the church, between the cross and the church. They had just danced one turn and were commencing another when a sudden gust of wind like a whirlwind swept down among the dancers. It blew off their hats and scarves and brought a sudden confusion. When it had passed, the young man in his elegant costume had vanished.

No one could give a reason why this had happened or what road he had taken. He never accompanied his friends to return the rented costumes, nor did he return to his house. He vanished forever, and no one ever knew or heard after that of his whereabouts.

Aside from the ordinary masks used in the *bailes de moros, de venado,*
and *de toro,* there are other masks found in Todos Santos. By chance I
discovered two of these hanging in the house of Domingo, my *mozo. (See
plate 22b.)* He and his wife Patrona told me that they had belonged to
their respective grandfathers and were used by adults only during special
fiestas, not dances. They were also worn by young boys on a certain fiesta
day.

Don Pancho asked Chimán Pascual Pablo some questions about masks
for me:

DON PANCHO

In what fiestas were masks used?

PASCUAL PABLO

In all fiestas.

DON PANCHO

Since when have masks been worn?

PASCUAL PABLO

Since the world was born.

DON PANCHO

Why were they worn?

PASCUAL PABLO

To hide the shame in one's face.

DON PANCHO

What do you mean?

PASCUAL PABLO

There has never been a time that people were not sly and lazy, that
people did not steal, or leave their wives for other women. So during the

fiesta of the pueblo they go out and walk about, wearing the masks to
hide their faces.

DON PANCHO

Is the custom of the masks an ancient one?

PASCUAL PABLO

Since the world was born.

DON PANCHO

Who orders men to wear masks?

PASCUAL PABLO

The *chimán,* when they are the sons of his table. The sons are those
who look for a *costumbre* from the table of the *chimán.*

6

*Costumbres and Fiestas*

The following rather detailed calendar of the *costumbres*[5] and fiestas
celebrated during the years 1946 and 1947 also constitutes a calendar of
a part of my stay at Todos Santos. The *alcalde* days are printed in capitals,
the *alcalde* of the year in heavy capitals.

*1946*

May 3: *imix*

Fiesta de la Cruz. Church filled with Indians with candles and offerings.
Dancing to marimba.

May 4: *IK*

Much ringing of bells. *Costumbre* by Prayermakers, Chimán Nam.

[5] For a list of the sacred places where *costumbre* is performed, see the Appendix, pp.
245 ff.

## May 5: *akbal*

*Costumbre* by Prayermakers.

## May 18: *ajmak*

Big ceremony in church to celebrate completion of work on church. *Costumbre* by Prayermakers, *principales,* Chimán Nam. Dancing and music.

## June 20: *t'ciik*

Fiesta Corpus Cristi. Last fiesta until September except for the ordinary *costumbre* of the Prayermakers and the Chimán Nam. San Antonio carried in a procession.

## September 11: *K'MANÉ*

Bells rang (and continued for twenty days—see next entry). People in church with offerings. *Costumbre* by Prayermakers and Chimán Nam.

## September 11 to October 1

Bells rang each day, and the Chief Prayermaker and Chimán Nam did a small *costumbre* every day for the twenty days with the exception of every fifth day, an *alcalde,* when they, with more Prayermakers, did a more elaborate *costumbre*.

## September 30: *batz*

On this night two specially appointed Prayermakers returned from Huehuetenango bearing a special box of candles for the fiesta of San Francisco, patron saint of the village, called Santo Todos Santos. One Prayermaker was of the year before, 1945, and the other of 1946. The candles were carried to the house of the latter and a skyrocket sent off to announce their arrival. To the house then came the *rezadores, mayores, principales,* the Chimán Nam, and a marimba player. They stayed all night.

## October 1: *K'MANÉ*

The candles were moved in a procession to the house of the Alcalde Rezador and laid in front of the *Caja Real*. There people stayed all day and night. In the procession they carried Santo Todos Santos and went to the four places.

## October 2: *aj*

Special box of candles moved to the church in a procession with the statue of Santo Todos Santos, in preparation for the fiesta of San Francisco. Procession from church to house of Alcalde Rezador without the saint, and afterwards *costumbre* at four places. Big drum and *chirimía* in procession.

## October 21: *K'MANÉ*

*Costumbre* by Prayermakers and Chimán Nam. Many people in church with candles and offerings.

## October 26: *NOJ*

*Costumbre* by *rezadores* and Chimán Nam.

## October 30: *imix*

Skyrockets at dawn; marimba.

## October 31: *IK*

Skyrockets; marimba. Dancers had *costumbre* at dawn at the *cerros*. This night they danced all night at the house of the Chief Prayermaker with all the religious body, the *principales,* the Chimán Nam. Commencement of fiesta.

## November 1: *akbal*

Santo Todos Santos Day. *Rezadores* sacrificed turkeys at the four *cerros* and blood at La Ventosa, El Calvario, Tres Cruces, the cross in front of the church, and Cumanchúm. Alcalde Rezador and Chimán Nam sacrificed turkey in front of *Caja Real*. Riders competed and dancers danced all day and night.

## November 2: *kets*

"Feast of the Dead." Both *ladinos* and Indians went to the cemetery to offer food, flowers, and *aguardiente* to the spirits of the dead. Dancing. End of fiesta.

## November 7: *t'coj*

Last day of twenty days of dancers, who danced all night and got very drunk.

## November 10: *K'MANÉ*

*Costumbre* by *rezadores* and Chimán Nam, for in twenty days they were to appoint the men who would take office in 1947.

## November 10–30

*Costumbre* every day by Alcalde Rezador and Chimán Nam.

## November 30: *K'MANÉ*

A special *costumbre* by Alcalde Rezador, First Rezador, and the Chimán Nam to implore that no more children should die of measles. Also *costumbre* by the *rezadores* at the four places. Church full of people with candles praying that the epidemic would be averted. That night the *principales,* the *rezadores,* and the Chimán Nam elected the *rezadores* and *mayores* for 1947. Also, the Alcalde Municipal was dismissed from office.

## December 1: *aj*

San Andrés Day. *Rezadores* and *mayores* notified of their appointments for 1947.

## December 5: *NOJ*

*Costumbre* by Alcalde Rezador, First Rezador, and Chimán Nam.

## December 10: *IK*

*Costumbre* by Alcalde Rezador, First Rezador, and Chimán Nam.

December 10–31[6]

Small *costumbre* every day and larger *costumbre* on the days *T'CE,
K'MANÉ, NOJ,* and *IK* (December 15, 20, 25, 30).

December 31: *akbal*

Dancing at the house of Margarita's father, who was Dance Captain for
1947. At midnight people went to the house of the retiring Alcalde
Rezador, and to that of the Alcalde Rezador for 1947, to congratulate
the latter.

*1947*

January 1: *kets*

Skyrockets before dawn; marimbas. At four in the morning, the new
Alcalde Rezador went to receive the *Caja Real*. New religious officials
changed places with those retiring and civil officials did the same, with
the exception of the Alcalde Municipal, who had not yet been elected.
About ten in the morning, the *Caja Real* was carried from the porch of
the school and placed on a table before the school. Dancers danced and
people worshipped. About noon, the *Caja Real* was carried to the
church by the new *rezadores* and to the house of the Alcalde Rezador.
That night he gave a dinner for the new *rezadores* and *principales,* and
the Chimán Nam; the Alcalde Municipal would have been invited had
one been elected. They ate the turkeys sacrificed that morning. Skyrockets.

January 6: *t'coj*

*Rezadores* and Chimán Nam did *costumbre* at the four places. (Fifth
day since they came into office.)

January 14: *NOJ*

*Costumbre* at the four places by *rezadores* and Chimán Nam. The
Alcalde Rezador told me that since he had taken office he and the
Chimán Nam had done a small *costumbre* each day in front of the

---

[6] Christmas, December 25, means nothing to the Indians of Todos Santos.

*Caja Real,* and the usual *costumbre* on every *alcalde.* On the twentieth day they were to have their big *costumbre,* during which they would make a tour of the *cerros.*

## January 20: *akbal*

*Rezadores* and Chimán Nam did *costumbre* at the four places.

## January 21: *kets*

*Rezadores* and Chimán Nam did *costumbre* at the four places.

## January 23: *kimex*

Big fiesta at night in house of Alcalde Rezador for the *mayores* and all others who worked for the church.

## January 24: *T'CE*

*Costumbre* by *rezadores* and Chimán Nam at the four places.

## January 28: *batz*

Chimán Nam postponed the twentieth-day celebration to January 28, as next day would be *K'MANÉ. Costumbre* by all the *rezadores, principales, mayores,* and a *chimán* from each *aldea.* They met that night at the house of the Alcalde Rezador.

## January 29: *K'MANÉ*

At two in the morning, the Alcalde Rezador sent *rezadores* to the four holy *cerros* and to Tiqnak to sacrifice turkeys and to La Ventosa, Cumanchúm, Timulé, and the cross by the church to burn blood. The Alcalde Rezador and Chimán Nam sacrificed a turkey in front of the *Caja Real* and then joined the other *rezadores* at the *cerros,* making a complete tour. At night the *rezadores* and *principales,* together with their wives, ate the sacrificed birds, drank *bebida,* and prayed in front of the *Caja Real.* The prayers at the *cerros* were to Santo Cielo, the four Alcaldes (especially K'mané), and the *dueños.* Prayers in front of the

*Caja Real* to Tata Soch. All the prayers were for the good of the pueblo, the people, the animals, and that the sickness *aftosa* (hoof-and-mouth disease) would not come from the frontier to harm the animals; also for seeds and crops, and that there would be no tempests.

### January 30: *aj*

The Alcalde Rezador brought me late in the afternoon a gift of two tamales and part of the breast of a turkey he had sacrificed that morning. "Señorita," he said, "if you eat these, good luck will be yours all the year. I went this morning early with a *mayor* to carry the turkey, copal, candles, and *pichacha* to the *cerro* Cilbilchax. We climbed slowly; this *cerro* has a view of Chiantla. Here I did *costumbre* and prayed to Dios del Cielo, the four Alcaldes, and the *dueños* that no sickness would come, especially that which is killing so many animals in Mexico, and for a good year for the pueblo, the people, the animals, and especially the seeds."

### January 31: *ix*

*Principales* went to the *cerros* to pray and burn copal and candles. No more big *costumbre* until March 9.

### February 3–28

*Costumbre* every *alcalde* day by Alcalde Rezador and Chimán Nam (February 3, *NOJ*; 8, *IK*; 13, *T'CE*; 18, *K'MANÉ*; 23, *NOJ*; 28, *IK*).

### March 5: *T'CE*

*Costumbre* by *rezadores* and Chimán Nam. Many people with candles in church. Last appearance of retiring *alcalde* and first of the five evil days.

### March 6: *k'nel*

*Costumbre* early in the morning by Chimán Nam and *rezadores* at the four places. *Costumbre* of *chimanes*.

## March 7: *t'coj*

*Costumbre* early in the morning by Chimán Nam and *rezadores* at the four places. *Costumbre* of *chimanes*.

## March 8: *t'ciik*

*Costumbre* early in the morning by Chimán Nam and *rezadores* at the four places. *Costumbre* of *chimanes*.

## March 9: *batz*

*Costumbre* early in the morning by Chimán Nam and *rezadores* at the four places. *Chimanes* went to the *cerros*. This was their big night when the *dueño de cerro* was to come. Alcalde Rezador received his *rezadores* at his house. They stayed all night, and at midnight the Alcalde Rezador sacrificed one turkey and prayed all night, keeping many candles lit. *Costumbre* of *chimanes* and the Chimán Nam in their own houses.

## March 10: *K'MANÉ*

First day of new year. *K'MANÉ,* Year Bearer for year. Skyrockets sent off at dawn to greet new *alcalde* for the year. Four turkeys sacrificed at dawn at the *cerros* and one in the house of the Alcalde Rezador. Blood offered at La Ventosa, Tres Cruces, cross by church, cross at El Calvario, Cumanchúm. *Costumbre* by *rezadores* and Chimán Nam at the four places. All the people went to the church with their candles, and to the *Caja Real*. The people prayed, saying: "Dios Espíritu of the *Caja Real,* Tata Soch, I implore you to give me good crops. May my cornfield, *frijoles,* and *chilacayotes* be plentiful. May you give rain when it is needed, but no tempests. May you guard all my animals from harm. Keep the pigs of the mountain away from my corn and the coyotes from my sheep. Give good health to me and my family, and shut the mouths of those who talk against me." Tata Julián asked me to burn my candle in front of the *Caja Real;* he prayed for me. Late in the afternoon a *rezador* brought me some of the turkey to eat.

## March 15–29

*Costumbres* for rain.

## March 15: *NOJ*

*Costumbre* by Alcalde Rezador and Chimán Nam.

## March 20: *IK*

*Costumbre* by Alcalde Rezador and Chimán Nam.

## March 25: *T'CE*

Much *costumbre* by *rezadores* and Chimán Nam at the four places.

## March 26: *k'nel*

Much *costumbre* by *rezadores* and Chimán Nam at the four places. Procession of saints twice to the four places.

## March 27: *t'coj*

Much *costumbre* by *rezadores* and Chimán Nam at the four places. Procession of saints twice to the four places.

## March 28: *t'ciik*

Much *costumbre* by *rezadores* and Chimán Nam at the four places. Procession of saints twice to the four places.

## March 29: *batz*

Much *costumbre* by *rezadores* and Chimán Nam at the four places. Procession of saints twice to the four places.

## March 30: *K'MANÉ*

Much *costumbre* by *rezadores* and Chimán Nam at the four places. Procession of saints twice to the four places. Four turkeys sacrificed at dawn at the four *cerros* by the *rezadores;* blood and turkey eggs offered at La Ventosa, Tres Cruces, El Calvario, cross at church, Cumanchúm;

and a turkey at the *Caja Real* by the Alcalde Rezador. This finished
*costumbre* for quite a while.

## April 4: *NOJ*[7]

Small *costumbre* by Alcalde Rezador at cross at church.

## April 17: *t'ciik*

Two processions for rain by *rezadores* and Chimán Nam.

## April 19: *K'MANÉ*

Two processions for rain by *rezadores* and Chimán Nam. At dawn
turkeys sacrificed at the four *cerros* and at the *Caja Real*. Alcalde Rezador asked me to dinner with the religious body.[8]

---

[7] Easter Sunday, April 6, meant nothing to the Indians of Todos Santos, but a fiesta was
held at Santiago Chimaltenango on April 5 and 6.

[8] On April 20, *aj*, I left Todos Santos. (Besides these fiestas, there was one in which
five young boys went from door to door asking for donations of corn. In his hands each
held a stick from the end of which hung a dead bird. These birds the boys would swing
back and forth as if they were alive. The corn which was collected they sent to a Catholic
priest in Chiantla as a present from the religious community of Todos Santos. I do not
recall the exact date of this fiesta.)

# 11

## Farewell to the Rezadores and Tata Julián

1

LUCK HAD BEEN with me when Tata Julián first called, to have his infected eyes treated. For about two months, I had to put drops in his eyes every few days, and on his visits he loved to look at *Life* magazine, smoke, and talk with me. In this way we became friends. When he was elected Alcalde Rezador it was wonderful news for me. Without his knowing it, I rechecked with Tata Julián the material Don Pancho had gathered in ordinary conversation. Voluntarily he told me of his *costumbres* and gave me other material I could never have obtained in any other fashion. He proved a loyal and generous friend, and I became very fond of this fine old man.

Tata Julián sometimes sent me presents of food and fruit. On several occasions, when he was entertaining the *rezadores,* he sent me pieces of cooked sacrificial turkey. The day before he first sent me turkey, he said, "Señorita Matilde, I shall send you some of the turkey tomorrow for it is my right to do so as Alcalde. I may be a stupid Indian but I have a heart and I like you."

Touched, I said, "Tata Julián, you are my friend and you know very well that you are intelligent, not stupid. That you are an Indian and I a *gringa* is not important, for in the eyes of God we are the same."

One day I asked Tata Julián who was the most important god. He answered, "First there is Tata Señor Dios in the sky; then Tata Soch, *dueño* of the *Caja Real*;[1] then the four Alcaldes del Mundo, of whom the most important is K'mané."

[1] To the Indians the Sky God was an abstract, non-personal god, while the spirit of the *Caja Real,* Soch, was a personal god as were the four Alcaldes del Mundo. To the *chimanes* it was the same except that their spirit was Santo Mundo.

233

"And el Dios Señor del Mundo, what of him?"

"He is the same as the four Alcaldes del Mundo."

"And what does the cross signify?"

"The world; it has existed since the world was born."

Chimán Pascual Pablo had told Don Pancho that the most important god was Santo Cielo, then Santo Mundo, then K'mané, then Imix.

On another occasion Tata Julián told me a story that he had learned from his father, who had heard it from his own father. It is the story of the origin of the world:

"The world was created in seven years, not in seven days as the *ladinos* say. There were many evil people on the earth then and they decided to kill God. God lived in the highest point of the palm tree. The tree was very tall and strong and had many leaves, and in the topmost point of this tree lived God.

"The evil people decided that to kill God they would have to chop down the tree, so they chopped and chopped, but still could not cut it down. Finally they found a snake, a huge snake. It was long and thick like a pine tree. It climbed the palm tree, it went around and around it, and it was going to kill God by swallowing him.

"A huge bird called a *sarchep*,[2] however, saw the snake climbing towards God and cried, 'God, you had better watch out.' God said, 'What can I do? He will eat me.' 'Do me a favour, God,' said the *sarchep*, 'make my feet like hands, but strong.' So God gave him big strong hands and he grasped the snake around the neck, carried it away and dropped it in the ocean. Then God looked down and saw the evil people below, so he made a wave of fire. It was like water, only it was fire, and it destroyed them."

Patrona, too, had heard this story from her father, but in a slightly different form. The animals as well as the evil people wanted to kill God. The bird did not drop the snake in the ocean, but ate it piece by piece. She related to me the following story which had been told her by her father:

"Before God was up in the topmost point of the palm tree, he went

---

[2] According to Tata Julián, a bird larger than an eagle that had lived in the time of his ancestors.

under the earth. Right above him, on top of the ground, was a rooster which crowed and crowed. From under the earth God said, 'Be quiet!' But the rooster crowed on and on, for he knew that God would soon come up. God then said, 'If you won't be quiet, I shall take you with me when I go up into the sky.' The rooster crowed on and on. All at once God came up through the earth and went up into the sky, taking the rooster with him. That is why, when roosters crow, they look up at the sky, for they are talking to God and they know what God is doing. That is why they crow at midnight[3] and every hour thereafter, for they know what God is doing and that the sun will soon come."

## 2

And now the time for my departure had arrived. I decided it was best not to go to Don Pancho's house the night he received his table. I felt Pascual might then suspect Don Pancho had been working for me, and I had much packing to do.

The next day, April 19, *k'mané*, Tata Julián, the First Rezador, and Chimán Juan Pablo came to call on me in the afternoon. I had asked Tata Julián to bring a *chimán* to cast the *mixes* for me, for I wanted to know if my journey would be a successful one and if my family were well. I gave them all coffee and cigarettes, and afterwards Juan Pablo cast the *mixes*. Tata Julián told me that all the *rezadores, mayores,* and visiting *chimanes* would eat at his house that night, that they would eat the turkeys sacrificed that morning. Then he talked of Don Pancho's becoming a *chimán*, a thing of which he did not approve. I wondered if Juan Pablo had told him how he had left Don Pancho's house the night before.[4] He asked me if I had gone to Don Pancho's to see him receive his table, and I said, "No." We smoked another cigarette and they left.

In the late afternoon as I was packing, with an audience of my neighbours, Tata Julián came again and said, "Señorita Matilde, I want you to come with me to my house."

---

[3] Actually, 1 A.M. All *costumbres* that commenced at "midnight" really commenced when the first cock crowed, which was about 1 A.M.
[4] See p. 148.

"But, Tata Julián, I am packing."

"Just for a few minutes," he said, with an air of mystery.

So I went. As we approached his house I could hear the marimba playing in Tata Julián's patio, and I could see many people, but I could not see their faces for it was rapidly becoming dark. "Pass within, Señorita," said Tata Julián.

Entering, I found the large room full of people, all busy. The women at the far end were cooking by the light of the fire and of *ocote* held by a boy. The First Rezador, my friend, came forward and greeted me, welcoming me, and so did all the others, both men and women. I instinctively felt that Tata Julián had told them that he had invited me, and he wanted them to welcome me. Many of them were my friends and I knew they would welcome me with pleasure, but there were some there who did not like me, and I knew it took great courage for Tata Julián to entertain me, against all rules, I was sure. For none except Indians were invited to these dinners, and only those who held some office.

Opposite the door in the corner stood the *Caja Real* on a table. It was decorated with cypress branches. The floor was covered with pine needles. On one side of the room was the table of the *rezadores,* a very long, narrow hand-carved table, of extremely heavy wood, probably oak. I could see that it was very old. It was covered with a white cloth, and on one side was a bench. In front of the *Caja Real* burned one good-sized candle, and on the floor in front was a clay pot with smoke of copal rising from it.

Tata Julián asked if I would like to say a prayer in front of it. I said, "Yes," and he said, "Señorita, if you would rather do it in your own language, you may."

I said my prayer—in English—and then the First Rezador said a prayer for me in Mam. Tata Julián then explained that he was asking Tata Soch to guard me on my journey, and to grant good health to me and to my family. I thanked him and sat on a bench to the left of the *Caja Real.* On one side of me sat a *mayor* and on the other the *chimán* Juan Pablo. I passed them and the others cigarettes. There must have been at least twenty-five men in the room, and a dozen women.

Two men held handfuls of pine sticks that served as torches. One stood at the other end of the room where the women were bending over two pots, the hugest I had ever seen. One was at least three feet high, and in this were steaming the tamales. The other pot was low and squat, and in this the turkey *masa* was cooking. The other man who held the torch stood near the table, to which Tata Julián soon moved. He sat down at the end on one side, the others following him. Including Tata Julián and Macedonio Pablo, the Alcalde Municipal, there were eleven people, all sitting on the one long bench. Two baskets full of bowls were put on the table and two men did the serving. They took several bowls, carried them to the women, who filled them with turkey *masa*, and then passed them around. They served me first, then Tata Julián, the Alcalde Municipal, and the *rezadores*, and after that the others. Baskets of tamales were continually being passed around. I unrolled mine from its leaf covering and dipped it in the gravy of the turkey, and I ate the turkey with my fingers. It was all delicious.

The setting of this feast was unforgettable: the young men holding the flaming torches that cast a glow on all who were near, the white tablecloth, the faces of the men at the table. Here there were wisdom and character and great dignity. Rows of gleaming golden corn hung from the ceiling and along both sides of the room. Everyone sat busily eating. Beneath the table one could see the men's red-and-white-striped trousers. From time to time Tata Julián would call out to me, saying "Eat well, Señorita," or "Little by little, eat well, Señorita Matilde." I was touched that he had invited me and sad that I was leaving.

Bowls were replenished, more tamales passed. The men had apparently told some joke, for they all roared with laughter. I felt I was the butt since, when they laughed, they looked at me. But I laughed with them. I felt sorry for the women and the men who were serving and holding the torches, for they were watching everyone eat and had nothing themselves. Coffee was served and after that *jícaras* of *batido*. They passed me a small one, holding just enough for me, and I said, "How pretty." For some reason this amused them; my remark was repeated and everyone roared with laughter.

The ceremony that accompanies the passing of the *jicaras* of *batido* is most impressive. One man passes them. He holds a *jicara* high in his right hand and says to its recipient the equivalent of "God bless you." The person who accepts it holds it high and says to all, sometimes repeating it for each person, "Greetings to the Ancient Ones." And all answer with the same phrase. I will always remember the sight of my Indian friends, drinking the *batido* out of the large carved gourd cups.

Finally the men who had held the torches and passed the food were relieved of duty, and they sat down to eat. I passed cigarettes to everyone, and then the bowls were collected. This was the time to leave, I felt. I stood up and said:

"Tata Julián, Señores, my stomach is full and satisfied by the delicious meal I have had. But my heart is sad, for tomorrow I leave Todos Santos. I am very fond of Todos Santos, and of all of you, and that is the reason my heart is sad. It was friendly and kind of you to ask me here tonight, Tata Julián, and I want to thank you and the others for giving me this pleasure."

"Thank you, Señorita," they responded.

"I shall often think of this evening," I continued, "when I am far away in my country. Good luck to all of you and may the pueblo of Todos Santos have a good year in every way. Thank you again."

I left, and they gave me *ocote* to light me on the way.

The next morning the party gathered to accompany me to Paquix. There were Domingo, driving a mule loaded with my cargo, Domingo's son Andrés, his neighbour, also Andrés, and Basilia and her brother Aj-Juan. I was on my white horse—the horse of the *dueña*—and my friends were on foot. I was touched when Tata Julián and his son came along to see me as far as Paquix. There a car met me, and Domingo and Basilia came with me as far as Huehuetenango, where they saw me off at the airport.[5] They were so intrigued by the plane that they were not sad. It was I who was sad.

[5] An airline had been operating between Guatemala and Huehuetenango only a few months.

# APPENDIX

## 1. STRUCTURE OF TODOS SANTOS

The village of Todos Santos has eight *cantones* or wards. The ancient Indian word for *cantón* was *ch'ipolaj*, meaning literally a district in the pueblo; that for *aldea* was *max*. The ancient name for the village of Todos Santos was Nam; for the whole Todos Santos township of nine *aldeas*, T'oj Nam.

The following are the *cantones* and *aldeas*, with their present-day names, their ancient names, and the meanings of the latter.

### Cantones of the Village

| Modern Name | Ancient Name | Meaning |
|---|---|---|
| Joya de los Pablos | T'oj Xak | Among the stones |
| Tuit Nam | Tuit Nam | Head of the pueblo |
| Tuit Chiip | Tuit Chiip | Head of the chipal plant |
| T'oj Witz | T'oj Witz | Among the mountain tops |
| Tuit Chililaj | Tuit Chililaj | Flat places on the mountain top |
| Tuit Xim | Tuit Xim | Head of straw |
| Joya de los Matías | Pop | Birth of water |
| Joya de los Jiménez | T'aj Bay | Below the road |

### Aldeas of the Township

| Modern Name | Ancient Name | Meaning |
|---|---|---|
| Chik'oy | T'ij Nak | Old trees |
| El Rancho (first subdivision) | T'oj Ch'ech | Among the *sacate* |
| El Rancho (second subdivision) | T's Puert | Narrow passage |
| T'si Xim | T'si Xim | Straw |
| Ch'aba | Ch'aba | Birth of the river |
| Chal Witz | T'oj Xak | Among the stones |
| Chausmil | Chausmil | End of a tree trunk |
| T'aja Witz | T'aja Witz | Below the mountain top |
| Maax | Maax | Between the straw |

239

## 2. THE INDIANS AND EDUCATION

On one occasion I asked Margarita Elón why she did not send her daughter to school. She replied, "Señorita, why should I send Marcelina to school? If she goes she will get sick. Here at home I teach her weaving and the ways of women. Why should I send her to school?"

My other neighbour, Patrona, wife of my *mozo* Domingo, said, "We did not send Andrés to school for there is much work for him to do here. When his father is away, who would bring me wood or look after the pigs and chickens? What would he learn in two years? When we have more money I shall send our other son, Margarito, to school and then on to Huehuetenango till he is educated. Then he can look after us when we are old." (*See plate 7.*)

My conversation with Tata Julián, the Chief Prayermaker (*see plate 12*), was as usual the most revealing. "Señorita," he said to me when I questioned him on the subject, "I do not send my grandchild to school because he learns more tending sheep and working with his father."

"But, Tata Julián, you are educated, you went to Guatemala City for education. Why not give your grandchild, too, an education?"

"Señorita Matilde, look at my hands. They are crippled with rheumatism. That is what comes from education."

"What do you mean, Tata Julián? I don't understand."

"Señorita, when I was a young man I was sent to Guatemala to college [high school]. Two of us were sent, two in fact from every pueblo. The government paid our expenses. We all lived in one place and all went to college together. The food was bad. It had no strength to it and we all became weak. Señorita, the *naturales*, as you know, are accustomed to sweat-baths. In the college we had to bathe in cold water. I went to the chief and said, 'Señor, it is the custom in my pueblo for the *naturales* to take sweat-baths. Here there is no sweat-bath. Will you give me permission to heat a little water for a bath?' He would not give me permission. After I had been there a year and six months, we all became sick with much *chor* [dysentery]. All of us were very sick, sick every day. They gave us just tea; no coffee. Many *naturales* died. We became so weak that we could not walk. More and more of the *naturales* died. Then my thoughts went back to Todos Santos. I knew that if I did not escape I would never see my pueblo again. Señorita, as weak as I was I escaped one night and I returned to my pueblo. I told my father all that had happened. He said, 'Go off to the mountains with the sheep and do not return till I send for you.' Señorita, they sent soldiers for me; they questioned my father. He told them he had not seen me for many months, that I was in Guatemala, Señorita. After that my hands began to hurt and they became like this. That is why I don't want my grandson to go to school."

## 3. THE FINCA SYSTEM

One morning early in January, 1946, Patrona, the wife of my neighbour Domingo, came to see me. (*See plate 7.*) Her eyes were swollen from crying. In very incoherent Spanish she told me that Domingo had signed a contract for himself and his son, Andrés, with Señor López, who owned the *tienda* in the village, to work on a coffee *finca* beyond Quezaltenango. She went on to say that she expected her baby in a month and a half, and how could she look after three children, get wood, and plant corn if neither Domingo nor Andrés was there to help her?

Domingo then entered the house and told me the whole story. The year before, he and Andrés were both sick for two months, so sick that they nearly died. In consequence he was not able to plant his corn. When he was better he could not work for he still had no strength. He had only a little corn. He therefore signed a contract with Señor López for money. He was to receive sixteen dollars and for this he and Andrés, aged fourteen, would both have to work sixty-four days picking coffee on the *finca*. They would have to walk there and back, which would take four to five days each way. At the *finca* they would be given huts, too poor to keep out the mosquitoes, and unground corn; nothing else. If they got sick they would get no medical care; and all this for less than one dollar a week apiece.

"If you will pay my debt to Señor López," Domingo continued, "I will work faithfully for you; have no fear of it. I will carry cargo for you from Huehuetenango; I will be your *mozo* on your trips." This is how Domingo became my *mozo*, my man Friday. When I went to Señor López to pay Domingo's debt, he said that he thought I was very foolish, Domingo was no good and would never pay off the debt to me. Needless to say, Señor López proved to be wrong.

But to give another experience. One week or so after Domingo became my *mozo*, a young woman with a baby a year and a half old came to see me because she was a friend of my maidservant Simona and had heard from her that I was a kind person. She was sick with malaria. Her baby was very ill with a temperature of 104°. She had just returned from working two months on a *finca*. In fact she had run away from it before her time was up because the baby was ill and because she did not feel well herself. I examined the baby and gave it some medicine, and then gave the mother some food. Before she could finish eating the police came and with them the agent with whom she had signed the contract, to lock her up in the *juzgado*. The agent demanded her arrest and insisted that she be shipped back in a few days to the *finca* to finish her contract. It made not the slightest difference to him that both mother and child were very ill or that it would be freezing cold in the jail.

I went later to see the Alcalde, but he was out so I saw the *secretario* instead. He told me that the woman owed five dollars and fifty cents which she had not yet worked out at the *finca* and one dollar and twenty-five cents for the bus from Quezaltenango to Huehuetenango. He would give her eight days to pay the agent, otherwise he would ship her back. I told the *secretario* that I would be responsible for her debt. She was then let out of the jail. I found out then that she owned no blanket, that all she possessed were the clothes on her back. Among other things she told me that the baby was by a *ladino* (not her lover the telegraph operator, whom I have mentioned elsewhere), that she had been living with him but when she became pregnant he began to lose interest and when the baby was born he discarded her. She had been working as a servant, but as she had to have things for the baby she ran into debt. Since the father of the child would give her no money, she had signed the contract. When it came time for her to go to the *finca* he finally gave her one dollar. She walked all the way to the *finca*, a journey which took her five days. This woman, named Basilia Elón (*see plate 8*), later became my servant, after I was obliged to discharge Simona for an indiscretion.[1]

I paid my servant one dollar and a half a month and bought her clothes.[2] Several of the old men who came to call asked why I paid her that much. I explained that sixty cents was not a fair wage. How could girls live on that? No wonder they had lovers. It was either that or running into debt. The old men looked at me and said nothing.

## 4. THE TODOS SANTOS COSTUME

(*Several of the plates depict details of costume. Below I cite the most notable.*)

If a man can afford to, he adds to his "Uncle Sam's Boy" striped trousers (*see plate 20*) wide horizontal red bars outlined by fine coloured lines, giving a plaid effect. His white cotton blouse has very thin stripes of alternating orange and green or red and green. The cuffs and collars are of the same colour and pattern as the trousers.

Over the trousers goes a black woolen garment, difficult to describe, I am afraid. (*See plate 20.*) From a wide waistband, three coat-tail-like strips hang behind— two hang free, giving an effect like a man's dress suit, and a middle strip goes between the legs like a breech clout and buttons onto the waistband in front by four buttons. When a man works, he tucks his tails under his waistband and rolls his trousers above the knee. The men wear any of three types of coat. There is a short wool tweed jacket that has narrow stripes of blue and grey and, around the bottom, a decorative band of a woven blue design. And there are two types of black wool tunic, one short, the other the long *capixaij*. The *capixaij* (*see plate 10*)

[1] For what happened to Basilia's child, see pp. 154 ff.
[2] For remarks on the usual wages of a maid, see p. 38.

hangs above the knee and has a fringe in back. All three coats are very warm and both wind- and rain-proof. Goatskins are slung on the back for protection when carrying cargo, and in front when gardening. During the rainy season, both men and women wear palm-leaf raincoats, so light that they can be rolled up and carried (*see plate 11*).

On their heads the men wear red bandannas, the store-bought kind having replaced hand-woven ones. These are tied over one ear in a fetching manner and crowned with straw hats, which have double crowns and brims for protection against sun and rain. (*See plate 21.*) The hatbands are usually of braided straw or leather. Those who are or have been dancers are entitled to wear plumes in their hats. The men all wear double-soled sandals, with nails in the soles, a leather thong between the big toe and second toe, and a high reinforced back to protect the heels on the rocky road.

The women wear *huipiles,* blouses made of woven cotton. (*See plate 9.*) These have fine red and white stripes, with a bib-shaped front of almost solid red, and a back with varicoloured designs of dots and lines. Around the neck is sewn a white cotton yoke like a collar, on which varicoloured lines of stitching radiate from the neck. A round design is sewn on the bottom of the yoke in front and in back. (The Todos Santos *huipil,* with its yoke, suggests the *huipil* of the Quiché women, to whom the lines signify the sun's rays and the round design the moon's. The Todos Santos women, however, have no knowledge of this meaning.) The skirt is of navy-blue cotton with pale-blue vertical lines about every six inches. Around the waist there is a stiff woven red sash called a *faja.* In cold weather the women wear shawls made of square pieces of cotton skirt material. They never wear wool. Their hats are similar to the men's, with shallower crowns. They usually wear their hair in two braids, encircled with ribbons and brought forward like a crown around their heads (*see plate 22a.*) The women wear sandals only on a journey and otherwise are barefoot.

The men used to weave most of the woolen material. Nowadays, much of it is imported. They often buy the material for their black coats from the Soloma or Santa Eulalia Indians. The women weave all the cotton material both for the garments of the men and for their own, except for their skirts, which come from Huehuetenango. They sew their own *huipiles.* Hats today are made in Jacaltenango or Concepción, and sandals come from Huehuetenango or Jacaltenango.

## 5. THE ORIGIN OF CORN

*The following corn legend was given by Pascual Matías, an old man of about ninety years:*

Corn was obtained by the *naturales* from the sources created by God. One of the sources is here in San Pedro Necta.[1] It is a mountain called Xepaxá.[2] It is to this mountain the people sometimes go to make offerings, if the season is poor for corn. No one has ever worked the land there. The corn grows on this mountain alone [i.e., without cultivation]. It produces ears which dry and then fall on the earth. No one takes them, for no one visits this place except to make offerings.

The *naturales* who lived near it used to eat roots and fruit before they knew of corn. It is said that, one day, a *natural* went to this mountain for food. While he was setting traps to catch birds he came upon a corn plant which was still green. This man did not know what corn was, and when he saw the grains he thought that possibly one could eat them. So he carried this corn to his family and they all talked about how to eat it: boiled, roasted on the coals, or raw? "How should we eat it?" they asked. "We will put it on the fire," said the wife, and as it was young corn, it turned out very well.

Thereafter the man went every day to carry back more corn to his house. After his house. He removed the leaves, and dried the kernels in the sun. Then, when a time, however, it became necessary for him to go quite a distance. So the man thought to himself, "Each day I have to go farther and farther. The mountain is covered with clouds and there are many animals who could devour me. It is better, therefore, if I look for the seed and plant it on my land. I had better not keep going to the mountain, I might not return; an animal might kill and devour me."

Thereupon he went to the mountain and found dry corn and carried it back to the rain came, he planted it. Very contented indeed was this man when he saw the plants grow; and when he saw it was really so, that the plants produced ears, he worked hard on his land. It was worth it. Every year he planted and other people do the same right up to the present day.

And so when the *natural* has no more corn for seeding he goes to Xepaxá. Here there is corn, small corn because it comes from the mountain, but corn which, if planted in cultivated land, grows well. Xepaxá is not the only source of corn. Omák, at Nebaj,[3] is also a source, and there are other parts of the world too where it is found. There has never been a time that God did not give food to all.

[1] A village about twelve miles (as the crow flies) west of Todos Santos.

[2] The *Popol Vuh*, sacred book of the ancient Quiché Maya, says (p. 165) that corn came from a place called Paxil in "the beginning when it was decided to make man." The scholar H. H. Bancroft believed (ibid., footnote 1) that Paxil was near Palenque.

[3] A village about forty miles (as the crow flies) east of Todos Santos.

*Many stories are told about the dangers to the corn crops. The following is one told to me by the Chief Prayermaker, Tata Julián:*

When I was a young man, there descended upon Santa Ana Huista[4] a plague of locusts. They ate up everything. Soon they were in Jacaltenango and on their way to Concepción. They ate everything in their path, leaving the country bare behind them. All the *rezadores* went to the *cerros* and prayed to the *dueño de cerro* to save their corn crops. In the afternoon the locusts had passed through Concepción. That night the *dueño* answered their prayers. He sent a storm of wind and rain, not enough to harm the corn, but just enough to drive all the locusts away."

## 6. SACRED PLACES

### 1

### Places Where the Rezadores and the Chimán Nam Perform Costumbre

| | |
|---|---|
| Cross outside church<br>Cross of El Calvario<br>T'ui Cumanchúm<br>*Caja Real* | Ordinary *costumbre* of Alcalde Rezador with the Chimán Nam, sometimes with the first, second or other *rezador*. |
| Inside church<br>Cross outside church<br>Next to store of Señor López<br>Near boys' school<br>T'ui Cumanchúm<br>El Calvario<br>*Caja Real* | *Costumbre* performed when there is a procession carrying the saints or the drum and when the *Caja Real* is carried on the first of the year. The saints are never carried into the house of the Alcalde Rezador where the *Caja Real* is, as far as I know. |
| Cross outside church<br>Cross of El Calvario<br>T'ui Cumanchúm<br>*Caja Real* | *Costumbre* performed on the first of day *k'mané,* after the *rezadores* have come into office; early on the morning of March 10, Mam New Year; and on the day of *costumbre* for rain. Also on other *k'mané* days as required. Only the Alcalde Rezador and Chimán Nam sacrifice the turkeys at these four places while other *rezadores* do the same *costumbre* at the following places, making a total of ten places. |

4 A village about fifteen miles northwest; Jacaltenango and Concepción are progressively nearer.

The four holy *cerros* and
Alcaldes del Mundo:
  T'ui K'oy
  T'ui Bach
  T'ui Xolik
  Cilbilchax
Chuyé (La Ventosa)
Tiqnak (Tres Cruces)

*Rezadores* sacrifice turkeys at the same time as the Chimán Nam and Alcalde Rezador do so at the above sites.

T'ui T'suts
T'ui Yembel
T'imol
T'ui Niyap
Batz Lom
T'ui Xak
T'inináp
T'imulé
Xepaxá

These also are places for *costumbre* and, together with the aforementioned ten plus the inside of the church, make a total of twenty places. Prayers and sacrifices are offered up at the twenty places on the first day of the new year of our calendar. *Costumbre* is performed by the Alcalde Rezador at T'ui Xak once a year for the seeds, and *costumbre* is performed at T'imol, which is in the *tierra caliente,* on January 1. On January 1 likewise a small turkey is sacrificed and eaten (cooked) at T'imulé.

2

## Places Used by the Chimanes Domingo Calmo and Rafael Calmo to Perform Their Costumbres

| | |
|---|---|
| Caballero T'ui K'oy | Caballero T'sipego |
| Caballero T'ui Bach | Caballero Tincoig[1] |
| Caballero T'ui Xolik | Caballero Tiqnak |
| Caballero Cilbilchax | Caballero Xemolak |
| Caballero T'ui Yembel | Caballero Xepaxá[2] |
| Caballero Punliak | Caballero Xemina Cruz |
| Caballero Chan Chuyé | Caballero T'ui Cumanchúm |
| Caballero T'ui Talchej | Caballero Chalajuitz |
| Caballero T'ui Soch | Caballero Xinakabiok |
| Caballero Xétajo | Caballero T'ui T'suts |

[1] With the exception of Tincoig, which he replaces with T'ui Lan, Chimán Pascual Pablo uses the same places.

[2] Xepaxá is called the Mother of Corn, and Indians make pilgrimages to it to pray for rain for corn. It lies west of Todos Santos. See the corn legend, p. 244.

3

Customary Sacrifices by Rezadores at Sacred Places

| Place and Direction from Todos Santos | Meaning | Sacrifice |
|---|---|---|
| T'ui Cumanchúm (south) | On the lime pit | Turkey |
| T'ui K'oy (north) | Head of an *olla* (pot) | Turkey |
| T'ui Bach (south) | (*not obtained*) | Turkey |
| T'ui Xolik (east) | Pass within or enter | Turkey |
| Cilbilchax (east) | Pick up green | Turkey |
| T'ui Yembel (south) | A full head | Blood |
| T'inináp (east) | (*not obtained*) | Blood |
| T'ui T'suts (south) | (*not obtained*) | Blood |
| Tiqnak (west) | Behind a *canac* tree | Turkey |
| T'imulé (west) | Behind the ruins | Small turkey |
| Batz Lom (west) | The last slab or tablet | Blood |
| T'ui Xak (east) | Head of largest rock | Blood |
| Chuyé (east) | (*not obtained*) | Turkey |
| Cross outside church | | Turkey |
| Caja Real | | Turkey |

## 7. CHART OF DAYS FOR CASTING THE *MIXES*
### (*as given by three different* chimanes)

| The Twenty Days[1] | Rafael Calmo | Pascual Pablo[2] | Macario Bautista, Chimán Nam[3] |
|---|---|---|---|
| K'MANÉ | Health, it is good, but not for marriage. | Good. God of *costumbre* of the *mixes*, of the table; prayers for all that is good. | *Costumbre.* Ask God for everything. |
| aj | Your son will come home; money, luck and good negotiations. | Good. If you solicit or ask from the people it will rain. God does not receive. | The young man is lost. Disputes. Burn copal. |
| ix | Lies; cunning; wickedness. You will not find or meet what you wish. | Bad. There is opposition, burn candles over yourself. | *Toj lama.* |
| tsikin | Gossip. There is nothing. | Good. It is against reason, but will be overcome. | A chicken. *Costumbre,* otherwise you are lost. |
| ajmak | Anger, disputes, robbery. *No.* | Bad. Protect yourself or the other one will win. | *Mej ben toil.* |
| NOJ | Someone is biting you; defend yourself. | Good. The *costumbre* is against you. Why are you bad, why do you deceive? | *Chiminimes.* The young man will die during the month. |

[1] The days printed in capitals are *alcaldes.*

[2] Pascual Pablo gave Don Pancho this chart for casting the *mixes* before the latter commenced his training as a *chimán.* Compare Pascual Pablo's information on type of day in the chart on pp. 251 ff.

[3] The Chimán Nam gave this chart unwillingly to Don Pancho. Some of it is, indeed, hard to make sense of.

## 7. CHART OF DAYS FOR CASTING THE *MIXES* (*Cont.*)

(*as given by three different* chimanes)

| The Twenty Days | Rafael Calmo | Pascual Pablo | Macario Bautista, Chimán Nam |
|---|---|---|---|
| *tcij* | A fight; your enemy is working against you. | Very bad. Look out for a dispute; he is very bad. | The *chimán* works evil. He is wicked. |
| *tciok* | Depart; danger. You are lost, a *costumbre* is necessary. | Bad. It is certain that you will fall into a dispute. | There is no work. It is a day of change. |
| *najpu*⁴ | It closes like a door, a little. | Good. You need *costumbre* with a table, but it will come out well. | It is necessary to plead with a woman. |
| *imix* | Ask for money, corn. You will be saved. You will meet what you wish. | Good. Need of *costumbre* with the Saint of the Corn, but it will come out well. | No one will steal your corn. The Gods will give. |
| *IK* | Bury the ones that you care for most, like your *tata* or *nana*. | Good. The Alcalde hears you; take your candles to God and you will be saved. | The day for the family to make *costumbre*. Very important day. |
| *akbal* | Will not die where he was born. Moves around a great deal. The *espiritu*. | Good. Who knows where? Obtained in a dispute. | Burn copal with the people. Your son is in the wrong. |
| *kets* | There is a fire burning against you. *Malaya* world. You need a *costumbre*. | Bad. There is fire in the sky against you. | Don't give fire. *Chimanes* do evil. |

⁴ Called *hunapu* by Macario Bautista.

## 7. CHART OF DAYS FOR CASTING THE *MIXES* (*Cont.*)
### (*as given by three different* chimanes)

| The Twenty Days | Rafael Calmo | Pascual Pablo | Macario Bautista, Chimán Nam |
|---|---|---|---|
| kan | You will die; nothing will come; no cure; carried away. | Good. There is still health in him. He will not die, he will live. | *Hua bi xin.* |
| kimex | (*No material obtained*) | Bad. He will die and be lost. No health. They will rob you. | *Chiminimes.* |
| T'CE | The Alcalde hears; it will turn out well. He wants a *costumbre.* | Good. The Alcalde hears you; everything will turn out well. You don't have to worry. | *Costumbre* for animals. |
| k'nel | You are a culprit. Already near; already ripe. Burn a candle bent double, in the middle of the night. | Good. This is the time. Yes, it is ripe. God will send it. | *Kan toil tuis k'nel.* |
| t'coj | Nine, nine days, pay your debt. You will meet what you wish.[5] | Bad. You can pay for your crime. It is open (clear), and you will come out well. | *Kil jo cho jol.* |
| t'ciik | Wicked like the dog of a gambler. With that there is. | Bad. Why do you work candles against people? It is your sin. | He is lost like a dog. |
| batz | Good for bargaining; life; health; return. | *Mayor casalera* of the world. Ask for everything and it will turn out well. | Day of *costumbre.* Pray for all. . . . |

[5] See p. 49, footnote 8.

## 8. THE CALENDAR[1]

| The Twenty Days[2] | Meaning of Name | Type of Day[3] | Type of Prayer |
|---|---|---|---|
| *K'MANÉ* | 1. Father of a child | 1,2,3. Very good | 1. For all things<br>2. For everything one wants<br>3. With candles |
| *aj*[4] | 1. Water<br>2. Ruler of seeds of all kinds | 1. Good | 1. With candles for all kinds of seed<br>3. For seeds |
| *ix* | 1. Cat<br>2. Ruler of dogs | 1,3. Bad | |
| *tsikin* | 1. Chicken<br>2. Ruler of chickens | 1. Good | 1,3. For chickens |
| *ajmak* | 1. Mountain<br>3. Day to dig potatoes and of animals | 1. Good | 1,2. For animals |
| *NOJ* | 1. Forest that smells good | 1,2,3. Bad | 2. *Chimanes* pray<br>3. Initiation of *chimán* |

[1] In the following chart I record the associations of the twenty days according to information furnished me by three different *chimanes,* just as they gave them to me. I have made no attempt to correct inconsistencies, repetitions, or anything else. In the three columns to the right, the key to the informants is: 1, Pascual Pablo; 2, Laureno Mejía; 3, Esteban Mendoza.

[2] The names in capitals are *alcaldes.* This list of the twenty days was given to me by the following *chimanes:* from Todos Santos, Esteban Mendoza, Pascual Pablo, Laureno Mejía, and Domingo Calmo; from Santiago Chimaltenango, Manuel Andrés; and the *chimanes* cited in footnotes 4, 5, and 6, with the variants noted.

[3] Totals of "bad" days: Pascual Pablo, 5 ("During these days the *brujo* tries to work his evil"); Laureno Mejía, 6; Esteban Mendoza, 5.

[4] Luis Elón, of Todos Santos, gave *aj juil.*

## 8. THE CALENDAR (*Cont.*)

| *The Twenty Days* | *Meaning of Name* | | *Type of Day* | | *Type of Prayer* | |
|---|---|---|---|---|---|---|
| *tcij* | 1. | Dispute | 1. | Good | 1. | For cats |
| | 2. | Ruler of cats | | | 3. | *Chimanes* pray against those who work evil |
| *tciok* | 1. | Dispute ending with a blow | 1,3. | Bad | 3. | *Chimanes* pray |
| | | | 2. | Bad; whoever is born this day will be poor | | |
| *najpu*[5] | 1. | Green corn | 1. | Good | 1. | For corn, money, for all things |
| | | | 2. | Bad | | |
| | | | 3. | Day of sickness and death | 2. | *Chimanes* pray |
| *imix* | 1. | Corn; ruler of corn and all crops | 1. | Very good | | |
| | 2. | Ruler of corn | | | | |
| | 3. | Day of corn | | | | |
| *IK* | 1. | Wind | 1. | Very good | 1. | Fiestas for corn |
| | | | | | 2. | For money |
| | | | | | 3. | Sick people are saved on this day |
| *akbal*[6] | 1. | Rain | 1,2. | Bad | 3. | With candles |
| | 2. | Ruler of the poor | | | | |
| *kets* | 1. | A flat place like a plain | 1,2,3. | Bad | 3. | *Chimanes* pray |

[5] Pedro Pérez, of San Juan Atitán, gave *anajpu;* Macario Bautista, Chimán Nam of Todos Santos, gave *hunapu.*

[6] Catalina Aguilar, of Santiago Chimaltenango, and Pedro Pérez gave *okbal.*

## 8. THE CALENDAR (*Cont.*)

| The Twenty Days | Meaning of Name | Type of Day | Type of Prayer |
|---|---|---|---|
| *kan* | 1. A cramp<br>2. Ruler of cattle and corn<br>3. Day of corn | 1. Good | 1. For all things, especially corn |
| *kimex* | 1. Pig<br>2,3. Ruler of pigs | 1. Day of sickness and death | |
| *T'CE* | 1. Horse; ruler of pack-animals and horses<br>2. Ruler of horses and all other animals<br>3. Ruler of horses, cattle, and all other animals | 1. Good | |
| *k'nel* | 1. It is ripe<br>1,2. Ruler of mules<br>3. Day of cattle | 1. Good | 1. For mules |
| *t'coj* | 1. Turkey<br>1,2. Ruler of turkeys<br>3. Day of turkeys | 1. Good | |
| *t'ciik* | 1. Dog<br>1,2. Ruler of dogs | 1. Good<br>2,3. Bad | |
| *batz* | 1. Mountain flower<br>2. Ruler of abundance for ears of corn, beans, money | 1. Much money, abundance of ears of corn, everything one wants | 3. Prayers and candles |

# BIBLIOGRAPHY

Boggs, Stanley H. *Guide to the Ruins of Zaculeu.* Huehuetenango: United Fruit Company, 1947.

Borbonicus Codex. See *Codex Borbonicus.*

Brinton, Daniel G. *Nagualism: A Study in Native American Folk-Lore and History.* Philadelphia: McCalla and Co., 1894. (Reprinted from the *Proceedings of the American Philosophical Society,* XXXIII [1894].)

Byers, Douglas S. See La Farge.

*Codex Borbonicus. Manuscrit Mexicain de la Bibliothèque du Palais Bourbon.* . . . publié en fac-similé avec un commentaire explicatif par M. E.-T. Hamy. Paris: Ernest Leroux, 1899.

Codex Dresdensis. See Gates.

*Códice Troano.* [Published under auspices of the Junta de la Relaciones Culturales of the Spanish Ministry for Foreign Affairs.] Madrid: Matev, Artes e industrias gráficas, 1930. [Note: Gates, in his edition of the Dresden Codex, says that this facsimile of the Codex Troano is "so cheaply and crudely done as to be worse than worthless."]

Dresden Codex. See Gates.

Förstemann, E. W. *Commentary on the Maya Manuscript in the Royal Public Library of Dresden.* ("Papers of the Peabody Museum of American Archaeology and Ethnology, Harvard University," Vol. IV, No. 2.) Cambridge, Mass., 1906.

Gage, Thomas. *The English American: A New Survey of the West Indies, 1648.* Edited with an Introduction by A. P. Newton. London: Broadway Travelers, 1928.

Gates, William. *The Dresden Codex: Reproduced from Tracings of the Original Colorings Finished by Hand.* Maya Society Publication No. 2. Baltimore: The Maya Society at the Johns Hopkins University, 1932.

——. See also Landa.

Goetz, Delia. See *Popol Vuh.*

Goubaud, Antonio. *The Guajxaquip Báts: An Indian Ceremony of Guatemala.* Guatemala: Centro Editorial, 1937. (Translation of article in *Anales de la Sociedad de Geografía e Historia de Guatemala,* XII [1935], 1.)

Hamy, M.E.-T. See *Codex Borbonicus.*

Hawkins, Laurence F. See Rodas.

La Farge, Oliver. [*S.E.*] *Santa Eulalia: The Religion of a Cuchumatán Indian Town.* Chicago: University of Chicago Press, 1947.

La Farge, Oliver, and Byers, Douglas S. *The Year Bearer's People.* ("Tulane University of Louisiana, Middle American Research Series," Publication No. 3.) New Orleans, 1931.

## BIBLIOGRAPHY

LANDA, FRIAR DIEGO DE. *Yucatan Before and After the Conquest.* Translated with notes by William Gates. Baltimore: Maya Society, 1937.

LINCOLN, J. STEWARD. "The Maya Calendar of the Ixil of Guatemala," *Contributions to American Anthropology and History,* Vol. VII, No. 38 (pp. 97–128). Washington: Carnegie Institution of Washington [Publication 528], 1942.

McGHEE, W. J. See THOMAS, II.

MORLEY, SYLVANUS GRISWOLD. *The Ancient Maya.* Stanford, Calif.: Stanford University Press, 1946.

——. See also *Popol Vuh.*

*Popol Vuh: The Sacred Book of the Ancient Quiché Maya.* English version by Delia Goetz and Sylvanus G. Morley, from the Spanish translation by Adrián Recinos. Norman: University of Oklahoma Press, 1950.

RECINOS, ADRIÁN. *Monografía del Departamento de Huehuetenango.* Huehuetenango: Tipografía Sanchez de Guise, 1913.

——. See also *Popol Vuh.*

REDFIELD, ROBERT. *The Folk Culture of Yucatan.* Chicago: University of Chicago Press, 1941.

RODAS N., FLAVIO; RODAS C., OVIDIO; and HAWKINS, LAURENCE F. *Chichicastenango: The Kiche Indians.* Guatemala: Unión Tipográfica, 1940.

SELER, EDUARD. [I]. "Ueber die Namen der in der Dresdener Handschrift abgebildeten Maya-Götter," *Gesammelte Abhandlungen zur Amerikanischen Sprach- und Alterthumskunde,* Band I, pp. 367–89. Berlin, 1902. (Originally in: Verhandlungen der Berliner Gesellschaft für Anthropologie, Ethnologie und Urgeschichte, 19 März 1887 [*Zeitschrift für Ethnologie,* XIX, pp. 224–31].)

——. [II]. "Zauberei im alten México," *ibid.,* Band II, pp. 78–86. Berlin, 1904.

[STADELMAN, RAYMOND.] "Maize Cultivation in Northwestern Guatemala" (Compiled by the Carnegie Institution of Washington from data collected in the field by Raymond Stadelman), *Contributions to American Anthropology and History,* Vol. VI, No. 33 (pp. 83–263). Washington: Carnegie Institution of Washington [Publication 523], 1940.

STEPHENS, JOHN L. *Incidents of Travel in Central America, Chiapas, and Yucatan.* Volume 2. New York: Harper & Brothers, 1853.

THOMAS, CYRUS. [I]. *A Study of the Manuscript Troano.* (U.S. Department of the Interior, Geographical and Geological Survey of the Rocky Mountain Region, "Contributions to North American Ethnology," Vol. 5.) Washington: Government Printing Office, 1882.

——. [II]. *The Maya Year.* With a prefatory note by W. J. McGhee. (Smithsonian Institution, Bureau of Ethnology.) Washington: Government Printing Office, 1894.

Troano Codex. See *Códice Troano.*

WAGLEY, CHARLES. "Economics of a Guatemalan Village." *Memoirs of the American Anthropological Association,* No. 58, 1941. (Supplement to the *American Anthropologist,* Vol. 43 [1941], No. 3, Part 3.)

# GLOSSARY

In general, terms are defined only in the senses applying in this book. References are given to passages in the text that give fuller explanation. The Mam words are followed by M in parentheses; words not so marked are Spanish or, in a few cases, Mayan.

## A

*ab ij* (M), year.
*aftosa,* hoof-and-mouth disease.
*aguardiente,* very strong local spirituous liquor made from sugar cane.
*Ahkin May,* Mayan high priest (Landa).
*aj* (M), water; young; second day in the Mam calendar (see pp. 251 ff.).—*a. ij,* young sun, title of a *zajorin* (q.v.).—*a. qia,* sorcerer, *brujo.*—*A. Walal Soch,* see *Soch.*
*ajmak* (M), fifth day of the Mam calendar (see pp. 251 ff.).
*akbal* (*okbal*) (M), twelfth day of the Mam calendar.
*alcalde,* an official; chief.—*A. Municipal,* leading civil official of the pueblo; mayor.—*a. del mundo,* chief of the world; (often simply *alcalde*) title of each of four days in the Mam calendar and of four gods identified with them (see Index).—*A. Rezador,* Chief Prayermaker.
*aldea,* hamlet, subdivision of a township.
*alma,* soul.
*alote* (M), young ear of corn.
*amapola,* poppy.
*Ambrosio,* see *Ténom.*
*anajpu,* see *najpu.*
*atole,* beverage made of ground corn added to boiling water.
*auxiliar,* auxiliary, a minor official of the pueblo.

## B

*Bacab,* Year Bearer of the Mayans (Landa).
*baile,* dance.—*b. de moros,* Dance of the Moors.—*b. de toro,* Bull Dance. *b. de venado,* Deer Dance.
*barranco,* ravine.
*batido,* ceremonial drink made of ground corn, sugar, and boiling water.
*batz* (M), twentieth day in the Mam calendar; see pp. 251 ff. As a deity, secondary to the *alcaldes* (q.v.); see *casalera del mundo.*

256

*bebida,* ceremonial drink made of ground cacao, ground corn, sugar, and boiling water.

*betch* (M?), kind of flower.

*bomba,* home-made bomb used in celebrating fiesta.

*bravo,* bullying.

*bruja, -o,* witch, sorcerer.

# C

*Caballero,* sir; in prayer, etc., honorific before name of deity. (Sp., knight.)

*caca,* droppings.

*Caja Real,* Royal Coffer; religious object of the Todos Santos Indians; see p. 66.

*cal,* lime.

*Calvario, El,* small chapel on outskirts of pueblo. (Sp., Calvary.)

*canac* (M?), kind of tree.

*canicula(s),* dog day(s), hot dry days in late July and August.

*canteco,* resident of Chiantla.

*cantón,* ward of the pueblo.

*capitán,* captain; leader of a dance or race team.

*capixaij* (M?), man's coat; see p. 242. (Cf. Sp. *capisayo,* garment worn as a cloak.)

*caporal,* handyman, attendant.

*casalera del mundo,* title of the deity associated with the day *batz.* (Cf. Sp. *casalera,* country-house; also *casal,* male-female pair. Its sense among the Mames is more like "Upholder of the World"; see p. 137.)

*cera,* beeswax (candles).

*cerro,* mountain top.

*chilane,* Mayan *chimán* (Landa).

*chilmol* (M?), chili pepper.

*chimán* (M), shaman-priest; grandfather, ancestor; see p. 24, f.n. 3, and p. 90.— *c. baj,* shaman-priest with knowledge.—*C. Nam,* shaman-priest of the pueblo; see *Rey, El.*

*chimolal,* see *t'chimolal.*

*chinchin,* rattle used in dances.

*chipal* (M), kind of plant.

*ch'ipolaj* (M), *cantón.*

*chirimia,* kind of flute.

*chor* (M?), dysentery. (Cf. Sp. *chorro,* a flowing.)

*Chucia Bank* (M), name of wife of Ambrosio Ténom, the mythical first *chimán.*— *Chucia Chuán,* title of a *chimán's* wife.

*chucho,* dog.

*cielo,* heaven(s).

*convento,* church building used as lodging for visiting priest.

*copal,* resin used for incense.

*copó,* tree the bark of which was used to make "paper" for Mayan codices.

*corazón,* heart.

*corral, chimán's* house, boothlike cubicle used for communing with Spirit.

*corrida*, race.—*c. de gallos,* Rooster Race, on Todos Santos Day.
*costumbre,* prayer, ritual, ceremony; see p. 16, f.n. 4. (Sp., custom.)
*cruz* (pl. *cruces*), cross.
*cuadrilla,* team, group.—*c. de corridores,* team of horsemen in a race.
*cuman* (M), honorific denoting superiority, before name of deity; cf. *k'mané.*
*curandero,* healer who treats illness by medical or magical means.

# D

*delito,* a transgression of the law.
*dios,* God.
*doblador,* fold of corn leaf used in ceremonies. (Sp., folder.)
*dueña, -o,* guardian, mistress, master; supernatural being supposed to dwell in a
   mountain or other natural formation; see p. 17, f.n. 6.—*d. de cerro,* mountain-
   top master.—*d. de pozo,* spring master.

# E

*ee,* see *k'mane.*
*ensayo,* rehearsal.—*e. general,* dress rehearsal.
*escuelix,* boy(s) who work for the religious body, clean out the church, etc.
*espíritu,* spirit.
*estoraque,* storax gum used as incense.

# F

*faja,* woman's sash.
*fiador,* sponsor, guarantor.
*finca,* farm, plantation, where Indians often hire out as workers.
*fiscal,* official who looks after the church, the needs of the visiting priests, etc.
*frijoles,* beans.
*fuego,* fire.

# G

*gaden* (M), *chimán's* chain of office.
*gente,* people.
*gringa, -o,* alien white person; see p. 16, f.n. 3.
*guacalito,* gourd cup.
*guaxakláj xau* (M), the Mayan ceremonial calendar used by the Mames.

# H

*haab,* Mayan calendar year.
*huipil,* woman's blouse; see p. 243.
*humo,* smoke.
*hunapu,* see *najpu.*

258

# I

*ij* (M), sun; day; seeds of corn.
*ik* (M), eleventh day (and an *alcalde*) of the Mam calendar; see pp. 251 ff.
*il* (M), *costumbre* performed for an offence or crime.
*imix* (M), tenth day in the Mam calendar.
*ine* (M), Todos Santos Indian's name for himself; see p. 16, f.n. 3.
*intendente,* mayor of the pueblo, civil chief (used formerly when a *ladino* only could hold the office).
*invierno,* winter; rainy season from mid April to mid November.
*ix* (M), young ear of corn; third day in the Mam calendar (see pp. 251 ff.).—*i. xwox, costumbre.*
*ixin* (M), corn.

# J

*jal* (M), old ears of corn.
*jicara, jicarita,* gourd cup.
*juez de paz,* justice of the peace.
*jun* (M), one.
*justicia,* justice.
*juzgado,* administrative building of the pueblo.

# K

*kan* (M), fourteenth day of the Mam calendar (see pp. 251 ff.).
*kets* (M), thirteenth day of the Mam calendar.
*kimex* (M), fifteenth day of the Mam calendar.
*k'mané (ee)* (M), first and most important day (and an *alcalde*) of the Mam calendar; see pp. 251 ff.
*k'nel* (M), seventeenth day of the Mam calendar.
*k'o* (M), rooster.
*k'oots* (M), vulture.

# L

*ladino,* person of Spanish culture and language as contrasted with one who follows the Indian way of life; see p. 16, f.n. 3.
*letra,* handwriting, learning, wisdom.

# M

*machete,* ax.
*malaya,* interjection occurring frequently in prayers, connoting reverence. (Cf. Sp. *mal haya,* alas, woe is me; also used in hopeful sense.)
*mam* (M), grandfather, ancestor.
*mar* (M?), *dueño* of the river.
*marimba,* musical instrument; see p. 212, f.n. 3.

*masa,* dish of ground corn boiled with chicken or turkey.

*mayor,* chief, minor official of the pueblo; minor religious functionary; one of the sixteen days in the Mam calendar other than the four *alcaldes.*

*mecapal,* leather headband used in carrying packs.

*mesa,* table.

*misa,* the mass.

*mix(es)* (M), turkey; seeds, beans, bits of quartz, etc., used by *chimanes* for divination (also *mix bel*); see p. 178.

*moja,* unexplained term; see p. 50.

*mono,* monkey; official of one of the dance or race teams.

*mozo,* male servant.

*mundo,* world.

*municipio,* township.

# N

*na, nana* (M), mother (a term of respect).

*nagual,* animal co-spirit; see p. 170.

*najpu (anajpu, hunapu)* (M), ninth day of the Mam calendar; see pp. 251 ff.

*nana,* see *na.*

*natural,* Indian's name for himself, in speaking Spanish; see p. 16, f.n. 3.

*nel* (M), Prayermaker.—*n. gat,* Chief Prayermaker.—*n. stol,* First Prayermaker.

*nim cruz* (M and Sp.), ancient wooden cross in front of church; see p. 23, f.n. 1.

*ninzuk t'uit nax* (M), Prayermakers.

*noj* (M), sixth day of the Mam calendar; see pp. 251 ff.

# O

*ocote,* splinters of resinous pine, burned for light.

*oj* (M), dispute without aid of a *chimán.*

*okbal,* see *akbal.*

*olla,* pot.

*ortiga,* nettle.

# P

*pacaya,* kind of palm.

*pach jaimes* (M), *corral* of *chimán.*

*palo de pito,* plant the seeds of which are used as *mixes;* see p. 178.

*pan dulce,* sweet bread.

*panela,* unrefined brown sugar.

*patrón,* patron.

*pelote* (M?), vulture.

*petate,* straw mat.

*pichacha* (M?), clay censer.

*pila,* fountain, communal well.

*policia,* policeman.

*Popp,* Mayan first month (Landa).

*pozo,* spring (of water).
*presentar,* to display.
*principal,* a religious official; see p. 56.
*pueblo,* village.
*pulsera,* healer who diagnoses by feeling the pulse.

## Q

*quetzal,* Guatemalan monetary unit, = U.S. dollar.

## R

*rancho, corral* of a *chimán.*
*regidor,* councilman of pueblo civil government.
*Remedio para Tristeza de Corazón,* "Remedy for Sadness of Heart," a patent
  medicine.
*rey,* king, kingly man.—*El. R.,* senior and most revered *chimán* of village.
*rezador,* Prayermaker.
*ropa,* clothing, costumery.
*ruda,* rue.

## S

*sacate,* grass, hay.
*salal* (M), *costumbre.*
*salve,* a part of the mass.
*san, santa, santo,* holy; preceding a name, saint.
*sarchep* (M), (mythical?) ancient bird.
*sebo,* tallow (candles).
*secretario,* secretary of the pueblo civil government.
*Señor,* (the) Lord; title of respect with religious names.
*silla bank* (M), title for god, spirit, of the *mixes.*
*síndico,* syndic of pueblo civil government; see p. 35.
*Soch* (M), Spirit of the *Caja Real* (also *Aj Walal Soch*); altar(s) on the *cerro* of
  T'ui Bach.
*soplar,* to fan, stir up (fire).
*susto,* fright.

## T

*ta, tata* (M), father (a term of respect).
*tambor,* drum.
*tata,* see *ta.*
*t'au witz* (M), *dueño de cerro.*
*t'ce* (M), sixteenth day (and an *alcalde*) of the Mam calendar; see pp. 251 ff.
*t'chi* (M), blood.
*t'chimolal* (M), act of sacrificing or offering ceremonially.
*t'ciik* (M), nineteenth day of the Mam calendar.

*tcij* (M), seventh day of the Mam calendar; see pp. 251 ff.
*tciok* (M), eighth day of the Mam calendar.
*t'coj* (M), eighteenth day of the Mam calendar.
*tenia*, tapeworm.
*Ténom, Ambrosio,* (mythical) first male *chimán.*
*tequin ij* (M), month.
*tesorero,* treasurer of the pueblo civil government.
*tienda,* store.
*tierra,* land.—*t. caliente,* hot country; see p. 37.
*t'ij* (M), old man.
*Todos Santos,* All Souls.
*todosantera, -o,* resident of Todos Santos.
*t'on dios ta* (M and Sp.), toast addressed to a man.—. . . *na,* to a woman.
*tortilla,* flat cake of ground corn.
*trago,* a swallow.
*tsikin* (M), fourth day of the Mam calendar; see pp. 251 ff.
*t'ui* (M), respectful prefix, used with holy place-names, etc.
*t'uit t'or* (M), *alcalde del mundo.*
*tzité,* plant the seeds of which are used as *mixes* (q.v.).
*tzolkin,* Mayan period of 260 days.

## U

*uayeb,* Mayan five-day period at end of year.
*uinal,* Mayan period of twenty days, month.

## V

*vara,* staff, stick.
*verano,* summer; dry season from mid November to mid April.

## W

*wanam* (M), heart.
*wanim* (M), soul.
*wen en ij* (M), month of twenty days.
*witz* (M), world.

## X, Y, Z

*xau* (M), moon, month.
*xim* (M), straw.
*x'nazal* (M), Prayermaker.
*Xoj K'au* (M), Year Bearer (New Year) Ceremony.
*xuk* (M), a custom to do with the fiesta dances; see p. 218.
*xwox* (M), copal.
*zajorin,* apprentice *chimán.* (Cf. Sp. *zahori,* imposter pretending to have occult powers.)

# INDEX

## A

Adrián, carpenter, 86
adultery, 69 f
afterbirth, 41
*aftosa* (hoof-and-mouth disease), 229
aged, attitude toward, 34, 54, 130
agricultural year, 188
agriculture, 29 f, 37, 39 f, 56, 59; *see also* corn
*aguardiente, passim,* esp. 39, 44 ff, 47, 64 ff, 83, 106 ff, 109, 128, 145 f, 200, 213, 216; *see also* drunkenness, toast
Aguilar, Catalina, *chimán,* 21, 114, 252 n
aim of book, 15
airplanes, 33 f, 238 n
Alcalde Municipal, 19, 33, 35, 36, 44, 59, 63, 64, 93, 147
Alcalde Rezador, *see* Rezador, Alcalde
Alcaldes del Mundo, *passim,* esp. 48, 67, 71, 77, 107 n, 137, 233, 234; *cerros* as, 246; days as, 100, 101, 188; *mixes* as, 178; *see also* calendar
*aldea,* 34 n, 35, 239
All Saints Day, fiesta of, 209 ff, 225; *see also* Todos Santos, Santo
altar(s): Catholic, 53, 81; *Caja Real* as, 64, 68; of *chimanes,* 24 n, 107 ff, 162, 195, 205 f; on T'ui Bach (Soch), 74; on T'ui K'oy, 74 n; pl. 14; *see also* table
Alvarado, Pedro de, 29 n, 93 n
Ambrosio, *see* Tenóm
ancestors, 23, 24 n, 54, 57, 66, 68, 99 n; *see also* Ancient Ones
Ancient Ones, 54, 67, 157, 238
Andrés, Manuel, *chimán,* 21, 105, 114, 178, 179, 251; divination system of, 182

## B

*bailes, see* dance(s)
bananas, 109, 113, 199, 205
Bancroft, H. H., 244 n
baptism, 42; with blood, 64, 146, 148; of *chimán,* 133 f
Basilia, *see* Elón, Basilia
bath, sweat, 38, 42, 84, 183, 217, 240
*batido,* 39, 109, 129, 237 f
Batz (Casalera of the World), *passim,* esp. 137, 188, 191
Bautista family, 57
Bautista, Félix, *rezador,* 55
Bautista, Macario (Chimán Nam, El Rey), 21, 55, 57 f, 90, 100 n, 190, 192 n, 252; divination system of, 178, 248 f; pl. 11; *see also* Chimán Nam
Bautista, Rosa, 19, 57, 109 ff, 133 f, 184; pl. 9
beans, 39; "sacred beans," *see* mixes
beards, 32, 129
*bebida,* 39, 42, 63, 228
bell of church, 43, 210, 223 ff; pl. 17
beverages, 39; *see also* aguardiente, batido, bebida
birth, 41 f; "of Don Pancho," 117 ff; "of table," 116 f
blood, *passim,* esp. 44, 66, 103, 111, 146 f, 195, 202 n, 207; staffs dyed

animal co-spirits, *see* nagualism
Antigua, 93
antisepsis, 184, 185, 211
Antonio, San, 224
*atole,* 39
*auxiliares* of pueblo, 35
Aztecs, 180

blood (cont.):
  with, 64; table sprinkled with, 146,
  148; of pine, 166 f
bloodletting, 183, 185
Boggs, Stanley H., 29 n, 254
Bollingen Foundation, 16
bombas, injury caused by, 185
bonesetting, 183
bride-price, 43
Bridge of the Bells, 89
Brinton, Daniel G., 170 n, 254
brujo(a), passim, esp. 122, 167, 168; author as, 17, 19, 51, 82 ff, 85, 185;
  chimán as, 69, 86, 90, 92; as nagual,
  170 ff; Stadelman as, 87
"bull-fighting," 122, 128, 132
"burial" (envoûtement), 122, 157, 159,
  160 f, 161 ff, 166, 169
burial practices, 51; see also funeral
  customs
burns, treatment of, 185
Byers, Douglas S., 54 n, 99 n, 215 n, 254

C

cacao, 39
Caja Real (Royal Coffer), 55, 64, 66,
  67 f, 228, 230, 232, 233 n, 236, 245,
  247; Alcalde Rezador's responsibilities re, 60, 61, 62; attack on, 67, 68;
  in election, installation of rezadores,
  63 f, 64 ff, 227; spirit of, 64, 66, 70,
  233 n; trial before, 66, 69 f
calendar, Mam, 15, 56 n, 71, 82, 99 ff,
  142, 188 ff, 251; of costumbres and
  fiestas, 223 ff; see also New Year, Year
  Bearers
calendar priest, see Chimán Nam
Calmo, Antonio, schoolboy, 174
Calmo, Dionisio, 93
Calmo, Domingo, chimán, 19, 54, 81,
  93, 158, 191 f, 246, 251; as brujo, 86,
  158 f, 205; ceremonies at house of,
  204 ff; divination system of, 182; as
  principal, 54, 56
Calmo, Domingo, mozo of author, 20,

86, 96, 100 ff, 107, 156, 168 f, 222, 238,
  240, 241; funeral of child of, 44 ff; as
  guide on mountain climb, 72 ff; pl. 5,
  6, 7
Calmo, Patrona, mozo's wife, 20, 42,
  56 n, 88, 155, 168 f, 183, 185, 222, 240,
  241; funeral of child of, 44 ff; pl. 7
Calmo, Rafael, chimán, 19, 51, 83, 84 f,
  93, 94, 153 f, 155, 158, 161 f, 185, 190,
  192 f, 246; as brujo, 86, 159, 160 f,
  168 f; ceremonies at house of, 193 ff;
  divination system of, 179 f, 248 f; as
  principal, 56, 59
Calvario, El, 53, 89, 218, 221, 230, 245
candle(s), passim, esp. 41, 44, 50, 61, 65,
  68, 70, 74, 81 f; bent double, 162; in-
  verted, 163, 167
caniculas ("dog days"), 31
canteco, 76
cantones, 35, 239
capitán: of race, 213 ff; of dance, 216 ff
capixaij, 38, 104, 242
caporales, 37
Carillo, Pascual, 20, 75 f
Casalera, see Batz
cat, as death symbol, 46
Catholicism, 15, 38, 42, 46, 53, 60, 68,
  69, 90, 175, 209, 232; status in Todos
  Santos, 53 f; see also church, Landa
  (esp. 39 n), salve
cattle, 30
celibacy, 57 f, 60, 101, 114, 123, 133, 163,
  214, 218, 191
cemetery, 160 f
centre of world, Todos Santos as, 54
cerros, passim, esp. 42, 51, 60, 61, 71 ff,
  84, 86, 88, 94, 97, 124, 125, 154, 164,
  209, 220, 228; as days (alcaldes), 71,
  77; dueños of specific, 76; as gods,
  190; as sacred places, 246; see also
  dueño de cerro
chain of chimán, 91, 92, 110, 136, 150 ff
Chajul, 99 n
chameleon, 46
Chanjón, Rio, 30, 186

chapel, *see* Calvario, El

Chiantla, 37, 45, 53, 60, 69, 76, 175, 209, 232 n

Chiapas, 101, 109 n

Chichicastenango, 84, 85, 88

chicken, *see* rooster

child(ren), 34 n, 72 f, 82, 84, 96, 114, 154 f, 170, 185, 226, 232 n; funeral of, 44 ff; belief as to fate after death, 51; pl. 7, 12, 19; *see also* escuelix

chili, in casting spell, 161, 167

*chimán(es)*, *passim*, esp. 25, 38, 41 f, 43, 47, 50, 67, 68, 73, 82, 86, 90 ff, 101, 124 ff, 211; author as, 17, 81 ff; calendar of, 188, 251 f; *corral* of, 107 (*see also* corral); cures for snake-bite of, 185 f; dance blessed by, 217, 219; divination by, 178 ff, 248 ff; Don Pancho's becoming, 83, 115–49, 235; and *dueño de cerro*, 76, 92 f, 93 f, 96, 97, 110, 126, 152; expense of becoming, 149; on five evil days, 190 ff; functions of, 150 ff; funeral of, 51 f; initiation of, 145 ff; New Year observance of, 67, 99 ff, 107 ff; "Night of the," 192 ff, 204 ff; race blessed by, 210, 214 f; regalia of, 51, 150 ff; at Santiago Chimaltenango, 105 ff; as soothsayers, 178 ff; as sorcerers, 170 ff; technique in casting spells, 160 ff; training of, 91 f, 93 f, 115 ff; types of, 90; woman as, 92 (*see also* Aguilar, Catalina); pl. 16; *see also* Bautista, Macario; Calmo, Domingo; Calmo, Rafael; Chimán Nam; Pablo, Pascual

Chimán Nam (calendar priest), *passim*, esp. 19, 24, 35, 36, 55, 59, 62, 63 ff, 113 n, 178, 209, 223 ff; attitude toward, 57 f; as *principal*, 56, 59; responsibilities of, 56 ff, 60, 90, 189; of San Juan Atitán, 21; *see also* Bautista, Macario

Chinabahul, 29 n

*chinchin* (rattle), 76, pl. 14

*chirimía* (flute), 55, 64 f; in calling snakes, 186

Christ, 130, 137

Christian feasts, 188, 227 n, 232 n

Christmas, 227 n

Chucia Bank, 112 n, 197

Chucia Chuán, 112, 203

church, *passim*, esp. 23 ff, 53, 60, 64, 66, 67, 81, 152, 156, 195, 209, 210, 217, 224, 227, 228; officials of, 55, 56; of Santiago Chimaltenango, 104, 114; pl. 1, 10, 13, 17

Chuyé, *see* La Ventosa

Cilbilchax (*cerro*), 71, 229, 246, 247; as day, 77

Cipactonal, Aztec god, 180

civil government, 35 f, 59; *see also* Alcalde Municipal

climate of Todos Santos, 31

clothing, *see* costume

Codex Borbonicus, 180, 254

codices (Mayan "books"), 39 n, 51 n, 66 ("long roll of skin"), 99 n, 100 n, 138 n; pl. 14

coffee, in funeral rite, 44; *see also* fincas

Coffer, Royal, *see* Caja Real

coffin, 50, 51

Comitancillo, 170

communion, 113 n

Concepción, 47, 87, 185, 191, 243, 245

confession, 191, 193

*convento*, 53, 175

copal, *passim*, esp. 61, 63 f, 65, 70; arrangement of balls of, 201; pl. 14

*copó*, 99 n

corn, *passim*, esp. 24, 30, 39 f, 42 n, 43, 60, 62, 69, 76, 102, 245; fiesta for, 232 n; legend of origin of, 74, 244 f; pl. 5, 14; *see also* batido, bebida

Corpus Cristi, 136, 175, 224

*corral* of *chimán*, 95, 107, 108 f, 133, 147, 148, 194, 195, 202, 203, 206

*corrida de gallos*, 209 f, 212 f; pl. 18

Cortesian Codex, *see* Tro-Cortesian Codex

cosmogonic lore, 24, 54, 77, 139 f, 234
costumbre, passim, esp. 16, 23, 24, 56, 57, 58, 60, 61, 62, 73, 86, 90, 120, 158, 189, 209, 231, 233, 235 n; calendar of, 223 ff; against disease, 84, 151 ff, 154 ff, 226; to cast spell, 160 ff, 163 ff; sacred places of, 245 ff; see also "burial," mixes, prayers
costume, 33, 38 f, 242 f; of dancers, 217, 218, 219, 220 f; of dueños, 93, 96, 175, 176, 220; of race riders, 210, 215; of Santiago Chimaltenango, 104; see also among plates
count, 42, 189, 190
coyote, 30, 72; as nagual, 171 ff, 173 ff
creation of world, see cosmogonic lore
crops, 59, 69; see also corn
cross: of chimán, 41, 90, 130, 137, 138, 148, 200; Christian contrasted, 23 ff, 90, 130, 148; costumbre at, 114, 152, 164, 195, 214, 217, 219, 225, 230, 231, 245, 247; divination by, 183; fiesta of, 223; motif of, 54, 102, 136, 138 n, 201, 234, pl. 14; and Santo Mundo, 24, 136, 138, 234; sign of the, 69; in sorcery, 167, 171; "the two crosses," 23 ff, 41, 51, pl. 1, 13, 15
crucifix, 90, 130, 148; see also cross
Cruz, Fiesta de la, 223
Cruz, Pedro, rezador, 55
Cruz, Raimundo, principal, 56
crystals, in divination, 178, pl. 16
cuadrilla: of dancers, 215 ff; of riders, 212 ff
Cuchumatanes Mountains, 29, 71, 73
Cuilco, 53
Cumanchúm, passim, esp. 23, 25, 31, 41, 42, 50 f, 66, 152, 157, 164, 174 f, 189, 195, 230, 245, 246, 247; pl. 15
curanderos, 152 f, 154 f, 183 ff
currency, 37 n
cypress, 63, 64, 236

D

dance(s) (bailes), 37, 88, 112, 203 f, 209,

213, 215 f, 227, 243; forming cuadrilla for, 216 ff; on stilts, 102; tale of dancer and dueño, 219 ff
day-count, 42, 190 f
"Dead, Feast of the," 226
dead birds on sticks, 232 n
death, 43 ff, 82, 84, 89, 93, 94, 96, 98, 114, 170, 177, 202 n; Lord of (Mayan), 49 n, 102, pl. 14; prediction of, 184
deer, 180, pl. 14
diet, see food
disease, illness, 37, 47, 56 n, 82, 84, 91, 113, 120, 124, 152 ff, 154 f, 166, 168, 183 ff; see also epidemic(s)
divination, 56, 102, 178 ff, 180, 248 ff; pl. 14, 16; see also mixes
divorce, 43
doblador, 195
"doctor," author as, see medical work
dog, 46, 102; author as, 159; as nagual, 170, 176; "talking like," 193
doll, see "burial"
Don Pancho (Francisco Palacios), 16, 18, 21, 51, 59 n, 76, 90, 91 ff, 93 ff, 100 ff, 110 f, 150 ff, 153 ff, 157, 163 ff, 165, 170, 181, 193 ff, 198 ff, 222, 233, 248; becoming chimán, 83, 115–149, 235
dreams, 45, 91
Dresden Codex, 99 n, 102, 108, 254; pl. 14
drought, 24, 102
drum, see tambor
drunkenness, 32 f, 36, 55, 85, 95 f, 149, 198, 206, 209 f, 212, 215
dueño (dueña) de cerro, passim, esp. 17 n, 50, 51, 74, 77, 90, 92, 94, 110, 151, 192, 206, 210, 212, 230, 233, 245; apparition of, 75 f, 89, 96, 97, 175, 176, 220 f; author as, 17, 51, 71, 85 f, 88, 96, 158 f, 238; chimán's concept of, 92 f, 94 f, 96, 97; fincas of, 92 ff, 96 ff; as god of dancers, 216, 217, 219; as god of race, 210; as nagual, 170 ff, 175; see also "spirit"

*dueño de pozo*, 75, 122, 133 f, 174 f
*dueño* of river, 120; *see also* dueño de
   cerro
dysentery, 37, 47, 240

# E

Easter, 232 n
eclipse, 56
economy, 37 f, 39 f, 241
education, 36 f, 240
El Calvario, *see* Calvario, El
Elón, Basilia, author's maid, 20, 21, 33,
   44 ff, 69, 82, 154 f, 159, 204 ff, 238,
   241 f; pl. 8
Elón, Luis, *chimán*, 84, 155, 251
Elón, Margarita, 20, 38, 42, 56 n, 154 f,
   216 f, 227, 240; pl. 5, 22(a)
El Rancho, 176
El Rey, *see* Bautista, Macario
end of world, 54, 77
*envoûtement, see* "burial"
epidemic(s), 17, 51 n, 56, 83 ff, 88 f, 90,
   96, 226
*escuelix*, 55, 175; pl. 12
*estoraque*, 130
evil, *passim*, esp. 51, 86, 92, 121, 151,
   157 f, 165, 234; defence against, 120,
   153; personification of, 140; spell,
   34 n, 82, 122, 160 f, 184; Tenóm's
   pact with, 143; *see also* brujo, five
   evil days
exhibitionism, 158

# F

fair woman, as *dueña*, 17 n
falsehood, and *Caja Real*, 69 f
family, organization of, 34
famine, 24
fasting, 101, 184
"Father, Great," 52
Feliciano, old man, 82
*fiador*, 122, 124 f, 133, 198
fiestas, 32 f, 56, 100, 175, 223 ff; Night
   of Chimanes, 192 ff, 204 ff; for *reza-*

*dores'* installation, 64; of Todos
   Santos, 209 ff, 224 ff; pl. 17, 18; *see
   also* Year Bearers
*finca(s)*, 33, 37 f, 168, 216, 241; agents
   of, 20, 209; of *dueño*, 92 f, 97
"First House," 67, 68
*fiscales*, 55, 60
five evil days, 101, 191 ff, 229 f; birth
   unlucky during, 42; *costumbre* during, 192 f
Florida, 106
flowers, 41 f, 148, 195 f; in cure of listlessness, 186
flute, *see* chirimía
fly, as symbol of spirit, 49, 52
food, 39 f, 49, 97, 107, 220, 237
Förstemann, E. W., 108, 254; pl. 14
four, *passim*, esp.: candle cut into,
   194 f; *cerros*, 77; copal balls, 116 f,
   146; *corral* poles, 107, 148, 203; cypress branches, 64; directions, 54;
   skyrockets, 149; *see also* Alcaldes del
   Mundo, cross
fowl, pl. 14; *see also* rooster, turkey
Francisco, San, 41, 54, 224 f
fright, cause of illness, 184
funeral customs, 43 ff

# G

games, 37
Gates, William, 39 n, 99 n, 108, 254; pl.
   14
gaze, of dead as bad luck, 48
goat, eaten to celebrate birth, 42
God, *see* supreme being
Gómez, Rafael, 216, 219 ff
Goubaud Carrera, Antonio, 21, 178 n,
   189 n, 254
greeting, form of, 23, 67
Gregorian year, 188
*gringos (gringas)*, 16 n, 17, 33 f, 233
*guacalito*, 109
Guardians of the Royal Coffer, see *rezadores*

Guatemala City, 29, 238 n, 240
guitar, 44 f, 108 ff, 145 ff, 204, 205

## H

hair: in casting spell, 161 f, 166, 169, 211; cut off by evil spirits, 157 f
Hamy, M. E.-T., 180, 254
handcuffs, in *Caja Real,* 67
Hawkins, L. F., 189 n, 254
healing, 90, 183 ff; *see also* curanderos, medical work
health, *dueño* who bestows, 76
heart: ailment, 82; "Remedy for Sadness of," 187; "transporting the hearts," 143 ff
herbs, use of, 167, 183, 184
Herrera family, 57, 171 f, 173 ff
hoof-and-mouth disease, 229
horse: in cosmogonic tale, 140; as *nagual,* 170; race, 209 f, 212 f, pl. 18; ridden by *dueña,* 17 n, 238
houses, 31, 38, 66, 126, 140; pl. 4, 5
Huehuetenango (town and Department), 25, 29, 34 n, 36, 37, 62, 64, 67, 84, 96, 154, 187, 224, 238, 240, 243
*huipiles,* 104, 243

## I

idol, 39 n, 51, 74; pl. 14
illness, *see* disease
Incas, 138
incense, 68; *see also* copal, estoraque
Indians, *passim,* see esp. Mames, Todos Santos Indians
*ine,* 16 n
infection, treatment of, 81, 183
informants, list of, 19 ff
inoculation, 85
Intendente, 23 f, 35, 66, 160 f; *see also* Alcalde Municipal
intermarriage, 33; pl. 19
interpreter, 54, 55, 63, 64
Isidro, San, 54
Ixil Indians, 99 n, 189 n

## J

Jacaltenango, 53, 54, 87, 91 n, 178 n, 191, 243, 245
jail, 24 f, 161
Jerónimo, Fernando, *rezador,* 55
Jesucristo, 51 f
*jicaritas,* 109
Jiménez, Sebastián, 194
*juez de paz,* 35
Julián, Tata, *see* Tata Julián
*juzgado,* 31, 43, 219, pl. 12; of Santiago Chimaltenango, 104

## K

K'mané, *passim,* esp. 178, 189, 190, 228, 230, 233

## L

labour, 37 f, 241
*ladinos,* 16, 18, 21, 23, 33 f, 38, 39, 51, 89, 90, 100 ff, 115, 163, 186, 203, 209; education of, 36 f; first to settle in Todos Santos, 57, 171; intermarriage, 33, pl. 19; in Todos Santos government, 23, 35, 38, 66; relation with Indians, 16, 18, 23 ff, 33, 37, 40, 44, 66 f, 68, 81
La Farge, Oliver, 32 n, 34 n, 54 n, 99 n, 178 n, 189 n, 215 n, 254
lamb, eaten to celebrate birth, 42
land system, 34, 40
Landa, Friar diego de, 39 n, 42 n, 51 n, 56 n, 57 n, 58 n, 60 n, 99 n, 100 n, 101 n, 107 n, 110 n, 111 n, 183 n, 189 n, 191 n, 254
language, 18, 22, 36; *see also* Mam language, Spanish
lasso, 45, 93
La Ventosa (Chuyé), 30, 40, 73, 75, 230
*Life* (magazine), 61, 233
lightning: in divination, 182; stroke of, 82
Lincoln, J. Steward, 99 n, 189 n, 254

listlessness, cure for, 186
locusts, plague of, 245
López, Rigoberto, Commissioner of Police, 160
López, Señor, storekeeper, 241, 245
Lucia, Santa, 41, 54

**M**

magic, 90; *see also* brujo, divination, mixes
maguey, 99 n, 180
maize, *see* corn
Malacatancito, 53
malaria, 37, 81, 113
*malaya*, 75 n
Mam language, 22, 36, 100, 104, 123
Mames (Mam Indians), *passim*, esp. 15, 29, 32, 36, 41; ancient capital of, 29; calendar of, 99 ff, 188 ff; *see also* Todos Santos Indians
Manuel, orphan and *nagual*, 171 ff
Margarita, *see* Elón, Margarita
marimba, 65, 212, 218, 236
market place, 31, 209; pl. 3
Maroka, *ladina* of Santiago Chimaltenango, 104 f, 114
marriage, 43; Indian-*ladino*, 33, pl. 19
Martalo, 93
Maryknoll Fathers, 53, 60 n, 209
*masa*, 69, 204, 237
masks, 222 f; pl. 22(b)
mass: Catholic, 53, 209; of *chimán*, 110, 112, 135 f, 146, 192; *see also* salve
massage, 183
Matheu, Julio and María, 21, 84
Matías, boy in tale of *nagual*, 174
Matías, Julio, *chimán*, 143 f
Matías, Pascual, 244
Matías, Roque, First Rezador, 55, 235 f
Matías, Viviano, *principal*, 56
"Matilde Robles," pseudonym of author, 48 f
Mayan elements, 17, 24 n, 29, 32 n, 36, 39 n, 46, 49 n, 99 f, 103 f, 107, 108,
109, 138 n, 188, 244 n; pl. 14; *see also* calendar, codices, Landa
"Mayan Nose," *chimán* at Santiago Chimaltenango, 107 ff
*mayores:* civil, 35, 44, pl. 20; as days, 190; religious, 55, 60, 63, 226, pl. 21
Mazatenango, 97
McGhee, W. J., 99 n, 254
measles, 51 n, 83 f, 226; *see also* epidemic(s)
medical work: of author, 17, 19, 81 ff, 84 ff, 87 f, 113; of *chimanes*, 183 f; of Don Pancho, 18, 83; of R. Stadelman, 97
medicine bag, 178, pl. 16
Mejía, Laureno, *chimán*, 251
Mendoza, Esteban, *rezador*, 55, 251
Mendoza, Fermín, *rezador*, 55
Mendoza, Juan, *rezador*, 55
Mendoza, Manuel, 171, 175 f
Mendoza, Mateo, *rezador*, 55
Mendoza, Telespio, 210
Mendoza, Tomás, *principal*, 56, 184
Mercedarian Order, 53
Mexico, 29, 73, 101, 109 n, 138 n, 229; *see also* Palenque, Yucatán
midwife, 41, 184, pl. 9
milk, mother's, 48
missionaries, 99 n; *see also* Landa
*mixes* (sacred beans of divination), 24 n, 42, 43, 51, 56, 83, 92, 101, 122, 155, 157, 166, 168, 178 ff, 185, 192, 235; Aztec parallel of, 180; chart for casting, 248 f; description of, 178; god of, 143; methods of using, 179 ff; pl. 14, 16
Mocá, 92
*mojas*, 50
Momostenango, 97, 205
money, 110, 120, 147, 157, 169; of dead, 52; offered by *dueño*, 75, 76
Monkey, race official, 214, 218
moon, 88, 243; eclipse of, 56 n
Morley, S. G., 32 n, 36 n, 57 n, 99 n, 102 f, 189 n, 254

moth, as symbol of spirit, 49
mother, 41 f; attitude toward, 34; "great mother who has many breasts," 48
mountains, 101 f; see also cerros, Cuchumatanes
*mozo*, see Calmo, Domingo, *mozo*
mule, in Indian economy, 37, 194
*municipio*, 34
muscles in leg, divination by, 183

**N**

nagualism, 159, 170 f, 171 f, 173 f, 174 f
name, choice of child's, 42
Nantejo, Juan, *chimán*, 91 n
National Indian Institute of Guatemala, 21
*naturales*, 16 n, 54
Navaho Indians, 16
Nebaj, 244
nettle, 201
New Year observances, Gregorian calendar, 64 ff, 188, 227, 246; Mam calendar, see Year Bearers
nine, significance of number, 49
number count, 189; see also count

**O**

*ocote, passim*, esp. 47, 73
Odette, first wife of Domingo Calmo, 208
Olintepeque, 93
Omák, 244
oranges, 194, 199, 205
*ortiga* (nettle), 201
owl, as death symbol, 46
Oxomoco, Aztec goddess, 180

**P**

Pablo, Estanislaos, *intérprete*, 55, 212 f
Pablo, Esteban, *rezador*, 55
Pablo, Feliciana, tale of, 88
Pablo, Francisco, 88
Pablo, Ireneo, *principal*, 56

Pablo, José, 56, 201 f
Pablo, Juan, *chimán*, 146, 148, 235
Pablo, Macedonio, 147, 237
Pablo, Manuel, 185
Pablo, Marcelino, author threatened by, 85, 87 f
Pablo, Pascual, *chimán*, 19, 54, 76 f, 83, 91 f, 112 n, 150 ff, 152 ff, 163 ff, 165 ff, 170, 184, 186, 190, 192 f, 222 f, 251; ceremonies at house of, 198 ff; divination system of, 178, 181 f, 248 f; as teacher of Don Pancho, 115–49
Pablo, Victor, 20
*pacaya*, 107, 109
pact, of *chimán* and *dueño*, 95, 98, 110, 151
*padres*, see Catholicism, Maryknoll Fathers
Palacios, Armando, Intendente, 23, 25
Palacios, Ester, wife of Don Pancho, 16, 21, 88, 149
Palacios, Francisco, see Don Pancho
Palenque, 109, 138 n, 244 n
palm tree, God in, 234
*palo de pito*, 178
*pan dulce*, 104, 209
Pancho, Don; see Don Pancho
Paquix, 29, 238
patriarchy, 34
*patrón*, author as, 96; of *chimán*, 152; *dueño* as, 96
patron saint: of Todos Santos, see Santo Todos Santos; Francisco, San; Lucia, Santa; of Santiago Chimaltenango, 110
Patrona, see Calmo, Patrona
Paxil, 244 n
Peresian Codex, 99 n
Pérez, Pedro, *chimán*, 21, 178, 252
Pérez, Tiburcio, 174
photography, 16, 30, 72, 158; as sorcery, 87
*pichacha, passim*, esp. 63, 65, 180, pl. 10
*pila(s)*, 31, 104; *dueño* of, 75; pl. 2
pine, *passim*, esp. 68, 107, 151, 194, 205,

236; sap of, 166 f; *see also* ocote
pineapples, 148
planting stick, 42 n, 102 f; *see also* staff
of office
pneumonia, 84
police, 35, 160 f, 212
*Popol Vuh*, 244 n, 254
population, 34 f, 35 n
potatoes, 29 f, 39, 40
Prayermakers, *see* rezadores
prayers, *passim,* esp. 59 f, 65, 69, 70, 109,
111, 194, 223 ff; by author, 69, 236;
for author, 68, 236; at birth, 41; in
*chimán's* training, 116, 118, 121; for
corn, 39 f, 60, 142, 245; for *corrida de
gallos,* 210, 213, 214 f; for dancers,
217, 219; for dead, 46, 50, 51, 142; for
divination, 181; by Don Pancho, 202;
to *dueño de cerro,* 74; for evil, 161,
162, 165; on five evil days, 192 f, 194,
196, 199, 202, 206 f; for good year,
61, 229, 230; personification in, 77 n;
for rain, 54, 60, 62, 74, 230, 244; to
rock on T'ui K'oy, 74 n; in sickness,
60, 84, 142, 152 ff, 226, 229; on twenty
days, 142, 251 ff; *see also* costumbre
pregnancy, 41
priest-kings, Chimán Nam as descendant of, 58
priests, Catholic, *see* Catholicism, Maryknoll Fathers
*principales,* 35, 61, 81, 85, 158; function
of, 56, 58 f
prison, *see* jail
processions, 64 f, 223 ff
prognostication, 155, 178 ff, 197, 235;
*see also* divination, mixes
property, 34
"psychological" complaints, 186 f
*pulseras,* 184 f, pl. 9
pyramid, *see* Cumanchúm

quaternity, *see* four
quetzal (Guatemalan currency), 36 n

Quezaltenango, 37, 82, 92, 93 n, 241
Quiché, 93 n, 189 n, 243, 244 n; conquest of Zaculeu, 29 n

### R

races, 37, 209 ff
rain: forecast of, 197; prayers for, 24,
54, 60, 74, 230, 231, 244; pl. 14
Ramírez, Abelino, *principal,* 20, 44, 54,
56, 67, 86
Ramírez, Manuel, *rezador,* 55
Ramírez, Ponciano, *see* Tata Julián
Ramírez, Victoriano, *rezador,* 55
Recinos, Adrián, 36 n, 37 n, 254
Redfield, Robert, 16 n, 254
*regidores* of pueblo, 35
religion, *passim,* esp. 15, 53 ff, 90 ff,
99 ff, 115 ff, 150 ff, 188 ff, 223 ff, 245 ff;
*see also* Catholicism, chimán(es), costumbre, dueño de cerro, prayers,
supreme being, etc.
religious body, *see* rezadores
*Remedio para Tristeza de Corazón,*
187
Rey, El, 58; *see also* Bautista, Macario,
Chimán Nam
Rezador, Alcalde (Chief Prayermaker:
Ponciano Ramírez or Tata Julián),
17, 19, 23, 35, 55 f, 61, 209, 219, 223 ff,
230; and *Caja Real,* 60, 61, 64 f,
67 ff; election of, 62 ff, 226; entertainment by, 61, 67 ff, 235 ff; function of,
60, 61, 189; installation of, 64 ff, 227;
judging adultery, 69 f; pl. 10, 12; *see
also* Tata Julián
*rezadores* (Prayermakers, religious
body), 67, 69, 73, 84, 113 n, 125, 209,
223 ff, 236, 245, 247; election of, 62 ff;
functions of, 59 ff, 189; installation
of, 64 ff; organization and list of,
55 f; pl. 1, 10
Ríos Hidalgo, Fortunato, 160
river: *dueño* of, 120; in *costumbre,*
121 f; *see also* Chanjón

"Robles, Matilde," pseudonym of author, 48 n
Rodas C., Ovidio, and Rodas N., Flavio, 189 n, 215 n, 254
Roman Catholicism, see Catholicism
rooster: sacrifice of, 59, 61, 70, 105, 111, 119 f, 146, 148, 152, 153, 156, 192, 194, 201, 202 n, 205 ff, 213, 214, 217; myth of crowing, 235; race, 209 f, 212 f; see corrida de gallos; pl. 18
Royal Coffer, see Caja Real
ruda (rue), in casting spell, 167
"Ry-Krisp," 88

S

sacred places, chart of, 245 ff
sacrifices, 247; human, 103; see also rooster, turkey
sadness of heart, treatment of, 187
saints' images, 53, 81, 245
Sakabech, 77
salt, in costumbre, 163
salve, at funeral rite, 44, 48
sanitation, 184, 185
San Juan Atitán, 21, 101, 170, 171, 173, 178, 183, 185, 186, 189, 252 n
San Martín Cuchumatán, 32 n, 34, 35 n, 40, 44, 182, 185, 199, 219
San Pedro Necta, 244
San Sebastián, 170
Santa Ana Huista, 245
Santa Eulalia, 54, 178 n, 243
Santa María Quezaltenango (volcano), 91
Santiago, 110
Santiago Chimaltenango, 16 n, 17, 21, 93, 178, 189, 232 n, 251 n, 252 n; New Year ceremony at, 100 ff
Santo Mundo, 24, 25, 77, 138, 139 f, 193, 233, 234; see also supreme being
sarchep, 234
Satero, dancer, 20, 37, 216
school, see education
school-house, 64, 65, 67, 227, 245

schoolmaster, see Villatoro, Gerónimo
schoolmistress, see Palacios, Ester
secretario of pueblo, 35, 42 n, 63, 241
Seler, Eduard, 103, 180, 254
serpent, see snake
servants, 38, 242
shaman-priest, see chimán
shame, hidden by masks, 222
sheep-herding, 29 f, 72, 75, 171 f, 173 f, 240; dueño for, 76; prayer for, 125
Simona, author's servant, 241, 242
sin, 51, 113, 114, 121, 142, 191, 193
síndico of pueblo, 25, 171
Sky God, 48, 77, 233
Sky World, 49, 51
skyrockets, 64, 65 f, 67, 109, 113, 145 ff, 149, 192, 218, 221, 227
snake(s), 87, 97, 103, 161, 234; curing bites of, 185 f; as nagual, 170; pl. 14
Soch: altar on cerro, 74; spirit of Caja Real, 55, 64, 66, 67, 68, 70, 229, 230, 233, 246
social organization of Todos Santos, 34
soldiers, 67, 68
Soloma, 53, 243
soothsaying, 90, 178 ff; see also divination, mixes
sorcery, 175 ff
Spanish, use of, 36, 63, 110, 123, 171, 199
spells, casting of, 47, 82, 92, 153 f, 159, 160 f, 161 ff, 163 ff, 166 ff, 168 f, 184
"spirit," 107, 110, 112, 114, 130, 135, 141, 156, 169, 192, 193, 196 f, 203, 207; see also dueño de cerro, Soch
spring, dueño of, tale about, 75 f
Stadelman, Raymond, 35 n, 40 n, 87 n, 97 n, 254
staff of office, 63 ff, 152, 180; pl. 10, 14; see also planting stick
Stephens, John L., 29 n, 254
stilts, dance on, 102
sulfa powder, 211
sun, 243; in lunar eclipse, 56 n
supreme being, passim (e.g., in prayers

as Dios, Santo Mundo, Sky Father, Tata Dios, Tata Grande, etc.), esp. 25, 48 f, 50, 52, 54, 77, 139, 143, 233, 234 f; *see also* Santo Mundo

*susto* (fright), cause of illness, 184

sweat-bath, *see* bath

swine, 30, 45, 168

**T**

table of *chimán*, 24 n, 84, 90, 116 ff, 131, 146 ff, 152, 166, 181, 198, 223; "transfer of," 126 ff

table-rapping, 152

Tajumulco (volcano), 17 n, 73, 86, 106

*tambor* (drum), 55, 64 f

tapeworm, 47

Tata Julián (Ponciano Ramírez, Alcalde Rezador), 17, 19, 23, 33, 53, 54, 55, 58 f, 61 f, 63, 88, 158, 185 f, 192, 233 ff, 240, 245; entertainment by, 64, 66, 67 f, 230, 235 ff; at funeral rite, 45 ff, 48 ff; judgment by, 69 f; medical treatment of, 17, 61, 233; pl. 10, 12; *see also* Rezador, Alcalde

Tecum Umán, 93 n

telegram, in Indian folklore, 50, 94

telegraph operator, 21, 160

Tenóm, Ambrosio, first *chimán*, 112, 122, 135, 138, 143

*tesorero* of pueblo, 35

Thomas, Cyrus, 102 f, 254, pl. 14

*tierra caliente*, 37, 73, 157, 168

toast, 47 n, 110, 238

Todos Santos Cuchumatán, pueblo of, *passim*, esp. 15, 29; age of, 54; civil organization of, 34 ff, 239; climate of, 31; deed to, 67; description of, 29 f, 38, pl. 2, 3, 4, 5; economy of, 37 f, 40; journey to, 29 f; language of, 22, 36; population of, 32 ff, 34 f; schools of, 36; social organization of, 34

Todos Santos Indians, *passim*, esp.: appearance of, 32, pl. 6–12, pl. 17–22; attitude toward author, 33 f, 81 ff;

character of, 15, 18, 32; costume of, 38 f, 242; language of, 22, 36; *see also* Mames; Todos Santos Cuchumatán, pueblo of

Todos Santos, Santo, 54, 209, 224, 225; fiesta of, 209 ff, 224 f, pl. 17, 18

Totonicapán, 217, 218, 220

township, *see* municipio

tree, in cosmogonic myth, 139

Tres Cruces, 230, 246

Troano Codex, *see* Tro-Cortesian Codex

Tro-Cortesian Codex, 99 n, 102 f, 254

tuberculosis, 154

T'ui Bach (*cerro*), 71, 76, 220, 246, 247; ascent of, by author, 72 ff; as day, 77; *dueño* of, 76 f

T'ui K'oy (*cerro*), 51, 71, 246, 247; ascent of, by author, 74 n; as day, 77; *dueño* of, 76 f; as sacred place, 246, 247

Tuit Nam (*aldea*), 89, 239

T'ui Xolik (*cerro*), 246, 247; as day, 77; *dueño* of, 76

turkey(s): egg of, 119, 128, 132, 145, 163 f, 166; as food, 39, 69, 84; as *nagual*, 170, 175; sacrifice of, 59, 61, 64, 66, 68, 105, 111, 153, 194, 195, 209, 228, 230, 233, 235, 247

twenty days, 142, 248 f; as gods, 190; *see also* calendar, Mam

typhoid, 84

*tzité* seeds, 178 n

**U**

Ubico Castañeda, Jorge, President of Guatemala, 114

umbilical cord, 41, 42, 93

"Uncle Sam's Boys," 38, 242

United Fruit Company, 29 n, 254

urine, in casting spell, 161 f

**V**

vaccination, 85

Valle y de Castillo, Jose Miguel del, lover and telegraph operator, 21, 160 f
venereal disease, 37
venison, see deer
Villatoro, Gerónimo, schoolmaster, 171, 174 ff
vinegar, in casting spell, 167
violin, 108 ff
virginity, 43
volcanoes, 74; see also Santa María Quezaltenango, Tajumulco
voting: for rezadores, 63; for civil officials, 35
vulture: as bad-luck symbol, 157; in cosmogonic myth, 140; as death symbol, 46

W

Wagley, Charles, 36 n, 40 n, 189 n, 254
wake, for dead, 43 f, 44 ff, 51
wasp, as spirit of dead, 44
water: dueño of, 75; dueño who bestows, 76; divination by, 183
wealth, attitude toward, 93, 96, 98, 126, 176 f, 203
weather, 56, 59; see also climate
weaving, 38 f, 243

whites, see gringos
whooping cough, 84
women, 34, 38, 41 ff; as chimán, 92, and see Aguilar, Catalina; defence against evil, 121, 142; greeting of, 67; as pulseras, 184

X

Xepaxá (cerro), 74, 244, 246
Xinabahul, 29 n
Xoj K'au, 99, 192; see also Year Bearers, ceremonies for
xuk, dance custom, 218

Y

Year Bearers: ceremonies for, 67 ff, 99 ff, 189, 190, 191 f, 204 ff, 230, 245; Mayan observance of, 102 f, 111 n, 189, pl. 14; ceremony at Santiago Chimaltenango, 17, 104 ff; see also Alcaldes del Mundo
Yucatán, 39 n, 56 n

Z

Zaculeu, ruins of, 29
zajorines, 90, 92